CROMWELL

AGAINST THE SCOTS

CROMWELL AGAINST THE SCOTS

The Last Anglo-Scottish War

1650–1652

John D. Grainger

TUCKWELL PRESS

First published in 1997 by
Tuckwell Press Ltd
The Mill House
Phantassie
East Linton
East Lothian EH40 3DG
Scotland

ISBN 1 86232 064 0

British Library Cataloguing-
in-Publication Data
A Catalogue record for this
book is available on request
from the British Library

The publishers acknowledge subsidy from

THE SCOTTISH ARTS COUNCIL

towards the publication of this volume

Typeset by Hewer Text Composition Services, Edinburgh
Printed and bound by Cromwell Press, Melksham, Wiltshire

CONTENTS

Illustrations and maps vi

INTRODUCTION 1

1. GARMOUTH AND WHITEHALL 5

2. THE INVASION OF SCOTLAND 16

3. DUNBAR 37

4. A REARRANGEMENT OF PARTIES 51

5. THE SCOTTISH RECOVERY 76

6. TORWOOD AND INVERKEITHING 94

7. THE INVASION OF ENGLAND 113

8. WORCESTER 128

9. STIRLING AND DUNDEE 147

10. THE FINAL CONQUEST 162

CONCLUSION 174

Notes 177

Glossary 187

Bibliography 189

Index 191

ILLUSTRATIONS AND MAPS

ILLUSTRATIONS

1. Charles II
2. Cromwell in 1649
3. Cromwell as ruler, on horseback
4. The crowning of Charles II at Scone
5. English cartoon of Charles II and the Scots
6. Dunbar victory medal, depicting Cromwell
7. The Battle of Dunbar
8. Alexander Leslie, Earl of Leven, Scottish Commander-in-Chief
9. View of Edinburgh, 1690s
10. View of Stirling, 1690s
11. General George Monck
12. General John Lambert
13. Neidpath Castle
14. Tantallon Castle
15. Dirleton Castle
16. Dunnottar Castle
17. The Honours of Scotland

MAPS

1. The English Invasion, 22–29 July 21
2. The Campaign Around Edinburgh 25
3. Dunbar, September 2–3, 1650 41
4. Central Scotland, Sep-Dec 1650 53
5. The Deadlock Broken, Jun-July 1651 99
6. The Invasion of England 112
7. Worcester 133
8. Scotland: The Final Conquest 152

INTRODUCTION

A FRIEND of mine, when I mentioned that I was writing a book about the 'last war' between England and Scotland, frowned momentarily, then grinned knowingly and muttered: 'Jacobites, of course'; a sideways look informed me that my title was too clever by half. Another friend, rather better informed, dismissed the Jacobites and thought I was studying the Tudor wars. Children at the school I was teaching in glazed over completely: a war between English and Scots was outside their comprehension; the class wiseacre commented audibly on sports; for all of them, their history was almost purely social and economic.

I also thought I was cheating to ignore the various Jacobite problems – surely Bonnie Prince Charlie at Derby constituted a real war? A little consideration convinced me that the '15 and the '45 (not to mention the '08 and the '19) were not wars on an international scale – though they occurred during such wars – but internal rebellions, and minor ones at that, on a level with the French Frondes, perhaps, or the IRA in Northern Ireland: destructive but futile. With those out of the way (and, all the more, such minor internal incidents as the Glencoe massacre in 1692 and the Covenanters of the 1670s) I was vindicated: the last Anglo-Scots war was the one which began in 1650 and petered out late in 1651 or early in 1652.

The need to justify a title is not a particularly good way to begin a book, but I want my readers to be under no misapprehension. This is not a romantic or a debunking account of the Jacobite failures: it is an account of a serious and thoroughly unpleasant international conflict, which resulted in the complete defeat of the Scots and their total subjugation by their ruthless neighbours.

One would have thought, as I did when I began wondering about it, that such an event would have attracted scholarly or popular attention long ago. Yet there is no account of the war. There are *partial* accounts, which are contained in books on other subjects. For example, biographies of Oliver Cromwell have chapters, usually, on the war, but their interest ceases when Cromwell came south in August of 1651. The war went on a good deal longer than that. The only military history, by W. S. Douglas, is *Cromwell's Scotch Campaigns*. It is out of print, was published at the end of the last century and is almost unreadable, so littered are its pages with footnotes of immense length. It also stops in August 1651. Histories of Scotland concentrate on a slightly earlier period, the revolutions of the 1630s and 1640s. So David Stevenson's *Revolution and Counter Revolution*, covering events between 1644 and 1651, largely ignores the military aspect of affairs to concentrate on internal politics, and stops without seriously considering the invasion of England or the rule of the English; that rule is considered by F. D. Dow in *Cromwellian Scotland* but without a serious look at the preliminary war. And English histories are even more myopic: the battle of Worcester is regarded as part of the English Civil War, whereas the great majority of the men in the king's army were actually Scots, and the English army was enthused at the prospect of beating out a foreign invasion. To regard the battle as part of the English Civil War is to distort the events of the whole previous year, and the course of the battle itself.

To some extent this is a justifiable position. The two countries had been part of the same monarchy for nearly half a century, and in a sense the war was the product of the preceding civil wars (in both England and Scotland), but they were two separate states (just as now they are distinct countries), with separate governments, and separate histories. Their joint monarchy, and earlier mutual interferences in each other's internal affairs, only blurs the outline of this separateness, it does not remove it. This war was a conflict between independent states.

The various accounts largely combine to allow the war to vanish, dropping between several historical stools, and so to deny the international aspect of this war – as well as failing to provide an adequate account of it. For the Scots it is a part of the failure of their Covenanting revolution, for the English it is an appendage to their civil war. The succeeding period of political union with England and Ireland, forged by the English on the anvil of Scots misery, is largely dismissed from consideration, an unsuccessful union prematurely born, which did not – could not – survive because of the violence of its origins, a child of rape. The real union came in 1707, a true marriage of willing partners. So goes the tradition ironically known as the 'Whig' interpretation, though some Scots might jib at the implication that the nation willingly sank its independence into a larger union in 1707.

So I present here an account, in narrative form, of a war between two independent states, both of whose governments were revolutionary in origin, though that was only a secondary element in the causes of the war. But it does mean that underlying the political surface there was, among many, even most, of the people in each country, a powerful feeling of alienation from the ruling groups. Those rulers were the men who had come out on top in the warfare and violence of the preceding decade and a half, and they were both few and deeply apprehensive of those they ruled. There were Royalists in England and anti-Kirkmen in Scotland, both of whom longed to displace their enemies from power, and it might be thought that a foreign invasion would provide an opportunity for a counter-revolution. Yet in neither country were there enough of these anti-government plotters willing to combine with the invader to overthrow the government in power. So when Cromwell invaded Scotland he could get no Scots help of any significance, and Charles II got little English help when he brought his Scots army south. The Bromsgrove blacksmith who commented to the fugitive king that he blamed Charles for bringing in the Scots invaders spoke for the vast majority of people, of all ranks, in both countries. No matter who ruled, the popular reaction was detestation of the foreigner.

This war is not, that is to say, a civil war, but a clear international conflict between sovereign states. It is the result of preceding events and attitudes, and it is made more difficult and complex than usual by the previous relationships between the two revolutionary governments. In the event, though, it was the more basic, visceral reactions of nationalism which prevailed on both sides, if with other ideological overtones. That both governments knew full well that their own existence, and in the case of the men themselves their very lives, were at stake on the outcome, added a powerful personal element, spiced as it also was by personal relationships reaching across the conflict. A Scots soldier at the Corstorphine confrontation recognised Cromwell, shouting that they had been on the same side at Marston Moor. He and the Bromsgrove blacksmith epitomised necessary elements in the story.

CHAPTER ONE

GARMOUTH AND WHITEHALL

June 24, 1650

THE war between England and Scotland which began in July 1650 was made as nearly inevitable as anything human can be by two events at opposite ends of their common island on the same day, June 24. In the north, at the small fishing village of Garmouth, at the mouth of the River Spey on the Moray Firth, King Charles II landed from the Dutch ship *Skidam*, setting foot for the first time in his kingdom of Scotland. On the same day, in Whitehall Palace, London, an English committee met, and their discussion centred on the reasons for the English invasion of Scotland which they had planned.

The king had had a hard voyage, rough physically and tough mentally. It had begun, in effect, back in January of the previous year, 1649, when his father, King Charles I, had been executed by his subjects for making war on them. The new king – as he claimed to be – had two overriding ambitions from then on: to avenge his father, and to secure possession of his empty throne. After seventeen months, the Garmouth landing was the first major step along that road. The road itself had already been difficult and unpleasant, and it would continue to be rocky, painful, long, and dangerous for the king; for many thousands of his subjects it was to prove fatal.

Scotland had been outraged that the privilege of executing its king had been usurped by its neighbour. That Charles I had been king of England (and Ireland) as well as Scotland, that the major share in the war against him had been borne by the English, that the Scots had had the man in their own hands and had sold him to the English – all this became irrelevant. As soon as the news of his execution reached

Edinburgh his eldest son had been proclaimed king of 'Great Britain, France, and Ireland', on February 5, 1649.[1]

The title was characteristically eccentric and needlessly provocative. There was no country called 'Great Britain': Charles I had been, separately but in his one person, king of Scots and king of England. No king of England had ruled any part of France (except the Channel Islands) for a century. And Ireland was never visited by any English or Scots king as its king between Richard II in 1398 and Dutch William in 1690. The collection of kingdoms the new king was credited with was a nonsense; it was also unnecessarily provocative to the English, for 'Great Britain' could only be interpreted as including England, and so the Scots seemed to be claiming the right to decide who should rule in England. It could be said that the last Anglo-Scots war began then, declared by the Scots on the English on behalf of an absent king whom they had never seen, and whom the revolutionary government never trusted.

Being proclaimed king did not, however, either make Charles II into a king or give him any power. The Scots attached conditions, in particular insisting that he had to subscribe to their Covenant, the religiously motivated revolutionary government which had been in power in varying combinations and factions since the 1630s. That was where the seventeen months between proclamation and landing had gone, into long, painful, and mutually deceitful negotiations. As Charles moved in slow stages from Paris to Scotland during that time, he was made to jump through ever more theologically strict hoops in a process he found intensely humiliating. Agreement after agreement he made with the Scots negotiators turned out to be no more than yet another step along the road to his complete submission. His personal habits, his amusements, his religious beliefs, his parentage, his father's conduct, his mother's Catholicism, were all criticised to his face.[2]

The voyage from Holland had seen the process continue. He was travelling in a Dutch ship loaned to him by the Prince of Orange, his brother-in-law, and he was cooped up in it with the Scots commissioners, who prayed at him interminably given half a chance, and indulged in minute criticism of his social, political and religious conduct. The ship was stormbound in the Heligoland Bight for a week, and during that week yet another negotiating screw was tightened. Then they crossed the stormy North Sea, making landfall at Orkney. As they came south they headed into yet another storm.[3] This was June, in a year whose weather was worse than even the wet and cold seventeenth century could easily recall. The new king could call nothing his own, not the ship he travelled in, nor the kingdom he was going to, and even his chosen companions were objected to by the sharp-tongued and insolent 'subjects' who laid down conditions for his rule which he had grudgingly to accept.

But this king was a lucky man. All his life he escaped the worst consequences of his extravagance and hotheadedness. He was sexually promiscuous in a time of widespread venereal disease, and escaped infection; he was hunted by a hostile English government in 1651, and escaped to safety overseas; he was saddled in 1660 with a new English constitution designed to hamper him with a perpetual Parliament, and escaped from it by the 1680s, despite being hampered by a family divided between Catholics and Calvinists. And now, the tempest which he encountered coming south from Orkney drove away a powerful English fleet under Admiral Popham which had been waiting for him in the Moray Firth. People on shore saw both fleets heading away from each other; Scotch mist ensured that neither fleet saw the other. Luck indeed.[4]

Before he landed, Charles at last signed the Scots Covenant, another turn of the screw, at the Commissioners' insistance.[5] But even that was not the end of the matter. In effect, neither Charles nor the Scots trusted each other, and in this they were both quite correct. Charles signed and swore to successive agreements with such strong mental reservations that he convinced himself he was only acting under duress; the Scots negotiators insisted on repeatedly tightening up the agreements because they could sense this reluctance in the king. The net result was that when he reached Scotland none of those in power would permit their new king to exercise any power.

On the other hand, he was personally popular. From the time of his landing he was welcomed, fêted, feasted, all the way south. He travelled from Garmouth by way of castles and cities, staying at the

Gordon castle at Bog of Gight, the city of Aberdeen, the powerful Dunnottar castle, the cities of Dundee, Perth, and Stirling, and in the end was lodged at Falkland Palace in Fife. Quaint customs dotted his route, like the doch and dorris the earl of Southesk made him drink, his leg hooked over the bolt of the doorway, at Southesk.[6]

The land he now ruled, at least in name, was governed by a revolutionary party, and it was their conditions he now had to meet. The Kirk party, as they were called, was a narrow group hoisted into power at the failure of the last party in power, the Engagers, who had led an unsuccessful invasion of England two years before, in 1648. The extremists, the Kirk party, had seized power by means of an armed uprising in the west of Scotland (the 'Whiggamore Raid' – the origin of the party term 'Whig'). With the main Scots army away in England the Kirkmen had seized Edinburgh and installed their own government in the capital. A purge had followed, and a compliant Scots Parliament had dutifully passed the Act of Classes, which provided the legal basis for the exclusion of the members of previous governments. These two parties were both opposed by the out-and-out Royalists, whose champion had been the marquis of Montrose. He had been the king's champion too, and had led an invasion of Scotland from the continent earlier in 1650. He had failed. His small army had been intercepted at Carbisdale in Sutherland by an even smaller force of the Kirkmen's troops, and totally destroyed. Montrose was captured and rapidly executed. As King Charles travelled south from Garmouth, he saw sections of Montrose's dismembered body displayed on spikes at Aberdeen and Dundee. This was a grisly reminder to Charles of his most devoted champion, and of his own responsibility – for Charles had failed to support Montrose, and had done nothing to save him.[7]

The continuing power in the Scottish government was located in the Committee of Estates, technically a standing committee of the Scots Parliament. It was composed of selected Members from the three estates of the Parliament: nobles, lairds, and burgesses. The Committee was the one permanent deliberative body in the kingdom's government, and it was wholly in the hands of the Kirkmen. The main offices were in their hands as well. The Lord Chancellor was John Campbell, earl of Loudoun, a skilful politician who had held the office since 1641, surviving all the twists of Scottish covenanting politics. Another Campbell, Archibald, marquis of Argyll, had also survived all along, but was no longer trusted by his fellows, though his chieftainship of the great Campbell clan gave him independent power. Sir Archibald Johnston of Wariston was the Clerk Register, ambitious but fearful, whose diary reveals the state a man can get into when he takes his religion too seriously, and loses his common sense.

It was with these leaders of the Committee that the king had to deal, and all power was in their hands. Charles had no hand in appointing office holders, and, distrusted, he was to be regularly subjected to further humiliations. The Scots Parliament was now a purged and obedient instrument of the Committee, whose only effective critic was the Kirk itself, in the form of the General Assembly and the Commission of the Kirk, a sort of ecclesiastical version of the Parliament/Committee system. But the Commission of the Kirk was more kirkly than the Kirk party. There was to be no hope for the king there.

In England, the English Parliament was also a purged body, but was somewhat less obedient to its Council of State – in effect the English version of the Committee of Estates. The Council was too large to work effectively, being about forty strong, though attendance was variable. It therefore operated through committees, some permanent, some *ad hoc*, and the recommendations of such committees were rarely questioned. The man with a foot in all these camps was Oliver Cromwell: M.P., General of the Army, member of the Council of State, and frequently appointed to the more important of its committees. His agility – political, military, rhetorical, religious – enabled him to dominate all these, though his control was never total. For, unlike Charles II, he was burdened with an active conscience.

On June 24, as Charles approached and landed on the Scottish mainland, the latest committee of the Council, of which Cromwell was a member, met. This was in fact a committee which Cromwell himself had suggested, and it consisted of himself and four other men, in all a conspectus of the new power which was ruling in England. Besides Cromwell, a country squire who had risen to power by his military and political ability, but basically a moderate conservative in politics, there were two other soldiers: John Lambert, a young Yorkshireman with a genius for generalship probably greater than Cromwell's, and Thomas Harrison, a former clerk and a Fifth Monarchist, both of these men being strong republicans. There were also two lawyer-politicians, Oliver St John, an opponent of Charles I ever since the quarrel in the 1630s over Ship Money, and Bulstrode Whitelocke, a lifetime moderate. Collectively these men were the most powerful group in England. They had come to meet the Lord General, the commander-in-chief of the New Model Army, another Yorkshireman, 'Black Tom', Lord Fairfax.

Fairfax had told the Council of State two days before that he would not lead his army in the invasion of Scotland which the Council planned.[8] This was not wholly unexpected news: issues of conscience tended to be very publicly known amongst this group of men, and Fairfax's conscience was more active than most. He had not made any decisive move until then, even though the invasion of Scotland had been planned for six weeks or more, but as the day of action approached, so did the need for him to make his decision. It was clearly painful for him. He was reputed to be under pressure from his wife, a notoriously outspoken lady, and from Presbyterian ministers in London,[9] with whom he and his wife sympathised, and who were vehemently opposed to an attack on their ideological brothers in the north. Despite the pressure, Fairfax was a man who made up his own mind, even if he took a long while to do so. When he did announce his decision to the Council of State, on June 22, Cromwell proposed his little committee to discuss it all with Fairfax in private.

They met in a room in Whitehall Palace, surely sitting round a table, a group of men who were personal and political friends, and who respected each other's qualms of conscience. Cromwell opened proceedings with a prayer, and Whitelocke made extensive notes.[10] Cromwell then began by inviting Fairfax to state his grounds for refusing to command. Fairfax replied in general terms, and the other four, one by one, asked him to be specific. So he was. 'We are joined with them [the Scots] in a solemn league and covenant,' Whitelocke recorded him as saying, 'and now for us . . . to enter into their country with an army and make war upon them is what I cannot see the justice of.'

He was referring to the alliance made back in the dark days of 1643, when the Scots had come south to help the English Parliament in its hour of need. The Scots' price had been English adhesion to their Covenant, and an English promise to institute Presbyterian forms of worship in the Church of England. Fairfax's words conjured up the memories of those days, and of the alliance which had been the foundation of the English Parliament's eventual victory. He was also implicitly calling up a threat, that a new conflict might break out in England, between the Presbyterians, led by Fairfax, and the rest. Such a conflict could only chill the hearts of all of them.

Cromwell smoothly agreed that 'if they have given us no cause to invade them, it will not be justifiable for us to do it'. Then he pointed out that the Scots themselves had already invaded England, meaning the Engagers' invasion which he and Lambert had defeated at Preston two years before. He went on to point out that the Scots were 'very busy at this present in raising forces and money'. What else, he was asking, were these forces for but to attack England? 'That there will be war between us, I fear, is unavoidable.' Better it were fought, in that case, in Scotland than in England.

Fairfax was unconvinced. He quite agreed that war was 'probable', but then he came to the heart of the matter. 'Whether we should begin this war and be on the offensive part,' he said, 'or only stand upon our own defence is what I scruple.' And he pointed out, accurately, that the new Scots regime of the Kirkmen had disowned the Engagers, and had deprived them of political rights. Politely, he did not mention that it had been Cromwell's own looming and forceful presence in Edinburgh which had helped the Kirk party reach that decision.

The confrontation between Fairfax and the committee was total. Fairfax insisted on the primacy of his conscience, the others on their right to invade Scotland. The discussion went on somewhat longer, but both sides were immoveable. Fairfax at last, in his fair and decent way, offered to resign his commission as Lord General. At that point there may well have been sighs of relief from the rest. Fairfax was not going to take the conflict in this committee outside. He was not prepared to invade Scotland, but neither was he prepared to stand in the way of the others doing so.

This was the crucial decision, but the argument went on, as such arguments do, for some time yet. The five tried to persuade Fairfax to stay, for he was immensely popular in the army, and his going might well cause divisions, even if he went quietly. It was suggested that he remain in nominal chief command while the invasion force would be commanded by Cromwell, but he would not. 'Everyone must stand or fall by his own conscience,' he said. The new English republic had lost the services of its most eminent and popular soldier. He attended the Council of State next day, to hear the committee's report, tendered his resignation, then returned to Yorkshire. His fundamental decency prevented him from taking the quarrel further. This made the war with Scotland, as Cromwell had said, 'unavoidable'.

Fairfax's resignation from the command-in-chief led to the appointment of Cromwell as Lord General. Heads immediately wagged at this. It was widely assumed that this had been Cromwell's aim from the start, and that all his arguments to Fairfax were therefore insincere.[11] Reading Whitelocke's notes, however, that is not the impression one gets. Cromwell was eloquent, and all five of the committee pressed Fairfax to stay. Of course, an imputation of insincerity can never be disproved, and it is certain that Cromwell must have known that, if Fairfax did go, he himself would be made Lord General in his place. But his reluctance looks genuine, as does his eloquence and his argument. He had just returned from a difficult and nasty campaign in Ireland, and one into Scotland would be as difficult, if not more so. There is little doubt, however, that Cromwell was the better man for the job. Fairfax had a tendency to berserker frenzy in battle, to revel in the fight for its own sake, whereas Cromwell was more thoughtful, and immensely more careful of his soldiers' lives. A half-hearted Fairfax fighting in Scotland against a skilled Scots army and commander would have been a recipe for an English disaster. For the Scots, on the other hand, Cromwell spelt political as well as military defeat. It took much more than mere military competence to conduct the Scottish campaign: it needed the ability to argue, to persuade, to intrigue – to be a politician as well as a commander – and these were abilities which Cromwell possessed, and Fairfax did not.

The six men knew each other well. As MPs, as soldiers, as

neighbours, as lawyers, as in-laws – St John was married to Cromwell's cousin – they had worked together for years. There was much in a discussion such as theirs which they did not need to say to each other. And the most glaring omission was any mention of Charles II, who was, at that very moment, landing in Garmouth.

For it has to be said that, by the standards of normal international behaviour, Fairfax was largely correct. England and Scotland *were* allies; the Scottish Parliament *had* disavowed the Engagers' invasion of two years before; war *was* only 'probable' – it only became 'unavoidable' once the English government decided to invade Scotland. All the arguments of the committee were irrelevant beside these solid facts. In all this, there was no cause for war, despite the military build-up on both sides.

And yet, above all the argument, and despite its not being mentioned, there was the problem of the king. Charles I had been mainly and above all else a king of England. His eldest son could not rest until he had regained that throne, and had avenged his father's death. For Charles II, his accession to the Scottish throne was only one more step on the way to those English goals, no matter how the Kirkmen might delude themselves that he was being made purely a king of Scots. The Council of State had decided that the invasion should be undertaken back in March.[12] They had information that the Scots were negotiating seriously to bring their king across from the continent, and that the Scots had made provision to recruit a new army of 5,440 horse and 13,400 foot.[13] It only needed suspicious minds, battered by years of civil war and rebellion, betrayal and conspiracy, and a memory of the Scots invasion of England in 1648, to put these facts together and conclude that the Scots' intention was for their king to lead that army in an invasion of England in order to put him on the empty throne.

To such men, habituated to the dangers of war over the past eight years, the obvious answer to such a threat was a pre-emptive strike. And it must be said that they were probably not wholly wrong. Invasion was surely Charles' aim, though the Kirk party, aware of their precarious position in Scotland, always denied that they harboured any ill will towards England. But they *had* protested at the execution of Charles I, they *had* proclaimed his son as king of 'Great Britain', they *had* brought his son to their kingdom and made him their king. They may well have done all these things for their own internal purposes: the Kirk party's position was known to be precarious, and it had been briefly propped up by English pikes at its inception, and this meant that it might not take much to overthrow it. And its enemies were the king's men, Royalists – what the Kirkmen called 'Malignants' – and Engagers. Annexing the new king to the Kirk looked to be good politics. But controlling him might be more difficult – hence the screw-tightening on the voyage. What was quite certain was that if the Kirkmen's Scots enemies gained power they would have no scruples about an invasion of England for their king.

Both sides had misconceptions about the other. The Scots had made provision to recruit an army partly in response to the threat of Montrose's invasion earlier in the year, and they hadn't done a great deal to recruit those numbers when the threat vanished. Both sides feared that the other would invade, and so prepared for defence. But such preparations can easily seem threatening – and both sides knew full well that the best defence is usually attack. Therefore they both feared a sudden attack. But both sides were also fundamentally hostile to one another for other reasons than fear. The Scots aim throughout the civil wars, since 1637, was to install a Presbyterian regime in England. This was still their aim. But the winners in the English civil war had been the Independents, represented above all by Cromwell, who were as unwilling to accept the Presbyterian straitjacket as they were to return to control by bishops. And, of course, at bottom, at the root of all this argument and dispute, there were the rival national feelings. The English soldiers who were stationed in Edinburgh in 1648 to support the newly installed Kirkmen's regime (commanded, as it happened, by Lambert) had been subjected to much hostility in the streets, their horses and equipment had been stolen, and they had been very glad to leave. The mutual dislike, mixed with contempt, which was a permanent feature of Anglo-Scots relations, rapidly rose to outright hostility at close contact.

All this, however, does not bring war unless both sides will it. The various elements in the crisis all came together in mid-1650. And the basic problem was that everyone in the dispute saw right on his side. Fairfax was right, and Cromwell and his committee were right; Charles II was right, and the Kirkmen were right. All appealed to God. The big battalions would decide.

CHAPTER TWO

THE INVASION OF SCOTLAND

July 22 – August 27, 1650

THE governments of both countries had made preparations for the war. Fairfax's resignation did not delay the English in the slightest. Parliament accepted his resignation, appointed Cromwell as his successor as Lord General, and accepted the declaration by the Council of State that the invasion was justified, all in a day. The declaration was published on July 4. Cromwell's lieutenant-general – second-in-command – was Charles Fleetwood, and the commissary-general was to be Edward Whalley. Both of these were relations of Cromwell, but he had numerous cousins, and nepotism was not involved. John Lambert was appointed major-general, and Thomas Harrison became major-general in command of the forces left in England.[1]

The invasion force had been listed for a month, and those not already at Newcastle were now ordered there.[2] It consisted of six regiments of horse and five of foot, a small force for the task, but it amounted to a good half of the forces available in England. Other forces were still tied up in the conquest of the last corners of Ireland.

The army the Scots had voted to raise back in February – nearly 19,000 men – had never actually been fully recruited, particularly among the foot, but the Act permitting the levy still existed; another Act was passed on June 25, so that in theory an army of 36,000 was authorised.[3] This was an enormous number for a state of Scotland's size and general poverty of resources, and nothing like that number was ever raised. The date is instructive, for the Act was passed before news of the king's landing or of Cromwell's appointment had reached Edinburgh. The Scots, like the English, already saw the war as 'unavoidable'. The war's ideological – as distinct from its nationalist – causes were also recognised, for the soldiers actually embodied were now to be subjected to an ideological test: a committee for purging the army had been set up on June 21, even before the new enlistments were agreed. The Kirk party was as scared of a hostile Scots army as the Parliament of England had been of their own; with the example of Pride's Purge of the Westminster Parliament before them, and of their own purging of their Parliament and the Committee of Estates, the Scots politicians in power voted to ensure that their army was to be rendered obedient to them and no-one else. And that included the king.

The commander-in-chief was Alexander Leslie, Earl of Leven, but he was too old, he said – he was about seventy – and too infirm for active command. He was left in place, but the command in the field went to his nephew, David Leslie, as lieutenant-general, a man who was just as ideologically correct. A thorough and intelligent professional soldier, the victor over Montrose at Philiphaugh, and joint-victor, with Cromwell, at Marston Moor, Leslie's preferred strategy was to let Cromwell's army come to him. He organised the fortification, with trenches and guns and forts, of a line from the sea at the fortified town of Leith on the Firth of Forth, to the fortified city of Edinburgh, with Edinburgh Castle as the impregnable anchor on the landward side. All men aged between sixteen and sixty in the counties along the North Sea coast between Leith and Berwick were ordered to be evacuated; all supplies were requisitioned. The English were supposed to march through a deserted land, inhabited only by a mob of women and children demanding to be fed.

Cromwell and the Scots spent a month longer in mutual preparation, starting at rumours of the other side's moves, and bombarding each other with declarations of intent and of righteousness. The Scots Parliament had already written to its English counterpart, naively asking whether invasion was intended, but not seriously expecting this to delay matters.[4] Now Cromwell wrote to the Scots to give reasons for his projected invasion, and he also set to work on a declaration of justification designed for publication.

This took some composing, it seems. One officer, Cornet John

Baynes, a Yorkshireman, wrote on July 11 to his uncle, Captain John Baynes, that the general and other officers had been striving mightily with the text for two days, but then, four days later, he commented that the first drafts, already printed, were burnt, and a new one prepared.[5] It appeared over the name of the Secretary of the Army, John Rushworth, in London on July 19, as 'A Declaration of the Army of England upon their march into Scotland, to all that are Saints, and partakers of the Faith of God's Elect in Scotland'. In nearly 4,000 words, much of it frothy religious rhetoric, there is a single sentence which refers to the English civil wars, but which is precisely apposite once more: 'We were engaged in a war with the . . . king for the defence of our religion and liberties'. Now, having removed that threat, the Declaration says, here is the same threat recurring, in a new king and a new religion, and so the English must engage in war once more.[6]

The war had already begun at sea. The English Parliament had decided to prohibit trade with Scotland during the war, but it took some time to get around to the details. As early as July 1, Captain Edward Hall, commanding the English squadron off the North Sea coast of Scotland, told the Council that he had captured a Scots ship out of Rotterdam, full of goods and carrying numbers of men and officers to Scotland. He had sent it into Newcastle, where Sir Arthur Haselrig, the governor, was to dispose of it. Two days later he reported chasing a group of five ships, capturing three, and driving the other two aground. One of them, a Dutch ship, was released after a search, and the others were sent once again into Newcastle. Two more were taken in the next few days by other ships of the English squadron. This activity, however, did not prevent one of Hall's ships sending a party ashore in the Firth of Forth for water. They were captured, and made to kneel and drink to the health of the king.[7]

Other English ships were employed to bring up supplies for the army. The Admiralty Committee of the Council of State was told that the fleet's victuallers had hired twenty-three ships in July to carry provisions north, and on August 1 the Council told the Navy Commissioners to hire as many as were necessary. Colonel Deane was asked to send more warships up from Plymouth to help in the blockade. Meanwhile, any Scots who were in England were sought out and investigated. A Scottish colonel, James Grey, was caught in London and brought before the Council of State, before being sent off to Cromwell.[8]

Cromwell had travelled north as soon as he received his commission as Lord General, being welcomed generously by the mayors and aldermen at Northampton, Leicester, and York, and at Durham he was entertained by the colonels of his allotted regiments and Haselrig from Newcastle.[9] He was now informed of the condition of Scotland, and it became clear that extensive preparations were under way. Early rumours of a pre-emptive Scots invasion had vanished, to be replaced by a more accurate appreciation of Leslie's intentions. Cromwell knew what they were, certainly by July 10 at Newcastle, and the Scots strategy of retreat and devastation was even known in London soon after. A Scots force, rumoured to be three regiments of horse under a Colonel Douglas, had been spotted at Coldstream, a border village on the Tweed fifteen miles inland from Berwick, and the Scots levy was known to be going well. On the arrival of the full English force, the regiments withdrew, having covered the levy and the evacuation along the invasion route. The English claimed they had fled.[10]

All this made the English expedition much more difficult than had been expected. Cromwell's force had risen already to eighteen regiments, but the Scots levy meant that he was still outnumbered. The Council of State in London, perhaps warned by Cromwell of the mounting difficulties, sent him a small battering train, and made arrangements for a regiment to march north through Lancashire to improve the garrison of Carlisle.[11] Leslie's strategy was already having its effect even before the English had reached the border. What had seemed straightforward in London had become a daunting problem in Newcastle.

But the troops were cheerful. They gave Cromwell a rousing welcome when he inspected them at Newcastle, voting to 'live and die' with him. On the other hand, some officers were clearly unhappy, probably suffering the same qualms of conscience which had assailed Fairfax. Colonel Bright tried to escape by asking for leave, was refused, and resigned; other, more junior, officers were dismissed. Bright's regiment were asked if they would accept Colonel George Monck as his replacement, but they refused, shouting that he had been their prisoner six years earlier, at Nantwich, before he changed sides to join Parliament. They did accept Lambert, however, who was Cromwell's next suggestion. Monck, one of Cromwell's favourites, was then given a new regiment, collected together from diverse companies in the Newcastle and Berwick garrisons. (Thus inauspiciously began the Coldstream Guards.) The temptation is very strong to see in all this an example of Cromwell's deviousness. He had succeeded in giving his two favourite subordinates a new regiment each, had increased his force by a regiment, had rid himself of a number of disgruntled officers, and had gained a reputation for democratic conduct with the soldiers which was thoroughly misleading but nonetheless valuable. On the other hand, perhaps he simply made a mistake in offering Monck to the regiment.[12] Monck may well already have been put in charge of the army's artillery train, though the appointment was not made official for many months.[13]

Cromwell, awaiting supplies, moved the army gently forward the sixty miles to Berwick, and on July 19 he held a grand review in the grounds of Lord Grey's Chillingham Castle. A muster revealed a strength of 16,354 men. Yet another 'declaration', this time directed to the 'People of Scotland', was published, to no discernible effect.[14]

What did have an effect were bloodthirsty remarks by the Scots, predicting what the English would do to any prisoners they caught. Folk memories in the borders and along the coast road to Edinburgh were powerful enough to make such predictions seem credible. Previous English invasions, and the behaviour of moss troopers who raided across the border in both directions, had been savage enough to sear local memories. A pained denunciation of such 'groundless and unjust reproaches, and many false slanders' was published by the English, and Cromwell issued a stern proclamation to his own army against violence and plundering. Having made a speech to his soldiers, warning of the difficulties ahead of them, he ordered his own regiment of horse to lead the march into Scotland. Colonel Pride's foot regiment was next. That combination, of Cromwell and Pride, should have been warning enough.[15]

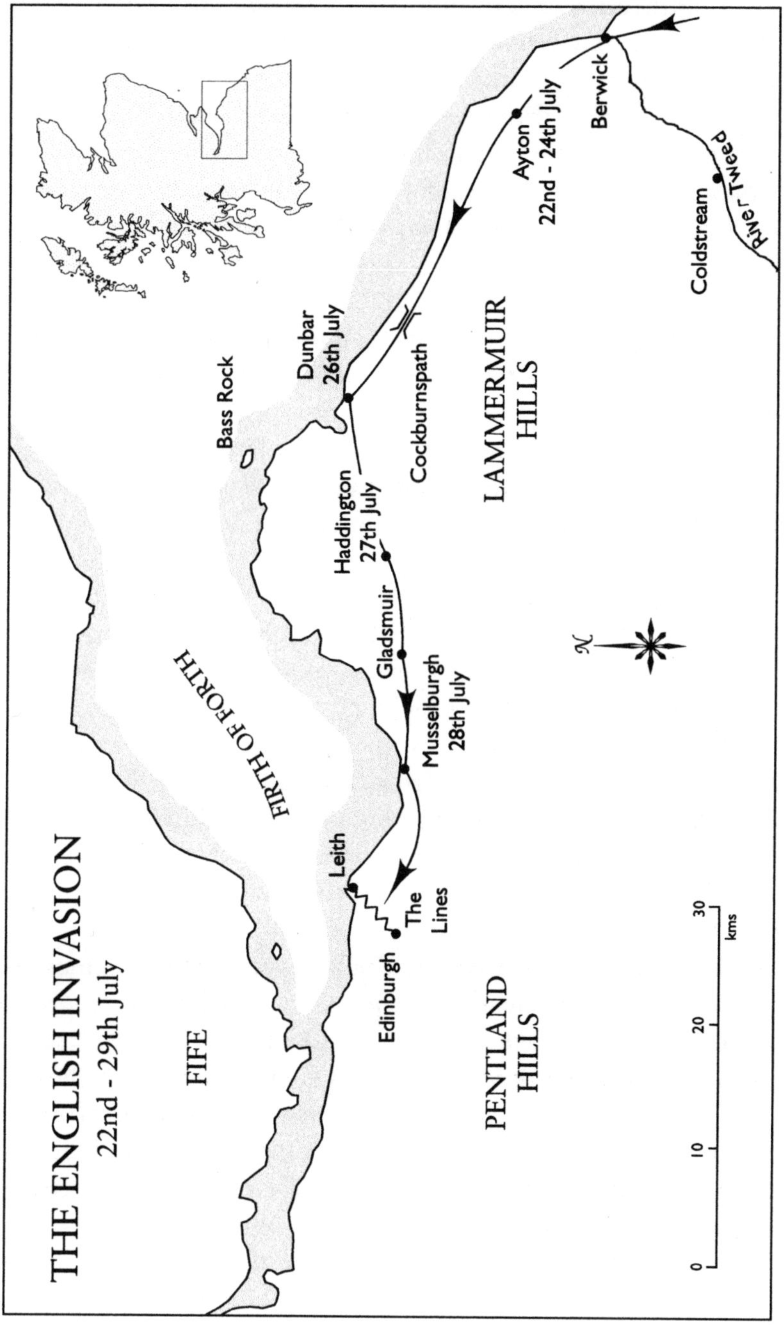
THE ENGLISH INVASION
22nd - 29th July
FIFE
FIRTH OF FORTH
Bass Rock
Dunbar
26th July
Haddington
27th July
Gladsmuir
Musselburgh
28th July
Leith
The
Lines
Edinburgh
PENTLAND
HILLS
LAMMERMUIR
HILLS
Cockburnspath
Ayton
22nd - 24th July
Berwick
Coldstream
River Tweed
N
0
10
20
30
kms

The English army took its time. After crossing the border, it camped at Ayton, four miles north. In front of it a line of beacons was successively fired, warning all Scotland of the invasion. Perhaps because of the implied threat in this the army camped at Ayton for three days, surely hoping for an immediate battle. But there were more resignations, by Major Barber, for one, as the army entered Scotland. However, nothing happened, and on the 25th the march was resumed, twelve miles to Cockburnspath. This was a narrow pass close to the coast, just the place for the Scots to make a stand. No doubt the three days had been partly occupied by a thorough reconnaissance of the whole area, not just the road ahead, but the inland territories as well. With the land stripped of its sustenance, one possible strategy for Leslie would be to hold his army inland, wait for Cromwell to push on north, and then march in behind him to cut his communications. Reassured, Cromwell could march on, and he went on to Dunbar, a useful, if small, port.[16]

Cromwell had left in Newcastle an agent, William Rowe, a former envoy of the Council of State to the Scots, as his Scoutmaster General, a combined intelligence officer and supply expediter. Rowe was busy about forwarding the laggard supply ships from Newcastle to wherever the army was, and he had his wife out searching Newcastle for materials for bedding for the army. He had a spy in Edinburgh to write to him, something presumably arranged while he was on the embassy there earlier in the year. Cromwell was thus not taken wholly by surprise at the actions of the Scots as the army approached Edinburgh.[17]

Some provision ships arrived at Dunbar, but provided no more than 'a pittance'. Supplies were already a problem. The English troops were shocked at the emptiness of the land. Lieutenant Hodgson remembered the cattle being driven away, and a correspondent in *Mercurius Politicus* went further, as befitted a journalist: 'though Scotland hath been often compared to a wilderness, yet it was never so like one as then'. So the English army had to rely on the supplies which could be shipped from England.[18]

Another day's march on the 27th brought the English to Haddington, eleven miles from Dunbar, and only twelve from Edinburgh.

From there Cromwell could see the Scottish outposts only six miles off at Gladsmuir, and rumours swept the army that there would be a battle there next day, on ground of the Scots' choosing. Next morning, a Sunday, a strong reconnaissance force of 1400 horse under the two major-generals, Lambert and Whalley, rode to Gladsmuir. They found only a small force of Scots cavalry, which prudently retired. Lambert and Whalley occupied Musselburgh, and the rest of the army followed. Only three miles now separated the two armies.[19]

The Scots had also had their troubles. Leslie's policy of retirement had scarcely pleased the inhabitants of the deserted territories, and it had been only partially effective. The English had managed to find some food, though not enough to feed the whole army, by any means. Meanwhile the women and children had been left to fend for themselves, and were at the mercy of the invaders, so that any food the English found was taken at the expense of those people. Some of the women found work baking and brewing for the invaders, and presumably fed themselves at the same time. Leslie was fundamentally relying on Cromwell's restraint, and on the discipline of his army, to preserve these women from harm. It might have been this which prompted him to refuse the offer by men of the Merse and Teviotdale to harry the rear and communications of the English army. He feared reprisals, no doubt.

This policy would change, but meanwhile the land was not being wholly abandoned, for many strongpoints, castles and fortified houses had not been evacuated, but were retained by their owners and garrisoned by their retainers. Much of the local supplies had gone into these castles. The English ignored these places on their march, for the moment, but if they became active centres of resistance, Cromwell's restraint might be relaxed, and the sufferers would be those women and children.[20]

The greatest of these strongpoints was at Edinburgh, where much work had gone into preparing the fortified lines which were intended to deny the English the cities of Leith and Edinburgh. Both places were walled, if in a rather antiquated fashion for the time, and a lot of effort had been expended on strengthening them. The city council of Edinburgh had been put in charge of the whole works back in June, soldiers had been allocated to the task, and the inhabitants of the city were ordered to provide the labour of a servant each to help. An especially vulnerable part of the castle, called the Spur, was demolished, but as time went on the matter became steadily more urgent. All the inhabitants of Leith – not just servants – were ordered to work on the fortifications on 14 July, and next day the local militia was embodied. Measures were concerted in case of a siege, and the castle was provisioned. But the urgency was still not sufficient. Orders were still being issued for work to be done on sections of the fortifications as the English began their march into Scotland, and again as they arrived in sight of the city. Nevertheless, under Leslie's supervision, the position had been made truly formidable. However, those self-same people who were supposed to provide servants to labour on the fortifications were also busily sending their portable wealth out of the city to safety further north. Confidence was not high.[21]

Skilful use of the hills nearby, and much digging, had strengthened the fortified position so much that Cromwell took one look at it and decided not to attack. There were trenches between the two fortified cities, beginning at Holyroodhouse and the Abbey Hill, just east of Edinburgh's Canongate, running roughly along the line of the present Leith Walk, and to the walls of Leith. Those walls had been strengthened, and were lined by nearly forty guns. Leith harbour was blocked by a heavy boom. To the south and east of Edinburgh were forward detachments of Scots forces on Arthur's Seat and on St Leonard's Crags. These posts were designed to prevent attacks on Edinburgh, and were also intended to block the route round to the south of the city. Looming over the citizens was the gloomy castle, separately garrisoned and provisioned, one of the most powerful in northern Europe.

On the morning of July 29, the English army marched out of Musselburgh to take up a position facing the Scots lines, in front of Restalrig and Jock's Lodge, with Arthur's Seat looming over them to their left, and a narrow approach between that hill and the Lochend Loch to their right. The first priority was to take Arthur's Seat, which dominated that end of the battlefield. An attack cleared the hill and two English cannon were dragged up to the top and began to bombard

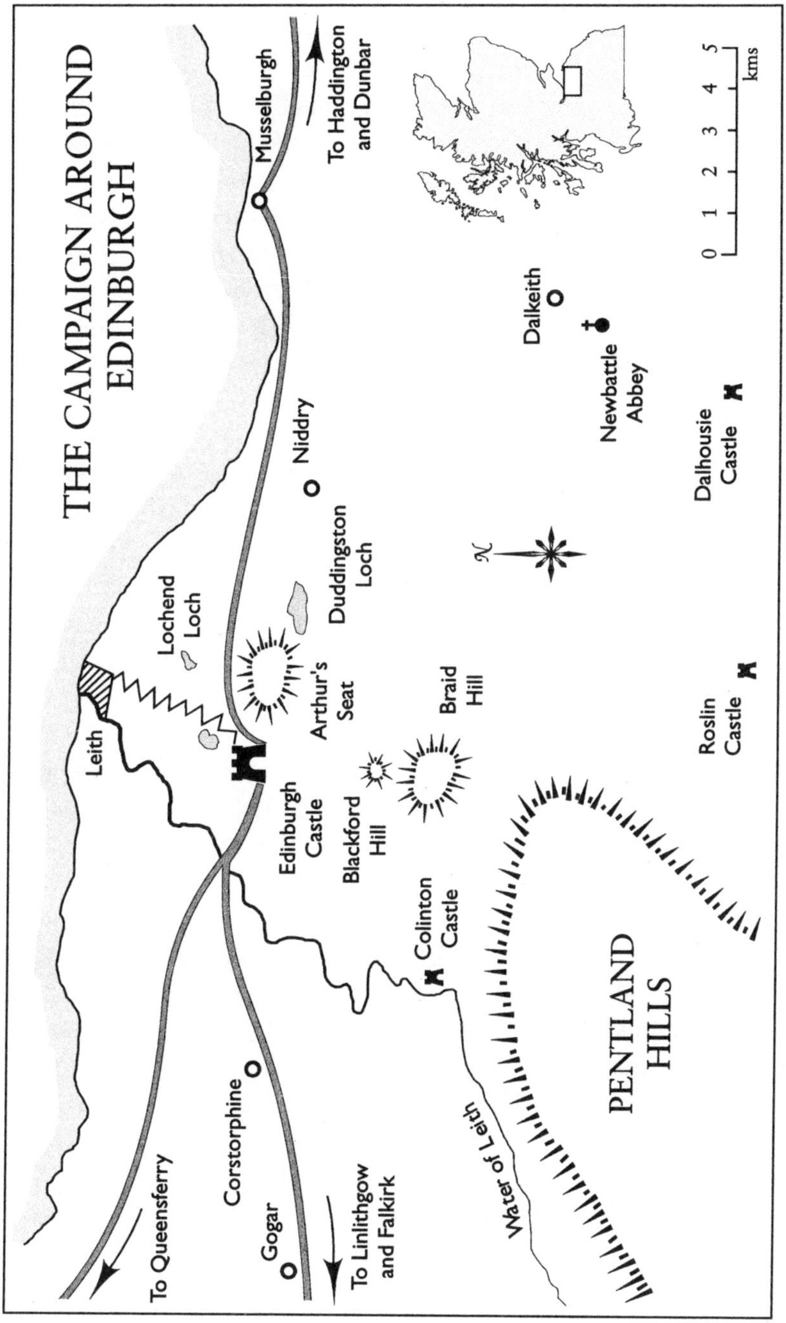
THE CAMPAIGN AROUND EDINBURGH
Leith
Lochend Loch
Musselburgh
To Haddington and Dunbar
Edinburgh Castle
Arthur's Seat
Duddingston Loch
Niddry
Blackford Hill
Braid Hill
Colinton Castle
Corstorphine
Gogar
To Queensferry
To Linlithgow and Falkirk
Water of Leith
PENTLAND HILLS
Roslin Castle
Dalhousie Castle
Newbattle Abbey
Dalkeith
N
0 1 2 3 4 5
kms

the Scots right, aiming at least in part at Scots troops stationed in the Quarry Holes of Calton Hill. After a while, a Scots regiment, commanded by Colonel James Campbell of Lawers, Chancellor Loudoun's son, retook the hill and captured the cannon, though they were retaken by the English almost at once. At the other end of the line, four English ships bombarded Leith. All this was to no avail. The Scots stayed in their trenches. The day was wet, and the rain continued all that night, with the English troops still out in the open, shelterless. By morning Cromwell had had enough. The trenches were too well planned and well manned for him to assault them, and his men were wet and hungry. In the morning he ordered retirement. Leslie had won that round, easily.

The English withdrawal was speedy, so much so that the rearguard became separated from the foot, marching ahead. Leslie sent out two cavalry detachments, one from Leith and one from the Canongate, to try to take the rearguard in a pincer. Hacker's regiment drove off the Leith force easily, but that from the Canongate was more successful against Captain Evanston and the 200 troopers who formed the tip of the tail of the English rear. Evanston and his men were rescued by Cromwell's regiment of horse, which drove the Scots right back to their lines, and there it was itself attacked by more Scots horse. Major-General Lambert's horse was killed under him, and he was wounded and captured, but then quickly rescued by Lieutenant Empson's troop from Hacker's regiment. Finally Commissary-General Whalley came up and drove the Scots back again, then successfully disengaged.

When the English got back to Musselburgh they found that the local people had returned and retaken their town. They had hidden from the English in the coal pits nearby and had come out when the English marched off to Edinburgh. In the two days since the English left, the people had crudely fortified their town, and now the English had to retake it. Major Haines of Lambert's regiment of horse did this smartly, killing thirty of the defenders in the process.

There was still no relaxation for the English. That night they were attacked in the town by a strong Scots cavalry force. Colonel Robert Montgomery, the son of the earl of Eglinton, a leading Kirkman, and Colonel Archibald Strachan, the victor over Montrose at Carbisdale, 'two champions of the church' as Cromwell remarked, led 800 horse by a roundabout route to Musselburgh. Some Englishmen with them fooled the guard picket, men of Lilburne's regiment, with their English accents, and the Scots rode deep into the town at the charge. Their aim, so it was said, was to take Cromwell himself – intelligent thinking by the Scots, if it was true, or perhaps by the English Royalists with them. But the noise was enough to rouse the whole English army, who cannot have been all that surprised at the raid. The musketeers of Lambert's foot regiment finally stopped the charge, and a counter-charge by a scratch force of English horse drove the attackers out of the town. On their retreat towards Edinburgh the Scots were again charged, by a patrolling English cavalry force, and lost a number of officers killed or captured. The captured officers were carefully and generously released next day by Cromwell, who put the wounded into his own coach for the journey to Edinburgh. He was, after all, waging a psychological campaign as much as a military one.[22]

Cromwell might sum up all this activity as 'a sweet beginning to our business, or rather the Lord's', but the whole thing had been distinctly ominous for the English. The Scots lines were impregnable. The Scots cavalry was clearly fully capable of raids and counter-attacks. The ordinary people were already sufficiently roused to fight for their homes against the veterans of the New Model Army. And after only a day standing to arms in the rain, the English army had had to retreat – or so the Scots might say. Above all, the supply problem weighed on all English minds. Cromwell ended the letter to the Council of State in which he reported the actions of July 29 and 30 by commenting that the Scots were 'hoping we shall famish for want of provisions', and then had to add, 'which is very likely to be if we be not timely and fully supplied'.[23]

The effects of all this on the armies was paradoxical. The English, who were the attackers, entrenched themselves at Musselburgh, and then discovered that the harbour was too small to permit the landing of supplies. This meant that there was no port west of Dunbar which they could use, and on August 5 the army marched back to Dunbar to collect supplies from the ships.[24] For the Scots, however, the result of their successful defence was even more serious. There was a powerful faction in the Kirk party which disputed Leslie's strategy. They considered that the pusillanimous defensive was to deny the power of the Lord, who was, of course, on their side. That being the case, large numbers of men were not required, only an army of staunch believers. They pointed to previous victories of godly troops against bigger forces, most recently Strachan's victory over the larger army of Montrose. It was this attitude which had led to the establishment of the Purging Committee in June, and this committee had been operating on a minor scale since then.

The apparent success of Montgomery and Strachan in raiding the English at Musselburgh encouraged the Kirk party further. The commission of the General Assembly of the Kirk, meeting in Edinburgh and Leith during the crisis of Cromwell's approach, was hot for a truly loyal and zealous army. The ministers who had been appointed as chaplain-supervisors to each Scots regiment were instructed to draw up lists of former Engagers in their regiments, and the Committee of Estates was urged to get rid of those who were not true covenanters. Then on July 28, with the English army at Musselburgh, the Clerk Register, Wariston, pushed forward another demand. He proposed a new sub-committee, one of ministers and generals, who would consult on the disposition of the Scots forces. General Leslie 'gave a sharp answer', as Wariston says – not surprisingly. The return of Montgomery and Strachan from the raid on Musselburgh caused much dispute. Wariston argued that a larger force, say 1500 horse, would have succeeded, and pointed out, no doubt with some relish, that he had so suggested beforehand. He got his sub-committee.[25]

Meanwhile the king had arrived. The news of his landing at Garmouth had been received in Edinburgh with a night-long celebration, which had been lit by the burning baskets and stools of the market women, but was regarded sourly by the Kirkmen, who were suspicious of popular emotion. Since then Charles had been living at Falkland Palace in Fife, across the Firth of Forth. The Kirkmen's pressure on him continued, and he was compelled to dismiss his Scots friends, whose Royalism was unacceptable to the Kirkmen, though his English Royalist companions, including the duke of Buckingham, were allowed to stay with him. But at least the treaty which the commissioners had made with him was ratified by Parliament, and a date (August 15) fixed for his coronation.[26]

Charles' main hope of real power, once all this was done, was the army. A levy such as the one the Scots had made was bound, in the political circumstances, to contain plenty of Royalists and Engagers. So the king wanted to visit his army. This was quite sufficient for the Kirkmen to want to keep him away, at least until they had purged the army of these 'Malignants'. William Ker, earl of Lothian, wanted to bring the king to the army officially, thus demonstrating that the Kirk party retained control of both, but the Committee of Estates dithered. Therefore the king came anyway, arriving at Leith on July 29, in response to an invitation from some of the officers in the army. Wariston saw Cromwell and the king equally as threats: 'at night the enemy came to Restalrig; the king to Leith'; and when the army greeted Charles exuberantly, Wariston complained about its 'exclamation and carnal courage'. The king's presence undoubtedly had much to do with the sudden aggressiveness displayed by the cavalry and the English Royalists as the English army began retreating to Musselburgh. This was, as Wariston said, 'ominous', for it would never do for the *king* to win the victory; it had to be 'the Lord's' – that is to say, the Kirkmen's – victory. So he argued that the king's presence with the army was a distraction from its real task, and persuaded Charles to leave.[27]

This experience put the Kirkmen on their mettle, and next day, having seen off the English and the king, it was the army's turn. The Purging Committee set to, and between August 2 and 5 dismissed about 3,000 soldiers as not being sufficiently godly. The test was, in fact, not religious at all, but political. Any men who had marched with the Engagers in 1648, or who were out-and-out Royalists ('Malignants'), were expelled. The purge removed at least eighty officers. Sir Edward Walker remembered them as the 'best men', but then he was an English Royalist. The price the army exacted for accepting this purge was the disbandment of the sub-committee which discussed the disposal of the forces, but the increased party commitment of the whole army was presumably reckoned to be worth it.[28]

The English waited at Dunbar for six days, while all this was going on in Edinburgh. In London the Council of State was already reacting to the apparent stalemate. Sir Arthur Haselrig at Newcastle was ordered to open up the route from Newcastle to Carlisle. Major Thomas Rippon was commissioned to raise four troops of dragoons to keep open the road from Berwick to the army's headquarters. The Council's Irish Committee was ordered to send 8,000 pairs of shoes to the army in Scotland, and the Ordnance Committee to send 2,500 sets of armour – 'backs and breasts and potts' – to Newcastle. Haselrig, again, was commissioned to raise a regiment of horse and two of foot, 'for opening the passage from Berwick to the army', and to prevent 'irruptions' by the Scots. A rumour that the Scots had sent a detachment to invade England provoked the Council to order the Yorkshire Militia Committee to call up one of its regiments and send it to Haselrig.[29] All this was the result of Leslie's strategy, and put much more pressure on the English government and army. There would be no rapid victory. It would all take time. Clearly, the war would be long.

How much Cromwell knew about the Scots upheavals in Edinburgh is unknown, but he certainly had informants in the city, and few of the ordinary people remained reticent when questioned. It is significant that he chose just this time, August 3, to write to the Commission of the Kirk, formally in response to the Scots reply to his initial declaration. It is a letter cloudy with religious rhetoric, aimed at sowing doubts in the minds of the Scots ministers, playing on the feelings of guilt which these men always had, and containing what is perhaps Cromwell's most famous sentence: 'I beseech you, in the bowels of Christ, think it possible you may be mistaken'. This is, in fact, the nub of his argument, as well as being virtually the only sentence in the letter which is immediately understandable.[30] The letter was addressed to the hardest heads in Scotland, however, and it had no result. Not yet, at least. But Cromwell knew what he was doing. It was yet another drip on the stone of Scottish resistance, wearing away at it.

Cromwell issued three days' rations on the morning of August 11 – he had already distributed some of his supplies to the townspeople – and the army marched out once more towards Musselburgh. There had been much discussion as to what they should do, and three alternatives had emerged: to fortify Dunbar and then wait for Leslie to attack them there, relying on the ships to keep up supplies; to mount a frontal attack on Leslie's lines; or to execute a flanking march to get behind Leslie's forces, cut his communications with the west, and so bring him out to a battle.[31]

All three of these had their attractions. Sitting at Dunbar would probably bring Leslie out, for there was already pressure on him to fight, but remaining on the defensive in a foreign land is difficult to maintain unless the enemy co-operates, and supplies were not reliable. An assault on the Scots' fortified lines was a good option, appealing to blunt do-or-die men, but it would be costly in lives, and Cromwell's army was not that large, nor could it be reinforced quickly; casualties had to be kept to a minimum. The time for an assault had, in fact, passed. If one was to be mounted it should have been when they first arrived. Having retreated once, it would now be a much more formidable undertaking, psychologically. It was thus a matter of the army's morale, and in that Cromwell was the expert. So his preferred choice was the outflanking march. Having re-supplied at Musselburgh, on the 13th the army marched round the inland flank of the Scots' lines and took up a position on the Braid Hills, due south of Edinburgh, about two miles off.[32]

The Scots had also been wondering what to do if the English entrenched themselves at Dunbar. One suggestion was to ignore the invader and march off against England. Wariston opposed this, as did Leslie, and, for the moment, so did the great majority of the Scots officers. No-one asked the king, but here was the beginning of the plan he was to put into execution a year later, under infinitely worse circumstances. At present, though, he was being harried unmercifully by the Kirkmen. They wanted to pin him down so that he could not move. They produced a declaration for him to sign, in which he was supposed to grovel in humiliation. He resisted, but gradually it became clear that, if he failed to sign it, his last chance to gain any power at all would vanish. And the approach march of the English army exerted yet more pressure on him.[33]

From his camp close to Edinburgh Cromwell fired off yet another appeal, this time to Leslie personally, with the intention of separating the king and the Kirk party. On the same day, the 14th, a group of English officers met a group of Scots officers on the sands between Musselburgh and Leith, each with an escort of a hundred troopers. But the Scots could not be persuaded to desert, even though they complained of being misled by the 'Malignants'. Nor did Cromwell's letter have the intended effect. Instead it was used by the Kirkmen to threaten the king, whose coronation had already been postponed in the face of the invasion crisis. Charles was making active plans to ride north, with the obvious aim of taking command of forces which had been gathered there, and which were known to be heavily Royalist in sympathy. The pressure of Cromwell's army brought both to their senses, however, and on the 16th Charles gave in, putting his signature to a new declaration of his loyalty to the Covenant. He had signed so many of these papers that yet one more would make no difference. *Then* he rode off to Perth, hoping that troops coming in from the Highlands would prove to be more loyal to him personally. Leslie stopped that scheme by ordering them directly to Edinburgh.[34]

By then Cromwell was once more on the move. On the 14th, the day of his letter, he marched the army back to Musselburgh for more supplies, and then, leaving a detachment to hold Stoney Hill to protect his base there, back again to the Braid Hills. There they camped on the old ground, but now the army had tents, for shelter in that appalling summer, and its control of the road back to Musselburgh would now permit re-supply to come up without having to march the whole army back.[35]

A short march on the 18th took the English to Colinton House, south-west of the city, on the Water of Leith. The house was taken, and thus another outpost established. Its English occupiers comprehensively wrecked the interior, according to a later claim for compensation. On his reconnaissance near there Cromwell was fired at by a Scot in a patrol. Cromwell shouted to him that he ought to be punished by his officer for such a wild and premature shot. 'I know you, Cromwell', the soldier shouted back. 'I saw you in Yorkshire' – at Marston Moor, when they had been fighting on the same side, against the father of the Scotsman's king.[36]

This incident highlighted both Cromwell's enormous energy – he always reconnoitred himself – and the Scots' problem. There was a substantial proportion of the Kirk party who were very uncomfortable at their political situation. They did not trust the king, with good reason, and they were not convinced of his attachment to the Covenant, again with good reason. Their alternative, however, was to adopt the position of the English republicans, or rather, to join the enemy, and this they could not do, for they were patriotic Scots. They resolved the dilemma, for the time being, by subjugating the king to the Covenant, hedging him about with covenanters, gradually stripping him of his own chosen companions, and portraying the English as sabbath-breaking monsters.

Cromwell seemed to be aiming at cutting the last land link between Edinburgh and the rest of the country, the western road towards Linlithgow and Falkirk. If he cut that road, the only link would be by water, by the crossing to Fife at Queensferry, or directly across from Leith, and the English fleet controlled the Firth of Forth as far as Queensferry. In fact, what Cromwell wanted was for the Scots to come out of their trenches to fight in the open, and his moves were designed to bring that about. He could not hope to cut the road for very long, given his supply problem. It was, again, a game of bluff. Leslie was short of supplies also, for he had a city to feed as well as an army. The price of food and drink in Edinburgh had already doubled, and there were complaints about its quality.[37]

There were stern discussions in the Scottish camp. The threat of a royal *coup* had not yet vanished, and Leslie did not know if he would be attacked by Royalists under the king from the north. He presumably had no illusions about the king's signature on the declaration. And now Cromwell's army was marching invitingly across his front, camped only a mile or so from the walls of the capital, an army smaller than his, and at the end of a difficult supply line. The suggestion was put to him forcibly that a march out to Dalkeith would cut the English communications. It was believed that Cromwell had lost 3,000 men through sickness already, which was an exaggeration, but not wholly wrong. And the closer he came, the more vulnerable the city seemed. There was another flurry of work on the fortifications, and anxious discussion of the numbers to be left as a garrison if Leslie took the army out.[38]

The result was that when Cromwell moved again, to threaten the western road, Leslie had to be seen to react. He pushed out a detachment to Red Hall, the house of Sir James Hamilton, on the Water of Leith about a mile downstream from Colinton House. This secured the main crossing of that river, and protected his flank for his next move. After another purge of 'Malignants' and Engagers, and a solemn day of fasting and humiliation, Leslie marched his army through Edinburgh along the western road to Corstorphine. The problems he faced were further highlighted by another meeting between officers from both sides the day before. On the English side the leading figure was Lambert, and on the Scots side Colonel Strachan. He was vehement against the king. The meeting, again, had no immediate results, but what was said could only encourage Cromwell to keep on chipping away at Scots unity.[39]

Cromwell's strategic move had succeeded, and the Scots had been levered out of their trenches, but their new position, behind two long narrow lochs on either side of Corstorphine village, was as strong as it had been in the lines. Cromwell watched the situation for three days, then reacted by attacking Red Hall. The place was strong. A six-hour bombardment by English artillery ensued, before Monck's new regiment broke in and took possession of the house. The whole affair looks like an attempt to bring the Scots army forward to defend the place. If so, it failed. But, having taken the hall, Cromwell now controlled the best crossing of the Water of Leith. Another fruitless meeting between English and Scots officers followed.[40]

On the 27th, therefore, Cromwell moved his army across the river even further to the west, crossing right across the front of Leslie's army, which, even if it had wanted to, could not attack, for it was blocked by the two lochs. The English clearly aimed to threaten the western road still further west, and so not merely cut the Scots communications, but take the Scots army in the flank as well. Leslie in turn shifted his army west, clear of the lochs to conform. For a time Cromwell and the army thought the moment of battle had arrived. The Scots army was drawn up north of the road, with the hamlet of Gogar at its centre, and the valley of the Gogar Burn in its rear, and its left wing anchored on a hill. The English were drawn up on higher ground to the south. Many of the English soldiers, convinced that the battle would be fought almost at once, threw away their surplus food and their tents – that is, they stripped for action. But then their scouts reported that the ground between the armies was too boggy. No attack could be mounted. Leslie had done it again.[41]

The artillery on each side fired several hundred rounds, and each side convinced itself that the other had suffered significant casualties. But the English could not stay. Their supplies were finished and they could not march further. The only recourse was to return to their bases. And now they faced an even worse problem. They could disengage, but their route to Musselburgh was by bad roads and over hills. The Scots, by contrast, could march by a straighter, shorter, better road, through Edinburgh. The English might well find that they could be attacked on the march, while in disarray, by a fresher, or refreshed, Scots army.

Leslie, on the other hand, also had his problems. His own forces were hungry, the purgings had weakened their morale, their leadership, and their discipline, and he feared that Cromwell would use his control of the Red Hall crossing to march into the gap between the city and his own forces at Gogar, or even to march on Edinburgh. There is no sign that Cromwell even thought of this, but Leslie could not be sure. So for the next two days the two armies marched eastward, each keeping a wary eye on the other's movements.

Cromwell moved first, crossing at Red Hall, to camp on Blackford Hill between his old camp on the Braid Hills and the city. Leslie moved rather farther (six and a half miles to Cromwell's five and a half) and camped that night (the 28th) at Calton Hill, at the eastern end of Edinburgh, his troops once more in the old trenches. He was thus in a good position to cut the English route to Musselburgh – but Cromwell was also in a position where he had a choice of routes, for he could, if he wanted, move south by the road to Dalkeith, and thence north-east to Musselburgh, well clear of the Scots.

Cromwell was fully aware of the possibilities. Scouting ahead, he decided that the likely battlefield, if the Scots came out, would be between Arthur's Seat and Musselburgh, so he posted two of his guns on a hill at Niddry, to dominate the likely ground. Next morning the English were moving early, and, sure enough, the Scots appeared on

Arthur's Seat. But once more nothing happened. This time a loch, Duddingston Loch, protected the English march, but they were clearly on the move earlier than the Scots, and Leslie had no wish for a battle. He was still convinced that he could remove the English army without serious fighting.[42]

These manoeuvres, over a period of five weeks, and over ground which is now covered by the suburbs of Edinburgh, had provided a major test for both generals and both armies. All had achievements to their credit. Cromwell had nudged and prodded at his opponent, inventively marching and manoeuvring, both militarily and in his intrigues. Leslie had stuck to his plan, clearly knowing full well that the English army was a more powerful force than his own. Twice he had forced the enemy to retreat. The English army, in bad conditions, at the end of a tenuous supply line, had performed very well, though its strength was wasting through sickness, and a trickle of desertions had begun. And the Scots army, despite the purgings, had been successful, and was now a more cohesive instrument, and still larger in numbers than its opponent.

The military contest so far was thus a draw, with a certain advantage to the Scots. But their political system of king-and-covenanting-Kirkmen was creaking under the strain, while there is no sign of anything but wholehearted support for Cromwell from the Council of State. It is difficult to estimate whether a victory or a defeat would be the more disastrous outcome for the Kirkmen. It was the presence on Scots soil of the invading army which provided the real support for the Kirkmen, enabling them to draw on national feeling. Victory would relieve the pressure, while defeat would discredit them. Leslie's strategy was both politically and militarily appropriate, and had so far been fully successful.

CHAPTER THREE

DUNBAR

August 30 – September 7, 1650

THE English retreat persuaded Leslie to change his strategy. The English had reached Musselburgh in a bad way. Cromwell sent off 500 of his men by ship to Berwick because they were too sick to march, and there were many others only slightly better off. Shortage of food, and, no doubt, bad food, for nearly seven weeks, had had its effect. Men were struck by the 'flux', dysentery. One soldier, as is the way with soldiers, blamed this on the local drink, which he thought not only had 'a filthy tang', but was 'laxative' as well. The condition of the English was well known to the Scots, and at one point Wariston decided that 20,000 English had died of it, but then he was always hysterical. Cromwell's strength at the muster just before the invasion had been over 16,000. It was down to a little over 12,000 early in September. At Musselburgh the stocks of food were low, for the army had been living on the supplies brought up from Dunbar nearly three weeks before, on August 11. It was also found that the Scotswomen who had been employed to bake and brew had been ordered out of their homes by Leslie.[1] Cromwell decided that he did not have enough supplies both to recruit his army and to recover its health, so he decided, apparently almost at once, to march on to Dunbar again.

To the Scots this looked like the retreat of a failed and desperate army. In this they were wrong, but they were also convinced that the casualties amongst the English were even greater than they had been. So when, on August 31, the English marched out of Musselburgh on the road to Dunbar, it seemed that the chance had at last arrived to drive the invaders out. Leslie's army marched out in pursuit. He was still not intending to fight, unless he could get the Scots into a position of overwhelming advantage. The English halted for the night at Haddington, and Leslie sent in a force to harry the rearguard in the evening. Any fighting was prevented when the moon was obscured by clouds. By the time the clouds had cleared away, the English were in their quarters. About midnight a party of Scots mounted musketeers beat up the quarters at the west end of the town, but were quickly driven off without much difficulty.[2]

One soldier, a cavalryman of Major Brown's troop, was captured and brought to General Leslie, whose practice it was to interview prisoners himself. The soldier was offered the chance to join the Scots, but refused. He was then shown the Scots camp, and released. Leslie, in other words, was trying his own type of psychological warfare – perhaps derived from a classical education which included Herodotos – and no doubt the size of the Scots army received due emphasis.[3]

The soldier's report did nothing to daunt Cromwell. Instead it may have convinced him that Leslie was at last willing to fight, and certainly the nearness of the two armies provided the opportunity, for they were camped no more than a mile apart. In the morning, Sunday, the English army filed out of the town and drew up in battle array in the fields to the east, where they said their Sunday prayers and sang their psalms. The Scots did not move. A little before noon, Cromwell gave up waiting, and, sending the carriages and guns off first, marched his army off towards Dunbar once more. Leslie followed, but at a discreet distance. He knew the ground, he knew the enemy's intention, and he now decided he had the English in a trap. Instead of harrying the rearguard – there was no fighting that day, other than some shots from two of the English guns when they thought the Scots were too close – Leslie aligned his army's march to the south of the Dunbar road, and, while the English were moving into the town, the Scots occupied Doon Hill, south of the town, where they could cut Cromwell's communications with the south. To make certain, Leslie sent a detachment off to seize the narrows at Cockburnspath.[4]

Cromwell's intentions in making for Dunbar had been multiple. He had hoped once more to bring Leslie out to a battle; he wanted a better base than Musselburgh, a port where supplies could be landed and stored; he was expecting reinforcements, who were being sent along the coast road, and Dunbar would be a good place to meet them. Once in the town he intended to fortify it, establish a magazine, and leave a garrison there. Whatever Leslie's hopes, Cromwell had no intention of going home.

Cromwell had thus achieved his main objective, which was to shift Leslie's force out of its impregnable trenches, once again. But Leslie had, as before, cannily used his local knowledge to get his army into a position where it could not be assaulted. Doon Hill was too steep for a force to attack up the slope – it still had the remnants of Iron Age hill-fortifications on the top. The Scots army was further protected by the steep sides of the Brock Burn, which flowed between the hill and the town and thus separated the two armies. Between the top of the hill and the sea, a mile and a half away, the land sloped down first to the southward road, and then there was a stretch of gently sloping, cultivated land, less than a mile wide, as far as the cliffs which formed the coast. The burn was fordable at three places between the sea and the ravine, near the cliffs, at the road crossing, and a little further inland at a place where a small cottage had been built. On the Dunbar side of the burn, about halfway between the road and the sea, stood a house called Broxmouth, belonging to the earl of Roxburgh, in a walled park of its own.[5]

The English tumbled into the town, 'a poor, shattered, hungry, discouraged army', said Lieutenant Hodgson. Another complained of the 'want of drink, wet and cold' which were 'our constant companions'. The army secretary John Rushworth said he sent 1,400 men off by ship, in addition to the 500 who had been sent by Cromwell from Musselburgh, and at least some of those 1,400 were sent from Dunbar, to the confusion of the Scots who saw the embarkation. Besides being hungry, ill, wet, and thoroughly miserable, the army had lost at least 2,000 men to this evacuation, and as many more to death by sickness and enemy fire in the various skirmishes and confrontations. Cromwell claimed that he was down to 7,500 foot and 3,500 horse at Dunbar, though others would add another thousand, which would presumably be the artillerymen. These figures show that Cromwell had lost a quarter of his men since the muster of July 19.[6]

It is certain that the Scots well outnumbered the English. Cromwell claimed the enemy had 6,000 horse and 16,000 foot, which, rather surprisingly, is exactly double, in total, the numbers he said he had. But others suggest an even higher number of horse. And this was after several purgings, which had removed several thousands of soldiers from the ranks, and several hundred officers from their commands. Yet three fresh regiments, perhaps those troops from the north whom King Charles had hoped to co-opt at Perth, joined Leslie as he marched to Haddington. Certainly the Scots were much the larger of the two armies.[7]

The English troops, grumbling and moaning in the enjoyable manner of all soldiers, were disposed into the fields between Dunbar and the Brock Burn as they arrived. The artillery was at first consigned to the churchyard, presumably because it was out of the way there. Guns took some time to emplace, and required the presence of lots of supplies. However, when it became clear that there was to be no immediate attack from Doon Hill, the guns were brought out and distributed more usefully, partly among the regiments, who had two of the smaller guns each. The main guns, the 'great guns' they were called, culverins and demi-culverins, were planted at a farmhouse, closer to the Scots, but still behind the line of the burn. This means that the English army was moved forward during the night of September 1, and was now camped closer to the burn than to the town. Someone had done some rapid scouting, and had discovered that the burn was only passable in its last mile, and that the ravine upstream provided good protection against any movement from the hill. No doubt, at the same time, Broxmouth House was occupied; it provided too convenient and defensible a strongpoint to be ignored, and its upper storey permitted a view of the whole of the terrain, including the hill upon which the Scots were camped. The small cottage across the burn was also occupied, by a detachment of thirty infantrymen from Pride's regiment and six troopers from Fleetwood's. All this shows the English army recovering its balance after the march from Haddington, a professional display of highly competent military administration.

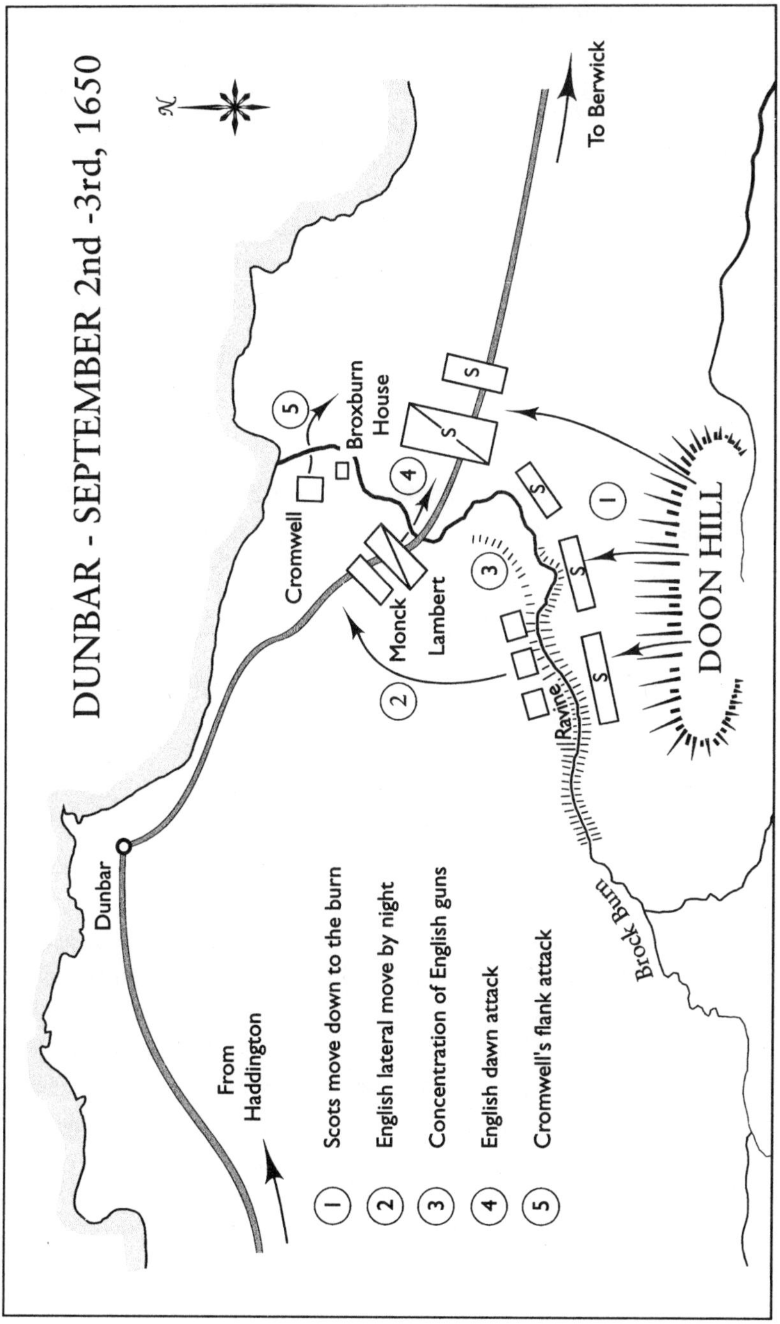
DUNBAR - SEPTEMBER 2nd -3rd, 1650
To Berwick
Broxburn House
Cromwell
Monck
Lambert
DOON HILL
Ravine
Brock Burn
Dunbar
From Haddington
1 Scots move down to the burn
2 English lateral move by night
3 Concentration of English guns
4 English dawn attack
5 Cromwell's flank attack

Next day, therefore, September 2, the English army was formed up for battle, the more cheerful no doubt for a night's rest, food, and the prospect of a fight. Cromwell had arrayed them in the traditional order, foot in the centre, horse on the wings. With Fleetwood and Lambert, Cromwell now stationed himself in Broxmouth House, the best place from which to watch the Scots' movements. He wrote a hasty letter to Sir Arthur Haselrig at Newcastle, warning him to be prepared in case the English were defeated, but telling him also to keep the danger secret from all except the Council of State. It is, for Cromwell, a notably incoherent letter, betraying great anxiety.[8]

The Scots had had a bad night, much more exposed to the weather on their hill than the English in their lower camp and the town. Their supplies are likely to have been low. They had been marching for two days, camping out for two nights, and Edinburgh, whence they had marched and which was their supply base, had not had much food available to give them when they started. Their position away from the road did not allow supplies to reach them easily, and there may not have been any attempt to provide any. They were in a position which they could hold for only a short time. In a sense the positions of the two armies had been reversed. It was now the English army which was safe and comfortable in its lines, with supplies from the sea and the better billets; it was now the Scots who were exposed to the weather, short of supplies, and facing the prospect of illness.

Therefore, it was now the Scots who were anxious, at last, to fight. The committee of ministers urged Leslie on, and he was by no means unwilling. A council of war met, and decided on the plan of action. It included the old earl of Leven, Leslie himself, and six senior colonels. Colonels Montgomery and Strachan were there, and another of the victors of Carbisdale, Gilbert Ker, colonel of a regiment raised by the ministers of the Kirk. Sir James Lumsden, lieutentant-general of the foot, and, like Leslie, a veteran of Marston Moor, Major-Generals Sir John Browne of Fordell and James Holborne, an Englishman, were the others. This was an exclusively military council: Leslie was not by any means forced to fight by the clerical committee, nor even by the council of war, as rumour had it later. He chose to fight, and he was backed up in that decision by all his senior officers and by that committee.

This has to be emphasised, because the influence of the ministers has been blamed for the decision. There seems no real evidence for this, and even Leslie did not use the excuse afterwards. He would not have left his Edinburgh lines if he had not been willing to fight at some point. Cromwell's destination was obvious from the beginning, and Leslie's own march was clearly aimed at Doon Hill from the time he left Haddington. The advantage of that position was clear to everyone, as also were its disadvantages. Once on the hill, Leslie knew he would need to move in a day or two, and, having come so far, he could scarcely retreat. The battle was on from the moment he decided to camp on the hill.[9]

The difficulty was that the Scots were now in a very awkward situation. The English were not going to attack up the hill, so the battle had to take place at the bottom of the hill, and, given the position of the ravine, that meant in the flattish area between the foot of the hill and the cliffs. So Leslie's first task was to get his forces to the low ground without allowing them to be picked off bit by bit by the enemy, or taken in the flank. So he had to guard the ravine, and he had to occupy the low ground in strength. All day on the 2nd he shuffled his forces downhill, watched carefully by Cromwell and Lambert in their eyrie in Broxmouth House. First Leslie moved part of his infantry down the hill to line the ravine, with a proportion of his horse on their left flank, inland. The rest of the horse moved down towards the low ground, adding itself to the end of the foot line, to form the conventional cavalry-infantry-cavalry line. But Leslie then fed more and more troops towards the low ground, first as far as the road, and then expanding the line gradually further and further towards the sea. The main mass of his horse were on this low ground, and the rest of the Scots foot moved in behind them. It was well and carefully done, the touch of a professional commander evident.

The isolated cottage, on the Scots side of the burn, which had been occupied by the thirty English soldiers the day before, was attacked in the evening, by two troops of Scottish lancers. The object of the attack was partly to remove the English outpost, but also, and perhaps mainly, to take prisoners for interrogation. It seems that Leslie had a suspicion that Cromwell was intent on escape rather than a battle, and he wanted to make sure. The six troopers of Fleetwood's regiment were quickly driven off, and three of the infantrymen from Pride's regiment were killed. When three of the foot were captured, the rest were simply driven off. There was considerable ill-feeling about this, for the English believed that they had been given quarter, but then they were 'cut and mangled in a most barbarous manner'. Pride's regiment were most annoyed.[10]

One of the prisoners, an old soldier, one-armed, was brought before Leslie, as the trooper had been at Haddington. 'Do you intend to fight?' the general asked.

'What do you think we are here for?' was the reply.

'Soldier,' Leslie went on, 'how do you intend to fight when you have shipped half of your men, and all your great guns?'

This was presumably the purpose of the interrogation. Ships moving out of the harbour with the English sick had no doubt started a rumour, and the removal of the guns from the churchyard, and the distance the Scots had to peer, through the rain, had exaggerated the scale of the English evacuation.

But this was an old soldier. He wasn't going to give anything away. 'Sir,' he replied, surely with a guileless look, pityingly, 'if you please to draw your army to the foot of the hill' – which movement he had been watching all day from his post in the cottage – 'you shall find both men and great guns also.'

All this free talk scandalised a listening courtier. 'How dare you answer the general so saucily?' he demanded.

'I only make answer to the questions demanded of me,' was the staunch reply.

Leslie obviously had no objection to straight talk. He let the man go, again as at Haddington. He returned to the English side and was taken to report to Cromwell. He had, he claimed, lost twenty shillings in the escapade. Cromwell gave him double. An old soldier, indeed.[11]

Leslie had got accurate information, but he interpreted it according to his preconceptions. He believed the English army was raddled with sickness, and that Cromwell was intent on saving what he could, beginning with his great guns. He believed the English were standing on the defensive, which was true enough at that time, and that they would stand still until he was ready to attack them. He knew the Scots army was double the English and it did not occur to him that the smaller army would attack the larger. So his deployments during September 2 were designed to get his army into a position to launch an attack next day. He ignored the actions of the enemy. He intended to attack next morning, and he expected the battle to be over by 7 a.m.

So confident were the Scots that there was some discussion about offering terms to Cromwell and his men before the fighting broke out. Some of the Scots suggested that the English should be offered their lives and their freedom, so long as they left their arms, ordnance, and ammunition, and should be allowed to march to England with their swords only. Others, the majority no doubt, were unwilling to let the English invaders and despoilers off so lightly. Discussion turned to the disposal of the prospective prisoners. 'They had thought of sending those they should take prisoners beyond sea.' All the ingredients of over-confidence were clearly present throughout the Scots army.[12]

Cromwell and Lambert – Fleetwood, more an administrator than a battle tactician, was apparently off organising – watched the Scots all day, ignoring the evident threat to Broxmouth House as the Scots came closer. Cromwell had ordered the army forward, so that its front lay along the line of the burn, but it was still arrayed in the old way, with cavalry flanking the foot. When Leslie began moving his forces he watched carefully, and finally, in the afternoon, it became clear to Cromwell what the Scot intended, and he quickly saw how to deal with it. He turned to Lambert and told him he saw 'that it did give us an opportunity and advantage to attempt upon the enemy'. Lambert had seen it too, at the same time. Cromwell called in Monck, who agreed with them. They went off to the town for a meal and a meeting of the council of war.[13]

Cromwell had decided to attack. Some of the colonels, who had not been able to watch the Scots' movements as he had, had decided that they were beaten. Some had concocted a scheme to send the foot away by sea, and have the horse break out by land. Cromwell left the argument to Lambert, who argued that the losses in such a move would be too great. He then went on to list the disadvantages of the Scots' position, and laid out the plan of attack. The key to the whole situation was the position of the Scots' left wing, where part of their infantry and a third of their cavalry were crowded into an awkwardly narrow space between the ravine and the slope of Doon Hill. There they could be effectively isolated from the rest of the Scots army, and pinned down by a much smaller force, which would appear to threaten them from across the ravine. They could also be bombarded by the great guns. That meant that the greater part of the English force could be used to attack the main Scots body in the low ground. The imbalance of numbers would thus be partly righted. The other colonels, once apprised of the possibilities, all agreed.[14]

By then it was dark. During the night the English army was reshuffled so that its main strength was concentrated on the low ground. The guns were manhandled forward and concentrated on a narrow front in a bulge of the land where the burn curled towards the Scots side. This was just beyond the mouth of the ravine, so that the guns commanded the junction of the Scots massed horse and foot on the low ground with the foot of the centre and left. From there the guns could fire into the Scots masses and at the same time prevent much of the foot from moving to the assistance of the cavalry on the low ground.

The attacking force was put under Lambert's command. Cromwell brought all his cavalry to the low ground, and put six cavalry regiments into the assault. Monck commanded a brigade of three-and-a-half foot regiments, having offered to do so when some opposition arose in the council to the planned role of the foot. This meant there had to be a lot of movement during the night: the horse on the right wing, inland, had to be brought across behind the centre to the low ground, some of the foot had to be shifted from the right to the left as well; the remaining foot along the ravine had to be spread out more thinly; the guns had to be manhandled forward into position, with all their paraphernalia of carriages, powder, and ammunition. Colonel Robert Overton, recently arrived, was given command of a brigade of one-and-a-half foot regiments which was deployed to protect the guns. Behind the 'van', as the assault force was called, were two reserve forces, Pride's brigade of three foot regiments, and the final two cavalry formations, Cromwell's own regiment and the dragoons, which Cromwell himself kept under his own hand as a last reserve.[15]

This deployment was an anxious time. Cromwell was remembered later riding about all night 'upon a little Scots nag', in and out of the light of the torches, supervising all the complicated movements. He was confident enough that the Scots were not going to make a move until morning, but there was always that final doubt, and if they attacked at night – they had done so at Haddington and at Musselburgh, after all – they would catch his force in total disarray. He was 'biting his lip till the blood ran down his chin without his perceiving it'.[16]

On the Scots side it was the misery of the night which was recalled, made the more so, no doubt, in retrospect. It was, of course, raining: windy too: 'a drakie nycht full of wind and weit'. They assumed that the English were as miserable as they were, and so unlikely to attack, and, of course, their minds were fixed on their own attack in the morning. The sounds of the weather could not wholly disguise the noise of the redeployment on the English side, however, and twice the Scots were further disturbed by alarms. When nothing happened either time, they took to assuming that all alarms were false. Major-General Holborne told the companies of musketeers to extinguish their matches, all but two per company, to save match. The council of war retired to get some sleep, officers left their units for shelter, cavalry unsaddled their horses, the infantry huddled into makeshift shelters made of the stooks of corn in the fields. All evidence of English preparations was ignored.[17]

Cromwell's aim was to attack at first light, but Lambert was not quite ready. A little later, about 4.30 in the morning, an hour before dawn, the first assault, by three regiments of horse, Lambert's, Lilburne's, and Whalley's, crossed the burn at the ford of the road, and fell on the surprised, weary, wet, unprepared Scots horse. The great guns opened up at the same time, firing into the Scots cavalry from their left. Two regiments of foot marched forward to seize control of the crossing, which presumably means that they rearguarded the assaulting cavalry, and prevented any attack on the flank of the horse from the Scots foot upstream. The Scots horse recovered, armed, saddled, and, even in their confusion, made a strong counter-attack. Lambert's three regiments were slowly pushed back to the burn, and the Scots foot came forward to get to grips with Monck's foot. The

Scots were assisted by being able to charge and push downhill. The English were slowly pushed back to the burn.

This was the crisis. The English assault force of five regiments had pulled onto itself most of the Scots force on the low ground, which amounted to over half of the Scots army. The guns – a nasty surprise for the Scots, since they had not been present the day before, and some at least thought they had been evacuated – were battering both the immobile Scots left and the centre and right. In effect the main body of the Scots was enfiladed, by the guns from upstream and by the assault force at the ford. As the Scots pushed the English back, however, Leslie lost control, clearly unable to see what was going on, and certainly unable to influence events. And anyway, the counter-attack of the Scots main force was proving successful, so it seemed.

Cromwell, on the other hand, was fully in control on his side of the burn. The battle was going the way, or one of the ways, he had anticipated. He had so far committed only Lambert's brigade of horse and Monck's foot. The two foot regiments initially used were reinforced, so it seems, by the rest of Monck's brigade in order to withstand the Scots pressure, but Cromwell was still on hand with his reserve, close by the action at the ford. He had his own regiment of horse, the dragoons, and Pride's brigade of three foot regiments. The fighting was concentrated at the road crossing, between Broxmouth House and the mouth of the ravine. Now Cromwell led his reserve behind Broxmouth House to the lower crossing of the burn between the house and the cliffs. This brought them onto the exposed flanks of the Scots, who were concentrating on pushing back Lambert's and Monck's assault forces at the middle ford. Pride's three foot regiments came into action successively, extending the English line, with Cromwell's regiment of foot closest to the burn, then Pride's, attacking all the more fiercely for the treatment their comrades had received at the cottage the day before, and then Lambert's foot regiment, formerly Bright's.

Cromwell carefully aligned each regiment before its attack. Lambert's was the crucial one, and 'he comes in to the rear of our regiment, and commanded to incline to the left', as Lieutenant Hodgson remembered, which movement allowed them to outflank the Scots line. It was sunrise as they were ready, and Hodgson 'heard Noll say "Now let God arise and His enemies shall be scattered"'. At this signal all three regiments charged as one, into the Scots infantry. 'I never beheld a more terrible charge of foot than was given by our army,' wrote the army secretary Rushworth, 'our foot alone making the Scots foot give ground for three quarters of a mile.' 'I profess they run', Cromwell shouted exultantly. He was remembered later laughing 'as if he had been drunk, and his eyes sparkled with spirits, carried on as with a divine impulse'. The whole army caught his excitement. Lambert's cavalry stopped retreating and charged the Scots horse, and Cromwell's own regiment of horse joined in. Monck's foot brigade advanced up the hill, with Monck himself 'at the head of them, with his pike in his hand'.

Pushing up the hill, the outnumbered English drove the Scots back and back relentlessly. The retreat destroyed such cohesion as the Scots retained. The cavalry broke and fled, blundering into some of their own foot in their confusion. Some went south along the Berwick road, others back over Doon Hill and towards Haddington. This spelt the doom of the Scots infantry. Charged by the English horse, they died in their thousands. Two regiments, that of Campbell of Lawers' Highlanders, and probably that of Sir John Holden of Gleneggies, stood and died in their places. One of them was destroyed by 'a troop of horse' which 'charged from one end to another of them, and so left them to the mercy of the foot', though it does not seem that much mercy was extended. But the lesson was clear to the rest of the right-wing foot, and they progressively 'threw down their arms, and fled', or surrendered. The unengaged left also fled, with their arms.[18]

Cromwell led a relentless pursuit. But his battle-exaltation did not let him lose control. He halted Hacker's regiment of horse and calmed them by getting them to sing the 117th Psalm. Shortest of Psalms, it was one most suitable for the moment:

> Praise the Lord, all nations,
>   extol Him, all you peoples;
> for his love protecting us is strong,
>   the Lord's constancy is everlasting.
> O praise the Lord!

Then he led them in a ruthless and disciplined destruction of the remnants of the Scots forces, for a distance of eight miles. Other English horse pursued the fugitives almost to Edinburgh. The Scots army was utterly destroyed. Between 3,000 and 4,000 died on the field, and 10,000 were taken prisoner, half of them wounded more or less seriously. No more than 8,000 demoralised and scattered survivors escaped, and only half of those rallied to Leslie in the next few days. All the Scots' guns and 180 colours were also taken. The English casualties were minimal: 'not twenty men', Cromwell claimed, probably understating. The prisoners included the Scots lieutenant-general of the foot, Sir James Lumsden, Lord Libberton, the Provost of Aberdeen, Alexander Jaffray, and several members of Leslie's own staff. Jaffray recalled that he had his horse 'shot under me, and I having received two wounds in my head, one in my right hand, and one in my back'. This was the price of defeat at an individual level.[19]

It was a superb victory, by an outnumbered, sickly army against a confident, well-led foe. And it was due, above all, to Oliver Cromwell. Of all his battles this was his masterpiece. His strategy in the campaign so far had been active without success, with almost all the cards in Leslie's hands – though his marches did eventually extract the Scots from their trenches – but at Dunbar his tactical brilliance shines like the exaltation he showed at the culmination of the battle. The secret had been to neutralise the Scots' superiority in numbers by the surprise attack out of the darkness, and by effectively ignoring at least a third of their soldiers, while at the same time using every man of his own. None of the English troops stood around doing nothing, all were employed usefully, whereas the Scots were far too crowded in the main battle zone, or were unused on the left wing. Plus, of course, Cromwell's timing of the decisive stroke, which he personally directed. And all done with the minimum of English casualties.

CHAPTER FOUR

A REARRANGEMENT OF PARTIES

September 4 – December 24, 1650

THE news of the battle spread. Cromwell did his bit. At least seven of his letters were dated from Dunbar on September 4: to the Speaker, to the Council of State; to Haselrig in Newcastle (enclosing the worried letter of two days before, which he had not been able to send); to his son-in-law Henry Ireton, the Lord Deputy of Ireland in Dublin; to Lord Wharton; to his wife in London; and to the father of his daughter-in-law in Hampshire. And these are only the known letters. Governor Fenwick of Berwick knew of the battle by rumour on the morning of the 4th, and for certain when he wrote to London about it in the afternoon. The people of Edinburgh discovered the defeat of their army when the Scots fugitives poured in through their gates, and Perth, where the king was, seems to have heard as early as the night of the 3rd. But other places in Scotland heard more laggardly. Peebles, not much further from the battlefield than Edinburgh, did not hear until the 5th, nor did Lanark. Many places, like Edinburgh, would have heard the news first from the lips of fugitives. The news reached London on the 7th, and had reached the royal Secretary Nicholas at Antwerp by the 13th, more or less accurately, apparently from London.[1]

But victory in the long-sought battle was not victory in the war. The Scots army might have been defeated or have fled, but the Scots as a whole would not admit defeat. Leslie reached Edinburgh, collected such forces as he could find – about 4,000 men, mainly cavalry – and moved rapidly on to Stirling. The magistrates and ministers of Edinburgh fled with him, or took refuge in the Castle. At Stirling, an inquest began immediately. Leslie was blamed at first, and replied by blaming the laziness of the army, and the negligence of the officers. He did not mention – he did not need to – that these lazy men and negligent officers were the survivors of the successive purges, and so were themselves the elect of the godly. He accepted his 'share of the fault', and offered to resign. There being no competent replacement, his resignation was refused, and no more was heard of casting blame on anyone. Thus Leslie was left in a much stronger position from which he could impose his strategy on the next phase of the war.[2]

Leslie was still the Kirk party's preferred commander, in default of any serious alternative, but the defeat at Dunbar began the process of breaking up their party. It was reported that the king had fallen on his knees to give thanks for the defeat of his army when he heard the news of the battle,[3] though since the source of this story was Colonel Strachan, one of the king's more virulent Scots opponents, this may be only a figure of speech or malicious gossip. Yet it was a fact that a substantial fraction of the Kirk party took the defeat as a clear sign, not that they were 'mistaken', as Cromwell had suggested, but that their alliance with the king was the prime cause of the defeat. The army, in other words, even after the purges, had been an impure instrument, and it should have been purged still more fiercely, beginning with the king. The remedy, in their estimation, was an ideologically purer army, and preferably one with no Royalist connections at all.

The main proponents of this view were Colonels Strachan and Ker, and Sir John Chiesly, a former commissioner of the Scots Parliament in London, and one of those who had negotiated with the king in Holland, with Johnston of Wariston ditheringly tending towards their view as well. In the desperate manpower shortage after the battle, a proposal to raise troops over and above the required legal levy from the west was revived. The organisation was the Western Association, modelled on the English parliamentary associations whose armies had been the foundation of the New Model. It had been formed in 1648, partly to resist the Engagers, and it was out of the west that the Kirk party had raised its army to seize power in the Whiggamore Raid. The Association had faded away, having served its leaders' purposes, but was now revived by their more zealous subordinates. It was now a union of the counties of the south-west Lanark, Renfrew, Ayr,

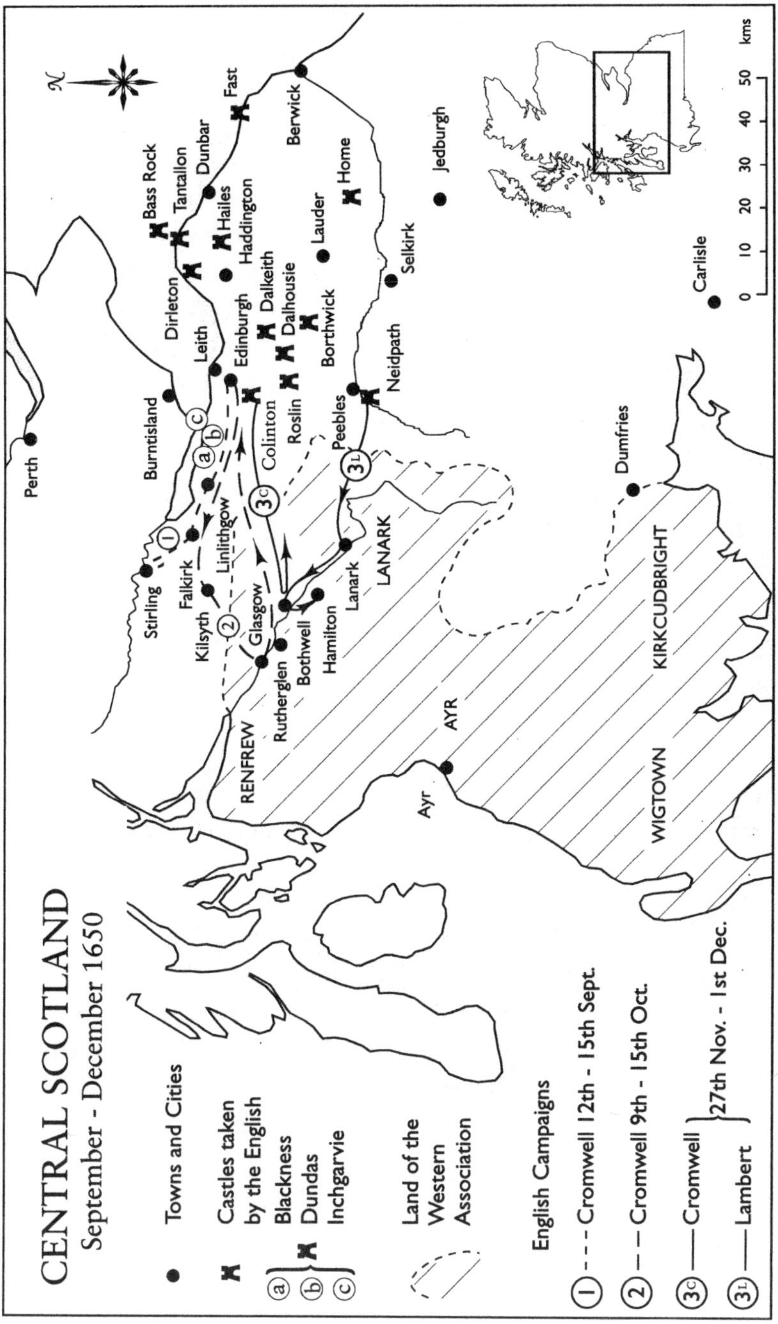
CENTRAL SCOTLAND
September - December 1650
Towns and Cities
Castles taken by the English
Blackness
Dundas
Inchgarvie
Land of the Western Association
English Campaigns
Cromwell 12th - 15th Sept.
Cromwell 9th - 15th Oct.
Cromwell
Lambert
27th Nov. - 1st Dec.
Perth
Burntisland
Stirling
Falkirk
Kilsyth
Linlithgow
Glasgow
Rutherglen
Bothwell
Hamilton
Lanark
LANARK
Colinton
Roslin
Peebles
Neidpath
Edinburgh
Leith
Dirleton
Dalkeith
Dalhousie
Borthwick
Bass Rock
Tantallon
Dunbar
Hailes
Haddington
Lauder
Fast
Berwick
Home
Selkirk
Jedburgh
Carlisle
Dumfries
KIRKCUDBRIGHT
RENFREW
AYR
Ayr
WIGTOWN
0 10 20 30 40 50 kms

Wigtown, and Kirkcudbright. Argyll, Bute, and Dunbartonshire, which had been in the original Association, now no longer participated, perhaps in part because of the marquis of Argyll's predominant local influence.

The Association had actually been revived some months before, as an anti-Royalist grouping. Despite the fact that it was composed of shires, its strength lay in the inclusion of such places as Glasgow and Paisley. In fact its revival is first recorded in the burgh records of Paisley, and one of the driving forces behind it was Patrick Gillespie, a Glasgow minister. Now it was given a new shot in the arm by the arrival of Ker and Strachan. The Committee of Estates, meeting in emergency session at Stirling, sent Strachan, Ker, and Sir John Chiesly to command their new force. The prospect of keen reinforcements was always welcome, but better still, from the committee's point of view, Strachan and Ker were now separated from Leslie. They had loudly blamed him for the defeat at Dunbar, and had refused to obey his orders. Since they had both fought valiantly in the battle, and had considerable support for their views, in the Committee and in the Kirk, it was easier to let them go off than to discipline them. Yet they were by no means welcomed wholeheartedly in the west. In particular the nobility were very suspicious of a force they did not control. The earl of Cassillis, another of those who had negotiated in Holland, and a senior member of the Committee of Estates, complained of the expense of the western levy, and kept his country of Carrick (part of Ayrshire) out of the levy; the earl of Eglinton, father of their dashing cavalry colleague Colonel Robert Montgomery, refused to have anything to do with them, and in fact disbanded men he had begun to recruit rather than serve with the two colonels.[4]

Demands inevitably emerged for a new purge of the king's household. Charles had already despaired to the extent that he had written to the Prince of Orange, asking him to send a ship on which he could escape if necessary, and this new threat to remove the last few congenial men around him drove him to extremes. His suggestion that the time had come to re-admit Engagers to the army was dismissed. He was further beset by the constant attentions of the marquis of Argyll, who had kept clear events until after Dunbar, and now re-emerged, pressing his ideas on the king. He received promises, and he managed to get custody of the regalia, the 'Honours of Scotland', but, since the king himself had no power, Argyll's efforts were largely wasted. They did confirm the king in his detestation of the man himself, however, in which sentiment he found himself in unaccustomed agreement with the Kirkmen.

The king was in despair. It was impossible for him to work with the Kirk party, since they would yield no power to him. So now he began to organise a conspiracy. At the same time, others, in Fife especially, drew different conclusions from the defeat at Dunbar. They pointed not to the impurity of the army, but to the purgings as the cause of their defeat. They issued their own formula for recovery: a reconciliation of Royalists, Engagers, and the Kirk party, and the re-opening of the army to the purged soldiers.[5] The hammer blow of Dunbar had thus exposed the cracks in the polity of the Scottish nation, and those cracks were widening steadily as time passed.

Meanwhile Cromwell and the victorious English army were finding that exploitation of their victory was by no means easy. On the day after the battle, in the midst of writing his victorious letters, Cromwell had released the wounded Scots prisoners, which disposed of half of them. He scarcely had enough food for his own army, never mind as many prisoners. But he could not simply release the fit men to fight again. So the unwounded – about 5,000 men – were then ordered south to be held by Haselrig at Newcastle. This was a distinctly unpleasant business. The prisoners were rank and file, separated from their officers. A considerable number simply ran away as soon as they could, before the English guards were organised, and this weeded out the more intelligent. The rest refused to move at first, until several were 'pistolled on the spot'. No food was provided for their journey, or at least what was provided sufficed for the guards with very little left for the prisoners. There were still some thousands who reached England. At Morpeth they were turned into a cabbage field for the night. They were so hungry that they devoured the cabbages raw, roots and all. Sickness inevitably spread among them. In Northumberland they were the responsibility of Sir Arthur Haselrig. Cromwell had written to warn him of their coming, pointing out that this was 'not every-day's work'.[6]

This was the problem. Caring for prisoners-of-war was not normal at the time. Usually they would have been ransomed, or exchanged, fairly quickly, if officers; or killed off, or released, or recruited, if private soldiers. But the ordinary Scots soldiers were in a new category. They could not be released, since they would immediately return to their own army. They could not be killed – certainly not by an instinctive humanitarian like Cromwell – for their deaths would only inflame the rest of Scotland, and the conquest was proving difficult enough already. They could not be recruited, for this was a war of nations, and these men were fighting for their country and their homes. Nor could Cromwell spare soldiers to guard them in Scotland, for he had few enough men as it was, and his supplies were barely sufficient for his own needs.

So he sent them to England, where they were someone else's problem, in the first place Haselrig's, then that of the Council of State. Cromwell clearly knew their probable fate, for he wrote to Haselrig a second time, on September 4, referring to 'your northern guests' and asking that 'humanity be exercised towards them', for this would be 'comely'. With that he seems not to have bothered about them any more.[7]

Haselrig was told by the Council of State, in a letter of September 10, that a committee had been set up to consider the problem. Meantime it was his responsibility. While various solutions to the problem of 'disposing' of the prisoners were suggested in London, Haselrig coped. He reported at the end of October that of the 5,100 men despatched south by Cromwell, he had actually imprisoned only 3,000 at Durham when they arrived. He had supplied food and coals for them, but they were still dying, and he mentioned 600 at Durham who were healthy, and 500 who were sick.[8] It is not clear whether the other 2,000 were alive or dead.

The Council had suggested in its first letter that some of the prisoners could be used in the coal mines. Six days later Mr Frost was directed to consult with contractors about shipping them overseas. By the 19th Haselrig was told to hand over 900 Scots to Major Samuel Clarke for transportation to Virginia, and another 150 to be sent to New England. They were to be 'well and sound and free of wounds'. By the end of October Haselrig had been able to deliver only 350 to Clarke, presumably because of the sickness amongst them. Another contractor, Isaac le Grey, undertook to take 200 to Virginia, and Colonel Rookby and Captain Johnson came up with a scheme to deliver 1,000 of these Scots soldiers for service in France. None of this actually materialised, except for the few whom Clarke collected. By October 9 the Council was wondering if Ireland might be the best destination. Clarke was bringing his allocation of men to London for onward shipping, and the Council wanted to ensure that they did not go where they could be used by any power hostile to the Commonwealth – which ruled out the Rookby/Johnson scheme. The men were still on the Thames on November 7 when a complaint was laid against Major Clarke alleging his ill-usage of the prisoners, but the accusation fizzled out when the Council demanded evidence from the accuser.

Cromwell had the idea that 2,000 of the prisoners would go to Ireland. The Council worried that the Highlanders 'by reason of their affinity to the Irish', might be too dangerous there. They suggested sending 500 'others' if there were so many. On November 11, Haselrig was told to deliver 150 prisoners to Augustine Walker, the master of the ship *Unity*, who would take them to New England. Walker sold his cargo for between twenty and thirty pounds each; sixty men went to the Saugus Iron Works at Lynn, the first iron manufactory in North America; another fifteen went, ironically, to Berwick, Maine; others to York, nearby. This accounts for about half the original cargo; probably the rest died, or, one hopes, escaped. The whole problem gradually faded from the Council's attention, as the prisoners died, as more escaped (though not many after they reached Durham), and as small groups were sent away. The last mention in the Council was that some of the sick men should be sent to the Blackwall pest house, the contractor to pay for their keep and recovery.

It seems likely that the majority of the 5,100 men Haselrig said were sent south from Dunbar died on the march or in prison in England. Of the rest a fair number escaped, mainly during the march to Newcastle and Durham, and most of the rest – but perhaps no more than a thousand, perhaps even less – were sent overseas, to Virginia and New England, and perhaps some to Bermuda. In one sense all this is an indictment of the general inhumanity of war; more austerely it is a telling indication of the inability of the English state to cope with a problem which, as Cromwell pointed out, was 'not every-day's work'.[9] But perhaps the Council would regard the whole affair as a success: few of the prisoners ever returned to Scotland to fight again.

Cromwell largely ignored the problem of the prisoners once they were in England, and there seems to be no indication that the Scots authorities bothered about them either. There are no official enquiries about them, perhaps in part because the Scots themselves had had the same fate in mind for the English had they won at Dunbar. Meanwhile the direct exploitation of victory began as soon as the prisoners had been sent south. Lambert was sent on to Edinburgh to secure the city, and then the rest of the army marched to Leith. All the work on the defences, which had continued until September 2 in Edinburgh, availed nothing in the absence of the Scots army to man them. Possession of the port of Leith now provided Cromwell's forces with the essential base for supply that he had needed since the invasion began. He garrisoned it temporarily with four regiments under Lieutenant-Colonel Paul Hobson. Edinburgh, however, was different. The city itself was his, but the castle still held out. The governor, the old earl of Leven, had fled to Stirling with all the rest, but the deputy governor, Sir Walter Dundas, was a strong Covenanter of the Strachan type, and was thought to be staunch. And so he was, for a time. Cromwell's early attempts to get him to surrender were futile.[10]

This caused Cromwell major problems. The Castle was impregnable, at least until the English army had a proper supply of siege artillery, and so it had to be blockaded. This tied up men, and the army was short of manpower, even though Haselrig sent up two regiments of recruits who reached Dunbar soon after the battle. The fortifications of Leith had to be repaired and strengthened, and Cromwell sent to Haselrig for masons to do the work. But it was even more necessary to press on into Scotland, to prevent the Scots from rallying. As it turned out, the delay of several days at Edinburgh, caused largely by the failure of the Castle to surrender, had been crucial. Cromwell detailed Colonel Overton as governor of Leith and Edinburgh with three regiments, and took the rest, on September 12, west towards Stirling.[11]

It rained. The army marched slowly, six miles the first day to Niddry Rows, then six more to Linlithgow. The heaviest guns were scarcely moveable and were sent back to Edinburgh. Falkirk was reached on the third day. He took Dunglass Castle, but the garrison of Callandar House, near to Falkirk, defied him, and he let it go. Another short march brought the army to within a mile of Stirling, and Cromwell summoned the town. His trumpeter was refused admission, for the very good reason that none of the Scots were confident of resisting his assault and so wanted to conceal their weakness. No more than 5,000 troops were holding the town and castle, and though Chancellor Loudoun was too pessimistic when he called them 'green, raw-levied soldiers', for most of them were survivors of Dunbar, he also admitted that Stirling 'is not yet fortified as it should be'.

Cromwell got his men to prepare for an assault, bringing up ladders and moving forward, but then he changed his mind and called them back. His army was too small to risk many lives in a potentially costly assault. It was perhaps a mistake. The Scots bluff was successful, but it was still a bluff. And the capture of Stirling, so soon after Dunbar, would have had a devastating effect on Scots morale. But there was that new army gathering in the west, and Edinburgh Castle lay untaken in his rear. William Rowe was even then writing to Cromwell with a summary of intelligence about the Scots forces. He thought Leslie had a force of about 6,000, mostly cavalry, escapees from the battle, and mostly in Stirling. He listed three more forces: Argyll with 9,000 men, Major-General Holborne with 7,000, and perhaps 3,000 in the north, a total possible force of 25,000 men, and that was without counting the forces recruiting into the army of the Western Association. And Cromwell's own army was, even with recent reinforcements, still no more than 13,000. The Council of State, even as they sent congratulations for Dunbar, also decided to send him reinforcements. Meanwhile Cromwell could not risk his present force. An assault would be costly, and a siege could not be mounted, since he could not surround the town. He ordered the army back to Linlithgow.[12]

A strong garrison of five troops of horse and six foot companies was left at Linlithgow, facing the defiant garrison of Callander House a few miles ahead near Falkirk. Linlithgow itself was to be fortified. This was yet another weakening of the field army. Back in Edinburgh, Cromwell sent out four regiments to garrisons in country houses round about. A good half, perhaps more, of his army was thus now being used up in garrisons, though they could be called out to march if needed. He met Colonel Deane, General-at-Sea, sent by the Council of State to supervise the blockade, and began plans to make a landing across the Firth of Forth in Fife. All the ships and boats along the south coast were to be gathered at Leith. On September 27, 2,500 troops were ordered there, but, once more, the attempt was cancelled before it began, perhaps because of the weather. But all these tentative movements did betray much indecision.[13]

The most significant of these moves was the garrisons sent to the countryside. Since Dunbar there had been a definite change in the English position in the land they had supposedly conquered. Maybe it was an official change of policy, more likely it was due to the scattering of fugitives from the battle, but the English soldiers were now encountering much more hostility in the lands between Berwick and Edinburgh than before. A letter published in the *Perfect Diurnal of the Army*, from an unnamed English soldier, complained of the women left in the evacuated lands being 'ill-favoured and dirty', stealing 'whatever they can lay their hands on', and murdering 'such single men as fall into their clutches'. Now there were plenty of men in the area as well, and a correspondent writing from Berwick reported in *Mercurius Politicus* that the post boy had been ambushed on the way to Edinburgh. 'Many such base injuries are daily offered us, which shows the inveterate and implacable malice of that nation.' In other words, a spontaneous guerilla warfare was developing, helped along by the general shortage of food, but rooted in nationalist outrage at the invasion. The same newsbook reported that 'not a man of note is as yet come in unto us'.

The countryside had been ignored by the English so far, but it was studded with antiquated castles, largely converted into more comfortable homes for the gentry in the past generation or so, but all originally built for defence. Local warfare had been endemic in Scotland until only two generations before, and it was still liable to break out in the north. So these houses were still defensible. In the manoeuvres around Edinburgh, it had taken a six-hour cannonade to break into Red Hall, and that was a small and unimportant house. So Cromwell's despatch of four regiments into garrison in the area around the city was an attempt to seize control of the Lothian area by holding these strongpoints. Some had fallen to the English in the collapse after Dunbar, now others were seized. Dunglass was one, another was called 'Cranford' by an English journalist, and Hailes and Colinton were perhaps others. There was little about this that was systematic, however, and the impression is of the expectation of a local Scottish collapse which had not occurred.[14]

Cromwell's real problem was his shortage of soldiers. The Council of State, after celebrating the victory of Dunbar, gritted its teeth and voted to send him reinforcements. A total of 6,000 more men were to go, according to decision of September 10, and by the 21st, as Cromwell was leaving Linlithgow in his retreat from Stirling, the details had been worked out. Colonel Fitch's regiment was ordered to Scotland, with an assorted group of horse, dragoons, and foot, from various sources. Others from the northern counties were to go to Carlisle, where Fitch, apparently separated from his regiment, was to command and lead an invasion of south-west Scotland. Two days later, Colonel Sexby's regiment was ordered to Scotland. Of all these forces, Cromwell himself was to receive a good deal less than the full 6,000, and it would take some weeks for any of them to reach him. The result of his victory was to increase the cost of the war.[15]

Scottish confidence had been revived somewhat by the sight of the English army's retreat from Stirling. The Committee of Estates had forthwith decided to implement its earlier determination that the king should be brought even more under its control. The presence of the slippery and distrusted Argyll with the King was another incentive. Argyll had extracted the promise of a dukedom from the king, and he had suggested that his daughter would make a fine queen, but he had not offered very much in return. That the king even talked to him was another measure of royal desperation, but instead of rescuing the king, the Committee blamed him, and by threatening yet another purge of the royal household they pushed him to breaking point.[16]

The Kirk party's monopoly of power had excluded many of the

royalist lords and gentry of the Highlands, and not all of them were as difficult to deal with as Argyll. The king had contacts with them, especially with the Gordon chief, Lewis, marquis of Huntly, but also the earls of Atholl and Airlie. These men, and others, had some military resources to hand, their followers having been largely excluded by the Committee from Leslie's army. Charles contacted them, and made plans for a seizure of power. The date was provided by the Committee, which decided that the king's own guards would be purged by Johnston of Wariston and Alexander Brodie of Brodie on October 3.

The plot was elaborate. The guards would arrest the two purgers, Wariston and Brodie; Highlanders would have infiltrated into Perth, where the king was staying, and Atholl would bring up his men to seize the town; Huntly and the other chiefs would gather, at a separate rendezvous; Lord Dudhope would seize Dundee from his home base at Cortachy Castle ten miles away. If everything went according to plan, it would be spectacular, and overnight the king would be in control of all Scotland north of Perth. But it was far too intricate to work. In particular, the king himself was fatally undecided about the whole thing. He still had the option of escaping to Holland, and gave instructions for some money to be transferred there shortly before the *coup* was to take place.[17]

The final group to be told were the Englishmen with the king. He told the duke of Buckingham on October 2, the day before the planned purge. Buckingham spread the news among the rest, who were horrified, and put it to Charles that it was all far too risky. At the same time, the Scots involved were pressing him to send the word out to act, fearing that they would be implicated by the many rumours which were circulating. Charles was undecided. He went out of Perth on the night of the 3rd, met Lord Dudhope, and then found that only a few of the expected Highlanders were at the rendezvous. Dudhope took him to Cortachy Castle, and from there the king retreated up the glen of the Southesk to Clova. He must have ridden over forty miles that day, and he had ended up in the middle of nowhere, in a dirty cottage, totally isolated from any of his supporters.

The result of all this was confusion. Some got the word to cancel, and did not move; others heard the call to action, and rose; some who rose discovered the cancellation, and went home; others heard that the king had ridden, and went to join him. And, of course, the word also reached the Committee of Estates, which was convened in emergency session by Chancellor Loudoun. They put the city of Perth on the alert, which foiled Atholl's projected seizure of the town, and sent to Colonel Robert Montgomery to gather up such troops as he could find in Angus and use them to prevent any Royalist rendezvous. They also sent Sir Charles Erskine of Scottiscraig to ask the king to come back, expressing amazement at his conduct, but also promising to work out a way to restore him to his other thrones of England and Ireland.

Charles had a most uncomfortable night in his hovel. Erskine reached him in the morning with the Committee's message, and then the arrival of Colonel Montgomery with 600 horse made the king's mind up. He returned to Perth. On October 7 he apologised to the Committee. It seemed that he had sunk even lower than ever. The Committee and the Kirk party had triumphed once more.[18]

Cromwell had heard of these events, called 'The Start' in Scots history. How much of the detail he had heard is unclear, but it was obvious something unsettling had occurred. He brought up a force of six regiments of foot and nine of horse to Linlithgow on October 9, and wrote to the Committee of Estates, describing their king as a hypocrite and a malignant, and blaming him for 'the calamity of war lying upon the poor people of this nation' – just the charges which had brought his father to the executioner's block. The Scots may well have felt that someone else was really to blame for their calamity.[19]

Without waiting for a reply, Cromwell then marched his army right across central Scotland, in front of Stirling, first to Kilsyth, and then to Glasgow. He wrote to the city to warn of his approach, and, just as at Edinburgh, the magistrates and many of the ministers instantly fled, to escape contamination. The experience of one who remained in the city shows that they were very sensible to do so. On Sunday, October 13, one of the ministers who remained, Zachary Boyd, sermonised mightily to a partly English audience in the High Kirk, inveighing strongly against the English invaders. As a result, he was then invited to Cromwell's lodging where he was 'overwhelmed . . . by a prayer of two or three hours' duration'. Not a fate to be courted lightly.[20]

Next day, on a rumour that Leslie was intending to mount an attempt to relieve Edinburgh Castle, the English started back to the east. The army marched back by way of a more direct route (that now taken by the M8 motorway). It marched fourteen miles the first day, over double its usual rate, and camped the next night, the 15th, at Blackburn, due south of Linlithgow. The alarm was false, so the opportunity was taken to occupy half a dozen more of the fortified houses in the area south and west of Edinburgh.[21]

This expedition, as usual, had had more than one aim. Partly it was intended to demonstrate to the Committee of Estates that Cromwell and his army could come and go more or less as they pleased, and that his retreat from Stirling had not been a defeat. The letter to the Committee was incidental to this. Certainly Cromwell hoped to exploit the recently revealed differences between the Kirkmen and the king, but those hopes cannot have been very strong. On the other hand, the appearance of a Western Association army was certainly a new development. The ideology of the Association, basically anti-Royalist as it was, was one which Cromwell could easily exploit. Both Strachan and Ker had shown already that they had much sympathy with the English republican position, and both men had already been involved in discussions with English officers, Ker in the conference on the sands in July, and Strachan before the Corstorphine confrontation in August. It was a messenger from Strachan who brought the story of Charles kneeling in thanksgiving at the news of the Dunbar defeat. Strachan had been wounded in that battle; the king's conduct in the Start was scarcely likely to win such a man over. So Cromwell's western excursion was also undertaken in the hope of winning the westerners over to the English anti-Royalist camp. He sent his trumpeter to suggest a meeting. This had one significant result. Strachan and Ker were with Wariston and Chiesly at Dumfries. The latter two prevented any meeting, but the two colonels were clearly still interested. The suggestion was thus unproductive in an immediate sense, but once more progress was registered in chipping away at Scots unity.[22]

Communications with the westerners thus had no immediate result.

The English force at Carlisle was apprehensive, but with little reason, for the westerners had no interest in invading England, only in reforming Scotland. Nevertheless Cromwell made sure. He sent two regiments to Carlisle to reinforce the garrison, and sent Commissary-General Whalley and Colonel Hacker with them – presumably their regiments were the ones sent. The strength of the Carlisle force – several thousands by now – is a measure of the size of the Western Association army, gathered in only a few weeks.[23] But that army was really no threat to Carlisle. At Dumfries, in fact, they were too busy to respond seriously to Cromwell's overtures. They had produced their own manifesto, called the Western Remonstrance.

This was the primeval Kirk party in politics. There was, the Remonstrance demanded, to be no truck with the king, at least until he proved himself a true and believing covenanter, and no invasion of England.[24] Presumably this was expected to procure the withdrawal of the English army. The Remonstrance was directed at the Committee of Estates, but it was already too late. The Committee had turned away from their extreme position in order to conciliate the king. His apology to the Committee on October 7, for the Start conspiracy, had been the first time he had attended any of the Committee's meetings, but from then on he attended regularly. At that time the Committee's main concern had been Cromwell's approach towards Stirling which began two days later, and the activities of the Highland Royalists who had been called out by the king, but who had proved to be much less willing to disband.

In the circumstances the Committee had to conciliate the Royalists. An offer of an indemnity was made to Atholl, who had already been told to disband by the king. Simultaneously Major-General Sir John Browne of Fordell was sent with a small contingent to enforce the disbanding of the others. But Browne was beaten in a surprise attack by Sir David Ogilvie at Newtyle in Angus, and the various Royalist chiefs insisted that they would only disband if an act of indemnity was passed for them all collectively. The Committee sent Leslie north with 3,000 horse to deal with them, but before he could do so, two envoys came to the king from the Royalists promising to obey *his* orders. They had coalesced into the 'northern band': Huntly, Atholl, the noted commander John Middleton, George Mackenzie, earl of Seaforth, the chief of the Mackenzies, Sir George Monro, the former Scots commander in Ulster, Sir Thomas Mackenzie of Pluscardine, a Dutch mercenary officer Johan van Druschke, and others: altogether, a formidable group who could, in combination, command a fairly strong force, and give it experienced military leadership.[25]

The effect of the Dunbar defeat on the narrow party rule of the Kirkmen, therefore, had been to break Scotland into five ideological-cum-geographical fragments. The south-west was loyal to the Covenant and also sympathetic towards the English republican invaders; the north was strongly Royalist, and the defeat of the Kirkmen's army at Dunbar had allowed them to reveal their power; in the west was the enigmatic and ambitious marquis of Argyll, who could command several thousands of his clansmen; in the centre, and still the strongest military power among the Scots, were the Kirkmen. They were in control of the Scots Parliament, the Kirk's General Assembly, and the functioning government of the Committee of Estates, and geographically they controlled most of the centre, Stirling, Fife, and the north-east, and the king was with them as well. The fifth fragment was that which had been conquered by the English, and was undoubtedly in the most desperate case of all.

The centripetal force exerted by the defeat at Dunbar had driven these various sections apart. It was no longer possible for all of them to operate together. At the same time, each of them was clearly too weak to withstand the English alone, so it remained to be seen which of them would link up. If the Kirkmen and the westerners joined, the king would be effectively finished, for it would be relatively easy for these radicals to make a peace with Cromwell at the king's expense. Lifelong imprisonment was his probable fate in such a case, unless he was able to escape by boat to the Continent. The alternative was a junction of the northern Royalists and the Kirkmen. In that event, it could only be under the banner of the king as the unifying force. And that would mean a continuation of the war, for the King's aim was still to become King of England and Ireland as well as Scotland, at Scottish expense if necessary.

As Leslie began his march north against the northern band, the

Western Remonstrance was presented to the Committee of Estates, on October 22. The Committee put off a decision, referring the remonstrance to a meeting to take place on November 14, and to the Commission of the Kirk, which was also to meet on that day. Meanwhile attempts were made to get the westerners to modify their terms. This revealed the fragility of the whole situation, for the Remonstrants reaffirmed their hostility to the king, while at the same time turning on the strongest advocates of an accommodation with Cromwell: Strachan was jailed and two other officers were cashiered.[26]

The Kirk party in the Committee was now in the surprising position of being the centre party, strong for compromise with those on either wing. However, the Remonstrants proved obdurate, as could have been expected. The Royalists, by contrast, had to deal with David Leslie, whose main priority was military unity in the face of the invader, and he did not have the rooted objection to the idea of the king as king which so angered the Remonstrants. Leslie met the northerners at Strathbogie on November 4, and signed an agreement by which the Royalist rebels agreed to disband in return for an act of indemnity for them all. So, by the time the Western Remonstrance came up for discussion finally on November 14, the Kirkmen already had an agreement with the Royalists.[27]

Cromwell, meanwhile, was having to cope with the breakdown of government and all authority in that part of Scotland which the English had supposedly conquered. Colonel Robert Overton had been appointed governor of Edinburgh and Leith, and commanders had been installed in control of garrisons at Linlithgow and near Stirling, but little had been done along the landward line of communications. Some of the 'great houses' in the area round Edinburgh had been captured, but their garrisons were liable to be removed in the event of a serious march, as to Glasgow. Overton had attempted to institute a benevolent regime in Edinburgh, with the intention of winning over covenanting opinion, and in accordance with the prevailing Independency and toleration of the English republican regime. Looming over the city, however, the Castle was an ever-present and occasionally active symbol of the defiance of the rest of

Scotland in the very heart of the capital. Cromwell had recruited Scottish miners from Prestonpans and Glasgow to begin a mine to enable him to take the Castle. By the time he returned from the western excursion to Glasgow, the mine had been going for three weeks and was said to be only fifteen yards from completion, but from then on the rock was impossible to penetrate. The arrival of mortars allowed a serious bombardment to begin about the end of October, from a position to the north of the Castle, west of the unfinished Castlehill Kirk. But the distance was great, accuracy was impossible, and the results were poor.[28]

Tension between the occupiers of the city and their victims was constant. The root of the matter was national feeling, but it often emerged as religious differences. Cromwell did not attend any of the city churches (unlike his practice at Glasgow) but held sermons and prayer meetings in the house of the earl of Moray in the Canongate, outside the city wall, where he was staying. Even meetings contrived with the friendliest intentions could go wrong when people behaved in their normal manner. An English officer at dinner with the magistrate upon whom he was billeted suddenly heard a guest preacher saying grace, and, as was normal practice, praying for the success of the Scots Covenant. The officer burst into arrogant reproaches. Another officer who had been ambushed by moss-troopers and had killed one of them, boasted of his success in public, and dared his Scots audience to say he was wrong to have killed his assailant. A bystander accepted the challenge, killed the officer with his sword, stole his horse as he fell off, and rode away freely. And this took place at the very gate of Cromwell's own lodging. Even in the city they occupied most heavily, the English were not safe. Defeating the Scots army had been difficult enough, conquering the land itself was proving to be an infinitely more complex problem.

The conduct of the ordinary English soldiers was reasonably polite and considerate, but they were inevitably resented. They were quartered in the larger public buildings, the University, the High School, some of the churches, and Holyrood Palace. They took what they needed, breaking up the furniture for firewood, and were generally careless with property. Holyrood caught fire as a result. Wariston thought it a judgment on the royal house.[29]

Resistance in the land around Edinburgh hardened. Groups of men, moving swiftly on horseback and based at untaken houses or castles, raided English posts, ambushed small English detachments, or simply took food. The English, adopting an old term from the border wars, called them 'moss-troopers'. By the time Cromwell returned from Glasgow, they were causing concern. One group, a party of Dutch mercenaries under Captain Augustine Hoffmann, and a second, under a captain called 'Sandy Kar' – Alexander Kerr – were especially busy.

Cromwell was moved to issue a fierce proclamation against such activities, using the sort of language and issuing the type of threats which would be familiar to any commander of occupation forces faced with resistance fighters. His men, he said, were 'spoiled and robbed, but also sometimes barbarously and inhumanly butchered and slain', and their assailants were 'not under the discipline of any army'. His anger is evident, and it was based in part upon his own strict conduct. He had been zealous in preventing plundering and indiscipline in his own army. He had told his soldiers 'that if any man should plunder, he would make him exemplary, and hang him at first proof, and would proceed severely against the officers that connive at or countenance them'. And this was not mere words: he *had* hanged English plunderers. So now he made exactly the same promise to the moss-troopers: 'I will require life for life, and a plenary satisfaction for the goods, of those parishes and places where the fact should be committed unless they shall discover and produce the offender'.[30]

More direct measures were required. His own army needed to be kept busy and the moss-troopers deprived of their bases, and these purposes could be happily combined. Several of the great houses in the Edinburgh area had already been occupied. Now a serious campaign was mounted to clear the whole territory round the city. Lord Lothian's house at Newbattle Abbey was in English possession by October 21, when Cromwell gave Lady Lothian protection against occupation and looting. Dalhousie, south-east of Edinburgh, was taken a week later. These two, close to Dalkeith and only half-a-dozen miles from Edinburgh, illustrate the precarious and narrow hold the English had on the hinterland.[31]

Both had been captured even before Cromwell's fire-breathing proclamation was issued. Others, more distant from Edinburgh, were also more difficult to take. Dirleton Castle, north of Haddington, was the base for Captain Watt, one of the more active of the guerillas. It was attacked in October, by Monck, and again early in November by both Lambert and Monck together, commanding 1,600 men. Monck, the artillery specialist among the senior commanders, had brought along two mortars, which had just arrived from Hull. The difference they made is shown by the contrast between Monck's two attempts. In the first he did not even attack; in the second, with the mortars, the castle surrendered after the fourth shot. The walls of these castles were old, but they were also thick and powerful enough to resist the low-trajectory cannon balls of the great guns; mortars, on the other hand, could fling their explosive shells over the top and into the living quarters. No guerilla fighters could cope with such treatment. The castle yielded sixty prisoners, and their horses, all of which were said to have been captured from the English. Ten English prisoners were released. The castle was then rendered unusable, and Captain Watt was shot.[32]

Lambert and Monck together were also sent against Tantallon Castle on the coast east of Dirleton. This was more a base for sea-raiders, and along with the castle on the Bass Rock a couple of miles offshore, it was a great nuisance to English shipping. Tantallon's landward fortifications, however, were immensely strong, and it seems that bases closer to Edinburgh were more urgent. Tantallon was left alone for the present. Roslin, however, not far from Dalhousie, in a strong position with the River Northesk enclosing it on three sides, was quickly captured by Monck a few days later. Cromwell himself moved out to deal with one of the strongest of the castles, Borthwick, offering decent terms to the commander on November 18.[33]

Borthwick was on the edge of the cultivated land; south of it were the thinly populated Moorfoot and Lammermuir Hills. It was also an apparently immensely strong place, protected by deeply entrenched streams on three sides, a massively solid pile containing, so it has been calculated, 30,000 tons of stone. It was commanded by its own laird, the 10th Lord Borthwick. Even more important was its position, and its symbolism. If Cromwell could control Borthwick, he would control the whole of the Lothians, with only Tantallon still holding out between Dunbar and Linlithgow. And that would free plenty of troops for more activity to the north and west. It was thus a crucial stronghold. Lord Lothian, on the instructions of the Committee of Estates, asked Colonel Ker of the Western Association to relieve the castle.[34]

The order was, of course, a deliberate test of the association's willingness to obey the Committee. The Western Remonstrance was even then being considered by the Committee, and by the Commission of the Kirk. The Committee had brought the king to heel, and had succeeded in squashing the Royalists of the Northern Band; now here was an ideal opportunity to deal with the westerners as well. In these circumstances Lothian was clearly chosen as the messenger because he could reinforce the order from the Committee by an appeal to family, for he was Colonel Ker's kinsman, a major factor amongst border families such as the Kers. But times had changed. Put on the spot, Ker refused to march, claiming that his forces were inadequate. This was probably true enough, for they could not hope to tackle the English, and most of them were newly recruited, but Ker did not stop at a simple military excuse. He added, gratuitously but significantly, that he did not feel the action would be advantageous, and then made comments indicating his lack of confidence in the king, and his unwillingness to serve him.[35]

Borthwick surrendered next day, November 22, giving the English control of the Lothians. Much more significant, however, was the clear breach now evident between the westerners and the Committee of Estates. The Committee decided on one more effort. Colonel Robert Montgomery was sent with a strong force of cavalry to take over the command of the western army in place of Ker. Montgomery had many qualifications for the job. He was a covenanter, an old colleague of Strachan and Ker, and was a noted cavalry commander himself; he was a son of the earl of Eglinton, who was a major magnate in the lands of the Western Association; he would, therefore, have a hereditary appeal; he could extend recruiting to Eglinton's lands; he could import a needed element of support from the local nobility into the movement; he was the captor of the king at Clova. A better choice could scarcely have been made.

Montgomery rode out of Stirling at the head of a force of 3,000 horse. If he succeeded in his mission by taking command of the westerners, he would have some 7,000 men under him. This would be a formidable force, if largely inexperienced. Together with the active sympathy of the people of the areas under precarious English control, he might dominate all southern Scotland, and carry the war back towards the east.[36]

Cromwell meanwhile had apparently come to the conclusion that the force under Ker had to be eliminated, and he plotted a trap for it. As soon as Borthwick surrendered, Major-General Whalley was sent south to Lauder with a cavalry force. This may well have been a bait for Ker, who was uncomfortable about his inaction. Ker brought his force to Peebles before November 27, possibly intending to attack Whalley. But on that day Cromwell launched two more forces. He took the major portion of the cavalry army on a march due westwards; Lambert, with 2,000 or 3,000 horse, rode south, directly for Peebles. Ker, however, retreated. Whalley and Lambert joined forces and followed him. Lambert also compelled the surrender of Neidpath Castle at Peebles, and then they rode west. By the 28th Lambert was at Lanark, and there he stayed for two days. Cromwell, meanwhile, with eight regiments of horse, rode west by the southerly route by Blackburn and Kirk o' Shotts, where a ninth regiment joined him. He reached Hamilton on the 29th, but he could not cross the Clyde because Ker had seized control of Bothwell Brig. The aim of this major operation was clearly to trap Ker's force between the two English forces, and Cromwell was perhaps never intending to cross the river. But Ker, who had a substantial force of five regiments, withdrew in the night, so breaking contact with Cromwell's force. The ambush had apparently failed. Cromwell turned back and began the return march to Edinburgh.

This is one interpretation. Another is that Cromwell's very obvious approach march was designed to attract Ker's attention, which it did, for he came north from Peebles to Bothwell. But Cromwell did not expect to fight Ker, assuming that the western army would not fight such a powerful force. By holding Bothwell Ker certainly prevented Cromwell from reaching him. Cromwell thus retreated, and Ker pulled back from the bridge, leaving it available for Lambert's force the next day.

Cromwell may not have heard of Montgomery's mission – the colonel set off after Cromwell's march began – but Ker certainly had. He decided that the best reinforcement for his position was a victory. The arrival of Lambert's force, which crossed Bothwell Brig and marched as far as Hamilton, seemed to provide a suitable victim. Ker thought Lambert had no more than a small detachment, and when Lambert camped just south of Hamilton, Ker decided to attack. Ker had about 1,600 horse and dragoons, camped at Rutherglen. He thought Lambert had 1,200 horse, but his actual strength was 3,000, double that of Ker. He marched by night, intending a surprise attack while the English were camped or scattered. But his approach, on a moonlit night over frozen ground, was detected by Lambert's men, who, in enemy territory, were thoroughly alert. The Scots advance force charged into the town and drove the English detachment out. But in the morning the main Scots force was caught disorganised, crossing a burn, and routed and scattered with contemptuous ease. Ker himself, his arm shattered, was captured, along with less than a hundred of his men. About as many were killed. The rest fled.[37]

This was almost the last gasp of the Western Association. Strachan, perhaps overcome with remorse, attempted without success to rally some of the defeated, who fled towards Ayr. Some probably headed north to join Montgomery, but neither of these men had any real power, and most of the men simply went home. Strachan gave up. He surrendered to Lambert since now the English were, to him, the least unsympathetic of all the surrounding factions. He was universally condemned as a 'hypocritical traittour' – ironically, since he was actually remaining quite loyal to his long-held beliefs.[38]

Strachan was taken to Edinburgh, where the Castle was still holding out. The mining had been unsuccessful, even when the conscripted Scotsmen were supplemented by imported miners from Derbyshire. A new battery had been put up, but the garrison was refraining from counter-action. It seems that the governor, Sir Walter Dundas, forbade firing without his express permission. He was also much troubled in his mind. He was of much the same political persuasion as Strachan. The defeat of the Western Association army was no doubt a clear sign to him of the folly of opposing the English. The arrival of Strachan gave Cromwell another weapon with which to belabour the unfortunate and perturbed governor. Before beginning his new bombardment, Cromwell summoned the castle formally on December 12. He adopted his usual tactics, emphasising the differences between the Covenanter governor Dundas, and the increasingly Royalist tone of the Committee of Estates. Dundas asked for ten days and the right to consult his superiors, but this was refused. Instead Cromwell suggested he consult with people closer to him, such as Strachan. Dundas agreed to this next day, but the people he nominated refused to give him any guidance. The bombardment began the day after.[39]

Dundas had been isolated for weeks. He did not know of events in the north, except as they were filtered through Cromwell's version. But now he received both news and supplies in a spectacular fashion. The Dutch moss-trooper, Captain Augustine Hoffmann, set out with 120 horse and supplies from Fife for Edinburgh. He scattered any enemies he found, killing eighty men and capturing six during his ride, while losing just as many. He rode right through to Edinburgh, and threw himself and his last thirty-six men, with the supplies they carried – 'all sorts of spices and some other things' – into the Castle.[40] Coming from the north, he could report to Dundas whatever he understood of events at Perth and Stirling. The result was scarcely what the Committee of Estates intended when the morale-boosting raid was authorised. Dundas was apparently dismayed at the news he heard, and he tried to reopen negotiations with Cromwell the very next day. He failed, and there was a delay in events because of a snowstorm. Then on the 17th the English bombardment began again, more fiercely than before. Dundas was caving in, and Cromwell was now at last able to begin serious negotiations for a surrender. Two officers were allowed out to the city, and, after a long night's talk, agreement was reached for the surrender of the Castle on December 24.[41]

Cromwell allowed generous terms, as he usually did. The garrison could march out with its arms and goods, the citizens could collect the belongings they had placed in the Castle for safe keeping, but the guns and the Castle became English. The surrender duly took place on the 24th, the day before a Christian anniversary neither side acknowledged. The English claimed that the supplies left in the Castle were enough for a much longer siege, but it was not the problem of supplies which had bothered Dundas. He showed his priorities by dismissing his men to their homes a few miles on the way to the Scottish lines, and returning to live in Edinburgh, to be reviled as a 'traiterous villain'. He had Strachan for company. These two men had put their ideology before their patriotism, just at the time when their countrymen were doing the opposite. For their pains both were found guilty of treason by the Scots Parliament, and expelled from the Kirk.[42] Meanwhile the soldiers out of the Castle who did return to the Royalist side were thrown into jail. Clearly it was a difficult time to be a Scot.

CHAPTER FIVE

THE SCOTTISH RECOVERY

January 1 – June 4, 1651

As if to compensate for the loss of the last foothold in their capital city, only a week later the Scots staged their king's coronation. With the war as a background, it was scarcely a happy occasion, and the grudging manner of the Kirkmen made it downright miserable. Preliminary fasts for the ceremony included one for the sins of the royal family: the man who actually placed the crown on the king's head was the seriously unpopular marquis of Argyll; the Chancellor Loudoun placed the king on his throne. The ceremony had been filleted of 'superstitious' elements like the anointing, but the king had to swear to uphold the Covenant as well as his Coronation Oath; and Charles was subjected to a sermon by Robert Douglas, a recent convert to the moderate view, who made it plain that the coronation did not alter the distribution of power in the kingdom. The English mocked the event, quoting the king as saying that 'I think I must repent too that ever I was born'. The whole event was a clear demonstration of the power still wielded by the Kirk party.[1]

Nevertheless the ceremony did mark a change. The king was no longer a harried victim, but a source of power in his own right. It was this which had driven Strachan and Ker and Dundas away into the arms – in one way or another – of the English invader. They could plausibly argue that they had been staunch in their views, while the Kirk party was shifting. Robert Douglas's uncomfortable sermon at the coronation may have been distasteful to the king, but it also showed the distance the Kirkmen had moved. It was in fact the despairing cry of a Kirkman drowning in a sea of Royalists.

This sea had begun to swell on December 14, when the Kirk

Commission had at last agreed that the crisis of the country demanded resort to a full levy of all possible sources of military manpower.[2] The destruction of the Western Association's army a fortnight before had helped them to this conclusion. The elimination of that radical force meant that the levy was now perforce extended to the Royalists. This did not necessarily mean a cession of real power to the king, for the appeal was not to party but to patriotism. Yet these men were party men above all. Few of them could mouth nationalist sentiments without putting them in party terms. Therefore the admission of Royalists into the army also opened the way to power for those same men, and above all for the king.

The next step in this process came on December 20, with the appointment of colonels to command the newly authorised levies. These men would be responsible for actually raising and organising their regiments. Inevitably they would attract Royalists. Former Engagers and old Royalists were included in the list, and even men who had fought with Montrose were permitted to bear arms again. The earl of Atholl, Lord Ogilvie, and the earl Marischal were commissioned as colonels and allowed to recruit regiments; all had been in rebellion against the Kirk party government as recently as October. The earl of Crawford-Lindsay, a former Engager, joined them. Highland chiefs of no known enthusiasm for the Covenant were admitted. The Act of Parliament ordered that the levy be applied to all men who could bear arms, and conditions and exclusions which the Kirk Commission had imposed were widely ignored.[3]

The gradual rise of the king to real power in Scotland meant that the danger of a Scots invasion of England was substantially increased. The sentiment of Strachan and Ker and their fellows, that the Scots should have nothing to do with foisting an unwanted king on their southern neighbours, was now at a discount, though not wholly absent. As the king became more prominent, the sentiment was bound to increase. It was fuelled by reports of widespread Royalist conspiracies in England, which were only waiting for a spark to light them. Embryonic organisations existed all through England; the earl of Derby still controlled the Isle of Man, and had much influence in Lancashire; a Royalist Western Association had a well-advanced organisation in the counties from Cornwall to Hampshire and Gloucester; other similar, but less competent, organisations existed in other areas. The king was in contact with all of them.[4]

The problem with conspiracies is that if they are small they are ineffective, if large they leak. Norfolk was the scene of one of the latter, in November. Meetings of Royalists had been held for months, with gradually more and more men becoming involved; an air of expectancy spread; rumours abounded. The parliamentary garrison heard all about it. But Colonel Rich at Norwich had apparently nothing concrete on which to act until November 28. Then, by accident, the word to rise was given. Four small groups gathered and moved towards Norwich, telling each other that there were 1,500 men there waiting to rise and join them. Colonel Rich called out the militia, brought out his cavalry garrison, and sent word to a detachment of dragoons at Lynn. There was no fight: the Royalists scattered and forty were captured.[5]

Here was food for thought for all sides. Norfolk had been a parliamentary county all through the civil wars, part of the formidable Eastern Association, yet now it could stage a rebellion. It was ineffective, but it had happened. If rebellion could happen in Norfolk, it could erupt anywhere. The republic's fright is shown by the savagery of the punishments: twenty men executed, a dozen jailed. For the Royalists, on the other hand, it was a fiasco of the first magnitude. Not only was there little secrecy, but there was little support, and virtually no organisation. Rumour ruled. And the punishments were a major deterrent to other actions of the type. Yet, once again, the fact that it was a rising in *Norfolk* could be held to be encouraging. Other areas were more traditionally Royalist. The basic Royalism of England could be said to have been demonstrated.

Also demonstrated was the even clearer fact that the English Royalists themselves did not have the strength to take on the republican government and its frighteningly efficient armed forces. There had been suggestions that the best way to spark a successful Royalist rising was to bring in a force of mercenaries – Hessians or Lorrainers, for preference – who could land somewhere on the east coast and form the tough, professional core of a new Royalist army. The rumours had reached the Council of State, who put the local governors on the alert. But there were no Hessians or Lorrainers, and no-one ever seems to have seriously believed that they existed. At the same time there was, paradoxically, a basic English hostility to the idea of the king returning to England at the head of a *Scots* army. If an army was to be the instrument of restoration it is difficult to see a more suitable one than that of the Scots – Charles was their hereditary monarch, after all. This readiness to contemplate the use of mythical European mercenaries but at the same time to recoil from using the actual Scots army is basic to the whole Royalist dilemma.

The fundamental reason, of course, was that the Scots would demand a political price; the mercenaries would not. The Royalists were instinctively rejecting the only foreign army which would have any chance of success, because they were not willing to pay the price in political dependence and religious imposition. The man who saw all this from the beginning was Edward Hyde, who always insisted that the Restoration must come about from within England. Without that invitation no Restoration would be in any sense permanent or stable. Yet how could the Royalist sentiment be voiced clearly when the republican government's army was so appallingly efficient and zealous? It was a dilemma which was quite inescapable, and insurmountable. Nevertheless, the vision remained: that the entry into England of a powerful force with the king at its head would bring Royalists springing out of the ground wherever he went. It was a vision which would only fade when it was tried and had failed, but it had to be tried if Hyde's alternative vision was to have its chance.

Before any possible Restoration of royal power in England at the points of Scottish pikes, however, the king had first to survive in Scotland itself. The kingdom of which Charles was now crowned king was sadly truncated. His capital was in the hands of his enemies, as was the southern and richer half of the country. On Christmas Day the English garrison at Carlisle had finally bestirred itself and moved into southern Scotland, occupying Dumfries and Kirkcudbright, and taking Kenmore Castle. The elimination of the Western Association army had removed any organised opposition in the area – though there had been fairly serious negotiations between the Carlisle commanders and the Association – but it had also let loose a scatter of belligerent Scots.

The problem of guerilla resistance had, as a result, spread westwards. Much of southern and south-western Scotland was relapsing into anarchy: 'the land mourning, languishing, left desolate, every part thereof shut up, and not safe going out nor coming in', the diarist Nicoll commented. Major-General Whalley had been sent to garrison the west, and was at Lanark for a time, with other garrisons at Hamilton and Ayr at least. But none of the garrisons was large, distances were long, and the country was difficult. For example, Colonel Hacker at Peebles was fighting moss-troopers late in December. Cromwell's army still only controlled the land within reach of its arms, and it would continue that way so long as an army and a king and a regular government survived north of the Forth.[6]

The winter had now fully gripped the land. A snowstorm had held up the siege of Edinburgh Castle in mid-December, and conditions became even worse in January. The shortage of grass prevented much in the way of military operations. Cromwell's march to Hamilton in late November had been swift and brief, perhaps partly because of the lack of food. But wild weather could also conceal movements. Captain Hoffmann had a force of 500 horse, and was active in harassing the English outposts. On January 11, a Scots force of about 800 horse marched out of Stirling to threaten Linlithgow, under the cover of 'tempestuous' weather. It was foiled in its aims, but only just, and turned back to Stirling.[7]

What may have been the English reply to this raid was an attempt by Monck to make a landing in Fife at Burntisland just a week later on January 18. This was a revival of the momentary scheme of Cromwell's in September. Monck commanded a force of 1,500 men in the enterprise, but he was unable to land. Some days later another attempt by the frigate *President* and other ships also failed when the leading ship got stuck in the entrance to the harbour. A week later Monck made an attempt to take Blackness Castle, on the Firth no more than two miles from Linlithgow, but failed again. About this time also a ship called the *John* was captured by the garrison of Tantallon Castle, the Scots base which Lambert and Monck had failed to capture in November. The cargo of shoes, boots, saddles, and beer for the army was a bad enough loss, but Cromwell himself had a personal cargo on board. It may be that other ships had been taken there recently as well.[8]

The Firth of Forth was thus only partly under English control. Tantallon and Bass Castles forced ships heading for Leith from England either to run their gauntlet – the channel between them was only a mile and a half wide – or to swing well to the north in order to avoid them; if they went north they could fall prey to Scots ships out of the Fife ports, and Burntisland, which Monck had attacked, was the best of the Fife harbours. Up river along the Forth the narrows at Queensferry were blocked by the Scots-held castle on Inchgarvie Island and by Scots guardships based there and on both coasts. Blackness was one of these bases, and Inverkeithing on the north was another. So all this English activity was not necessarily an invasion of Fife so much as an attempt to gain control of the Firth to make the approaches to Leith safer.

The failure to land at Burntisland, nevertheless, did provoke some serious rethinking, though the only evidence for this is in its result. On February 10 the Admiralty Committee of the Council of State approved a plan to concentrate at Leith fifty flat-bottomed boats, which had to be built specially at London and Newcastle. They were to be manned by a captain and five seamen each 'of approved fidelity to the commonwealth'.[9] The suggestion for this can only have come from the Englishmen at the Firth, in the light of their failures with bigger ships. It also indicated a much firmer intention to be able to land in Fife if necessary. Cromwell was widening his options.

This ineffective military activity went on against the background of information from the Scots side which was both encouraging and ominous. Reports of the new levy greatly exaggerated the Scots numbers. Cornet Baynes reported that the Scots were raising 60,000 men, and that the intention of this army was to invade England. Cromwell certainly had more accurate information than that. One of his spies, John Mosse, was caught in Perth about this time. Cromwell disowned him and offered to exchange him. The Scots asked for Sir James Lumsden, the lieutenant-general of the foot captured at Dunbar, which shows the value of the intelligence the Scots thought he was supplying, but Cromwell refused. Cromwell also had other sources. Wariston had come to Edinburgh to get the Scottish Records, captured in the Castle, which were to be released in accordance with the terms of surrender, and Wariston talked a lot. Cromwell strung him along so much that he came under suspicion on the Scots side. He was also very much of the Strachan and Dundas persuasion, as Cromwell well knew.[10]

The news Cromwell heard was not just of the recruiting of the new army. A mutiny of troops in Stirling had brought Major-General Holborne under suspicion – he was English, which may have been enough – though he was quickly cleared. Here was one of the dangers of the Royalist rise to power. The old army was the Kirk party's army, and many men clearly did not welcome the new, and perhaps arrogant, recruits. At Stirling a corporal was reported as saying that 'going as they did in taking in malignants, he would rather join with Cromwell than with them'. This was the issue raised by Strachan and Ker and Dundas, still very much alive in the Kirk and the army. The faction in control, who favoured the compromise with the Royalists, were now known as 'Resolutioners', and were opposed by 'Protesters'. All during January of 1651 protests and messages of support came in from synods and presbyteries from Ayr to Aberdeen. Inevitably the argument drove the various proponents further apart, and the Resolutioners became steadily more Royalist.[11]

This was the political background to Cromwell's next campaign. He had successfully brought over several prominent men, and a military move now could well have a useful effect. On February 4 he marched his army west again, first, in more wild weather, to Linlithgow, then on to Falkirk, and further on to Kilsyth. The Scots army stayed in its warm shelters, and it was the weather which drove the English back to their bases. It also had a more useful effect for the Scots, for on his return to Edinburgh Cromwell fell ill with an ague, probably from exposure to the appalling weather. He was ill, with short periods of recovery, until late May.[12] His illness coincided with a period of relative quiescence in the campaign, but the two should not necessarily be seen as cause-and-effect. The reason for both was the winter weather. And even so a number of significant developments did take place in that time, which cumulatively cleared the way for the final confrontations.

The weather, as the English had discovered, restricted large movements, but it did not prevent relatively small expeditions. The Scots moss-troopers were as active as ever, but their bases could also be dealt with. In the Borders, Colonel Fenwick, the governor of Berwick, came out to attack Home Castle, a centre from which raiders could levy contributions from Kelso, Coldstream, and all south-west Berwickshire. The lord was not present, but his governor, James Cockburn, was defiant, asking such generous terms that Fenwick refused. Cockburn was perhaps not quite sane; certainly he did not fully appreciate the dour seriousness of men like Fenwick – though Fenwick himself was of a Border family. Cockburn answered Fenwick's summons with a jingle:

> I, William of the Wastle,
> Am now in my castle,
> And awe the dogs in the town
> Shan't garre me gang downe.

This would have been gloriously defiant if it had been backed up by military sense. As it was, Fenwick's own soldiers enterprisingly found a way to seize a dominant position, and Cockburn's resolve crumbled.[13]

There was considerable activity all through the Borders at this time: the Kirk session at Peebles could not meet at all in February 'because the enemy are going up and down': an English patrol was ambushed at Jedburgh, and ten men killed. The blame was laid on a moss-trooping leader called Richardson who was publicly threatened with 'exemplary punishment'; a Scots laird was fined a hundred pounds sterling for not trying to catch raiders; two Scots who ran away rather than fight their fellow countrymen had their houses burnt down; two parishes were fined three hundred pounds each, which was the equivalent of what the moss-troopers had levied; Selkirk was fined five hundred pounds for sheltering moss-troopers, and when a mass meeting voted not to pay, the town found itself occupied by a force of English cavalry, which jailed the magistrates until they agreed to pay up. 'The famine among the Scots poor draws on apace.'[14]

Neither side could now withdraw. Far too much was at stake. The whole English republican regime demanded a victory and conquest. Defeat of its army and its great general in Scotland would stimulate all the latent Royalist sentiment in England, and the dream of Charles II, to be borne to London on a rising Royalist flood headed by a Scots army, would become that much closer to reality. For the Scots it was equally clearly a matter of political, religious, national survival. No possible compromise between Royalist independence and English conquest now existed. And between these positions 'the famine among the Scots poor draws on apace'.

Victories on a small scale were sought in default of a final conquest. Home Castle was satisfying, Tantallon all the more tantalising. The capture of the ship *John*, with Cromwell's own trunks on board, may have been the trigger for the decision to besiege the castle, but this would have had to be done sooner rather than later anyway. On February 13 Monck rolled up to its gates with two regiments of foot, some great guns, and a mortar. The governor of the castle, Alexander Seaton, burnt the small town of thirty houses before the gates to give his men a field of fire. (The English commented that the town was one of the prettiest they had seen.) Monck had to use his great guns to batter down the outworks, and only then could he bring his mortar into action. The castle was simply a wall, the other three sides being cliffs precipitously falling to the sea. The strength and thickness of that wall made the mortar less effective, but the great guns successfully battered at the wall until it crumbled into the ditch. Seaton hung out a white flag for a parley, but Monck refused anything less than surrender. On February 21, after eight days, Seaton at last submitted. The prisoners were less than a hundred, with only a dozen horses, but fifteen or sixteen guns and 120 arms were taken.[15]

Again as at Home Castle, his victory was trumpeted rather more than it deserved, in the absence of anything better. Only Fast Castle, on the coast between Dunbar and Berwick, was now a significant Scots post, and that fell a few days later. Bass Castle, expected to follow Tantallon, held out. At last the English could claim the road to Edinburgh was clear.[16]

Nevertheless Edinburgh was still uncomfortably close to the front line. The Scots controlled the south bank of the Firth from Queensferry westwards, and regularly mounted raids out of Stirling as far as Linlithgow, the most advanced English garrison. Early in March all this was demonstrated when the Scots landed a force of cavalry at Blackness, no more than two miles from Linlithgow. Clearly the intention was to begin raids into the lands between Edinburgh and Linlithgow, though the Scots also expected Blackness to be the next English target. Putting cavalry in there was therefore extremely provocative, since such troops were only suitable for raiding. The Scots expectation was therefore fulfilled.[17]

Blackness was very powerful, by reason partly of its walls but mainly because of its situation on the end of the ness, the cape, largely protected by water.[18] To capture the castle, it was first necessary to control the Firth, and that in turn meant dealing with the Scots guardships which were based at Inchgarvie, the island-castle which blocked the narrows at Queensferry. Monck was now Cromwell's acknowledged expert. He took his time organising everything, but at last on March 29 a combined operation began. Three English frigates sailed up river and captured one of the Scots watch-ships stationed at Inchgarvie. They were shot at from the north shore and from Inchgarvie, but passed the narrows safely. They then bombarded Blackness from the water side. Next day Monck marched his land force from Edinburgh: 1000 infantry, formed of a company of foot from each regiment, and the artillery. Batteries were constructed, and the bombardment began. There were signs that the Scots were mounting a relief force under Major-General Massey, so Cromwell sent out a force of horse to cover Monck, and the rest of the foot then followed. This display effectively deterred the relief, and without its help Blackness fell, on April 1.[19]

The Scots attributed this rapid English reaction to treachery. Wariston had arrived at Leith on the 29th, and he was blamed, as also was an English spy at Perth, Alexander Hamilton.[20] In fact, it can more plausibly be attributed to the vigilance of the English scouts and the garrison at Linlithgow. They must, after all, have been alerted to look for some such activity by the Scots while the siege went on. On the other hand, it was certainly secret information, perhaps from Hamilton, which had led Cromwell to warn Colonel Robert Lilburne at Ayr that a party of Royalists were on their way from the king to the Isle of Man. Lilburne mounted a raid on Greenock to intercept them.

Most of the party escaped, but a Royalist agent, Isaac Birkenhead, was caught, and his papers with him.[21] He had been travelling back and forth between Man, Lancashire, and Scotland, and his papers revealed an extensive network of plans for a Royalist rising in the north-west of England, involving several rendezvous, an invasion from Man by the earl of Derby, and the assistance of a force of cavalry from Scotland under the command of two Englishmen, the duke of Buckingham, and Major-General Massey.[22]

Once again, as in Norfolk, this was not wholly a surprise to the Council of State, or to Cromwell. The Council was informed of 'a perilous plot' on March 12, after the study of Birkenhead's papers, and it responded by ordering troops into Chester, North Wales, and Lancashire, and by ordering all soldiers on leave from the army in Scotland to return to their regiments. More troops were to be raised and Worcester's defences were to be slighted.[23]

The papers also led to another agent, Thomas Coke, captured in London on March 29. His papers, and his tongue, told of preparations in other parts of the country. Both Coke and Birkenhead talked fully and rapidly, with names, dates, and details, in successful efforts to save their lives. Throughout April the implicated men were rounded up. Most were soon released, having given heavy pledges of security to deter them in the future. Most, indeed, were not deeply implicated, but had been interested sympathisers waiting for someone else to move first.[24] The rising, if it had ever taken place, would probably have been more formidable than the Norfolk fiasco – though it could scarcely have been feebler – but now it was unlikely ever to happen at all. It was yet another blow to the king's plans. As the prospects of an English rising receded, so the king's dependence on the Scots grew. But many of the Scots were indifferent or hostile to the English adventure.

For the moment the Scots army was small and scattered. Like the English invaders, the Scots were marooned by the weather and the lack of supplies. They had tackled the problem in a party spirit. The Committee of Estates was still dominated by the Kirkmen; the Royalists established a new committee, whose purpose was 'for Managing the Army', that is, recruiting and supplying, but not the conduct of military manoeuvres. It was heavily Royalist in personnel, but its members worked hard to produce the wherewithal needed by an army. They regularly went out as commissioners to enforce their committee's instructions. With the end of winter and the arrival of the warmer weather, the growth of the grass, and the greater availability of food, the numbers of soldiers concentrated at Stirling gradually increased.[25]

A source of recruits which was very tempting but tantalisingly difficult to reach was the south-west, thinly held by the English, strongly covenanting in sentiment, and reasonably well populated. For the king it was also the road to England, which had to be controlled before his army could reach to the south. In early April the local magnate, the earl of Eglinton, with his three sons, began to move in that direction. Eglinton and two of the sons intended to go by way of Dumbarton, and across the Clyde estuary. The spy Alexander Hamilton may well have given notice of this, but it was Captain Crook of Haselrig's regiment of horse, quartered at Eglinton itself, who took action. He had news of Eglinton's route, presumably from a local informant, and under his own initiative he rode through the night to intercept the party. He did so at Eglinton's house near Dumbarton, capturing Eglinton himself and one of his sons, but Eglinton's eldest son got away. The raiders captured forty horses and a thousand pounds' worth of booty, but the really satisfactory result was the prevention of Eglinton's recruiting in the west. He was said, no doubt with some exaggeration, to be able to raise 5,000 men.[26]

Eglinton's youngest son, Colonel Robert Montgomery, rode south out of Stirling on 14 April, covered by a Scots raid in force towards Linlithgow. This raid amounted to a successful skirmish, in which the garrison's commander, Major Sydenham, was badly wounded. Colonel Montgomery was similarly successful, but not quite as he would have hoped. Cromwell was warned, and he had prepared his own counter-stroke. On the 16th he drove in his coach to Leith. Wariston, who was watching, thought the army was intending a landing in Fife, for some of the flat-bottomed boats ordered in February had recently arrived. Perhaps he was intended to think so, and any Scots spies in Edinburgh with him. Cromwell was greeted uproariously by his army at Musselburgh, 16,000 to 18,000 strong. They clearly knew something was up.[27]

Having thus fixed Scots attention, the march was due west again. The camp on the night of the 17th was at Blackburn, sixteen miles from the starting point at Musselburgh, and at Hamilton on the 18th, another twenty miles on. This was swift marching, clearly designed to counter Montgomery's foray. Then they marched on to Glasgow, only eleven miles, on the 19th. And there the army stayed for eleven days.[28] If Cromwell thought that Montgomery's raid was the preliminary to a Scots invasion of England, he had clearly prevented it, though it was probably not so intended, at least not immediately. At the least, very little successful Scots recruiting would have been possible with the English army in the west.

Cromwell attended anti-English sermons in the High Kirk on Sunday the 20th, but when he sent to the ministers to invite them for a discussion they shied away. No doubt word of Zachary Boyd's terrible experience of being prayed into the ground back in December had got about. But you did not defy a man like Oliver Cromwell so easily. The English officers had a day of prayer as preparation, then on the Wednesday the refusing ministers found that the soldier-messengers were absolutely insistent on their attendance on the Lord General. By then, of course, persuasion was out of the question. Cromwell and Lambert and the others debated with James Guthrie and Patrick Gillespie, two of the inspirers of the Western Remonstrance, and former colleagues of Strachan and Ker, but they got nowhere.[29]

Glasgow had been in a sort of no-man's-land between the various armies. It was in Lanarkshire, and so part of the Western Association, and its ministers had been active in inspiring that Association's revival. The collapse of the Association left the city at the mercy of the English garrison at Hamilton commanded by Colonel Lilburne. When Cromwell marched across to Glasgow the first time, in December, all the magistrates and many of the ministers had fled, and before they came back the Hamilton garrison had demanded that the city pay 'a cess upon pain of present plundering and sacking'. In the emergency, the citizens met and appointed a committee 'free of all blemish of malignancy' who were given powers to control local taxation and to use the proceeds to buy off the English blackmailers.

This, of course, amounted to a declaration of independence of all parties, and the returning magistrates and ministers were deeply unhappy at their loss of power. So long as the committee could hold the threat of the English over the city, however, they had no need to give up control. Cromwell's arrival changed all this. There was no question of paying Lilburne's blackmail while the whole English army was quartered in the city, and the Provost and his deposed supporters decided that the time had come to rid themselves of the upstart committee.

The English did nothing to sort out the local government of Glasgow, but when the two groups began to fight they did intervene to keep the peace. On the 29th the Provost and the President of the Committee came to blows outside the Tolbooth, and had to be separated by the soldiers on duty there. The Provost then consulted with the ministers, equally deprived of power, and a plot was laid. The President was asked to meet with the Provost and his Council. He attended at the Provost's house, waiting outside, but was not called in. Inside, the Council took due note that the President was not attending their meeting as required, and then agreed that he was contumacious, sentenced him to punishment, and marched out to jail him. The Council Clerk and the President of the Committee walked through the town arguing. Outside the Tolbooth the Clerk, believing he had public support, tried to put the President under arrest. The Clerk was wrong. A crowd gathered to defeat him and once more the English soldiers on guard at the Tolbooth intervened. The *coup* had failed.[30]

In such circumstances Cromwell could be perfectly content. Glasgow was most satisfactorily in confusion, with a clear preference among the citizens for a quiet life. On the 30th, somewhat short of supplies, he gave the order to begin the march back to Edinburgh, using the southern road. He called in at two houses on the way, in the process demonstrating just why it was that the Scots wanted the English to leave. At Allanton he visited the house of Sir Walter Stewart, where Lady Stewart gave him a drink of Canary wine, and Cromwell was heavily pleasant to her and her son. The boy came close enough for Cromwell to stroke his head, not a gesture calculated to reassure any parent. Lady Stewart, a Royalist, 'abated much of her zeal' for her opinions while Cromwell visited. This was eminently sensible of her, but the tension of the visit shows clearly through the bland English report. Cromwell went on to Lady Kilsyth's house. She was more staunch in her beliefs, and tried to persuade some of the English soldiers to desert. Cromwell was furious. He replied by burning her house down, contents and all. Whatever means of persuasion he used, on Kirkmen or Covenanters or Royalists, Cromwell was a foreign invader, terrifying women and children in their own homes, and destroying property in all directions. Such a man was bound in the end to drive his enemies to cooperate with each other.[31]

The army was back in Edinburgh by May 2, disappointed at not having encountered the Scots. Many of the English garrisons in the west were now withdrawn, and Colonel Lilburne was sent to the south, to the area of Jedburgh and Kelso in Tweeddale and Teviotdale. His practised ability to live off the land in Clydesdale was now to be exerted on the borderlands. The west was now largely clear of English power. Their concentration at Carlisle amounted to a dozen troops of horse and half as many of dragoons. Lilburne and other local garrisons in the south were alerted to move at a day's notice to reinforce Carlisle, and Cromwell urged that Major-General Harrison should go across to the west, perhaps making Penrith his headquarters.[32]

All this was clearly bait for Charles and the Scots. These two had been gradually closing on each other since Dunbar, and a distribution of general commands in March showed that a serious spirit of co-operation among Royalists, Kirkmen, and Engagers had finally arrived. It also produced an army top-heavy with generals. The king was in theoretical chief command, and the earl of Leven was still the nominal commander-in-chief, with David Leslie the actual commander. In addition, there were now two other lieutenant-generals, the Engager John Middleton for the horse, and the Kirkman Holborne for the foot – but Holborne had once been dismissed after a mutiny of his soldiers at Stirling, and was under suspicion of contacts with Cromwell. Four major-generals were also appointed, Sir John Browne of Fordell and Robert Montgomery for the horse, and Walter Scott of Pitscottie and Thomas Dalyell of the Binns for the foot. For an army of less than 10,000 this was a lot of top brass. But of the making of generals there was no end: the duke of Buckingham now became lieutenant-general

Charles II. Prince Charles in 1648, aged 18, by David des Granges, showing the sensuous lips, spade-nose and cow-eyes which were to captivate women for the next forty years. A more unsuitable king for Covenanting Scotland could scarcely be imagined. It is a sign of the desperation of both sides that they came together and tolerated each other for a year and more, until their mutual defeat. But Charles escaped; Scotland was captured. *By courtesy of the National Portrait Gallery, London.*

Cromwell in 1649, by Robert Walker, recently victorious in the struggle to eliminate the king. From then he was compelled onward to the conquest of Ireland, then Scotland, and finally his own Parliament. This portrait shows him at that point in his life where he could still, just, have retired to be another country gentleman - as Fairfax did - but his participation in the regicide drove him ever on. It seems doubtful that Ireland and Scotland would have suffered conquest had it not been for Cromwell's power of command. *By courtesy of the Scottish National Portrait Gallery.*

Oliver Cromwell, shown most suitably on horseback, for he was a cavalry general. It is also the traditional posture of the ruler in European political iconography; further, the picture is an adaptation of one by van Dyck of Charles I. Like the man's policies and his government as ruler of the British Isles, this portrait was subject to many alterations and adaptations by the engraver, P. Lombart.

Dunnottar and the Scottish Regalia. Dunnottar Castle, on the North-Sea coast south of Aberdeen, was another of the almost impregnable and inaccessible medieval fortifications which held out against English conquest. It was here that the Honours of Scotland – Crown, Sword and Sceptre – were concealed until the castle was about to be taken. Then they were hidden in a nearby village. The castle was one of those of the Earl Marischal, who was captured at Worcester. The whole is perhaps a metaphor for Scotland's situation by 1652: nobility captured, castles taken, honours buried. Dunnottar *Crown Copyright: RCAHMS.* Regalia *Crown Copyright: Historic Scotland.*

commanding the English Royalist contingent, with Daniel Massey as his major-general. This was perhaps reasonable, on the assumption that large numbers of Englishmen would join the invaders on their march. Johan van Druschke, the Dutch mercenary, was another major-general. Cromwell, with an army twice the Scots' size, made do with only two generals besides himself.[33]

The reason for this multiplicity of generals, of course, was the continuing rivalry, even hostility, between the differing factions on the king's side. By this time there was only one barrier holding back a full Royalist takeover, the Act of Classes, passed in 1648 to exclude the Engagers and the Royalists from power, and which could only be repealed by the Scots Parliament. The Committee of Estates tried desperately to avoid giving it the chance to repeal, and the Commission of the Kirk avoided a direct answer when appealed to on the issue. The meeting of Parliament which should have taken place in April was prorogued first to May 21, then again for two more days. In fact, of course, the Act had been breached in the observance repeatedly already, but its formal repeal would be a significant symbolic move. Pressure became too great. The Kirk Commission laid down conditions, but they were easily met. They were embodied in a new Act passed by Parliament on May 30, where those excluded by the Act of Classes had to sign a band before being admitted to office. Then the Act of Classes itself was repealed. The Royalists cheerfully signed the band and then ignored the guarantees. In this, of course, they were only following their king's example. And then a new Committee of Estates, dominated by Royalists, was elected. The counter-revolution had brought the king at last to real power. The change was given added point by the arrival at long last of the levies from the Highlands at Stirling. They had been rumoured to be arriving for months, and their numbers had been as uncertain as their location. Now they arrived, overwhelmingly Royalist, but not so numerous as had been hoped.[34]

The difficulties of stockpiling supplies had prevented the full concentration of the Scots forces. The problem was that the area under the king's government was generally poor. The more troops gathered at Stirling, the more food was needed there to feed them, so that it was impossible to develop a magazine of supplies as a reserve.

The contrast with the English forces is demonstrated by two contrasting comments in May. When Cromwell brought his army back from Glasgow on May 2, he was able to order, immediately, the distribution of a week's supplies to the whole army, which numbered about 18,000 men. Two weeks later, at Perth, the Managing Committee had to confess that it had only six days' supply in hand for an army half that size.[35]

As a result some of the Scots troops were stationed in Fife and towards Dundee, the better to extract food from the farming population without the need to transport it any distance. The English flatboats at Leith were clearly a threat to Fife, and detachments were spread along the south Fife coast as a deterrent.[36] Nevertheless, despite all the difficulties, the Scots army was gradually gathering: its detachments were tolerably close together, and could be concentrated in a fairly short time; its chain of command was clear, if long and top-heavy; its supplies were accumulating; and its Royalism determined its destination.

Colonel Montgomery's activities in the south-west had left the English garrison at Hamilton too exposed, and on June 1 Commissary-General Whalley took eight regiments of horse west to collect the garrison and escort it back to the English lines; Colonel Alured finally withdrew from Dumfries early in June, retreating to Carlisle; Boghall Castle beside Biggar in Clydesdale was reoccupied by Scots troops. That invasion of England which had been threatened in April, and again in May, and had been discussed by both sides since the war began, had now become possible.[37]

All this marked a significant recovery by the Scots. After Dunbar Leslie could gather only 4,000 men; now, despite losing castles in the south-east, and despite the defeat at Hamilton, the army had recovered to 10,000 men at Stirling, more raiding with Montgomery, and still more spread through Fife, once more outnumbering its English opponent. The skilful use of cavalry – as opposed to the incoherent activities of moss-troopers – had driven the English back to a line from Carlisle to Edinburgh, providing the Scots with a clear field for manoeuvres and recruiting in the south-west. This was a notable achievement, due in part to the alliance of Kirkmen and Royalists, so painfully constructed during the winter. But it would still be necessary at some point to tackle the full English army. That had been reinforced, and was full of high spirits – for the reverse side of the Scots success had been the deliberate English withdrawals which enabled Cromwell to concentrate his forces. The Scots problem remained: their resources in population and supplies bore no comparison with those of their enemies. It would need something extra to tip the balance either way. An English rising would do – but this was now, after Norforlk, and after the capture of Birkenhead and Coke, very unlikely.

Another item which might tip the balance was the elimination of Cromwell. His illness since the February march to Kilsyth had lingered on for months. He was liable to a relapse if he went out. He was also uncertain about what to do. An assault on Stirling was as obnoxious an idea as ever. Another expedition to the west was possible, but would be likely to be as unproductive as those in the past. The arrival of the new flatboats in the Firth of Forth meant that the invasion of Fife was now a serious option, but that coast was guarded. Much discussion went on, and much praying, and the inactivity in early May was blamed on the lack of forage. Then Cromwell's illness struck again, and for a week and a half he was laid up. Doctors were sent from England, but he had more or less recovered by the time they reached Edinburgh. Then at the end of May he promoted Lambert and Monck to be lieutenant-generals – Fleetwood had returned to England in April – and made Colonel Deane, the naval expert, major-general. It was a sign. The general was recovering his health and vigour. And the comparable Scots recovery of strength, and of control of the west, spelt danger.[38]

CHAPTER SIX

TORWOOD AND INVERKEITHING

June 4 – July 31, 1651

THE long, bitter winter and the slow, cold spring had delayed all growth. It was only in early June that both sides came to the conclusion that serious military activity had become possible. Cromwell came out to hold a grand review of his forces in 'Edinburgh Fields' – the English term for, presumably, the open land east of the city – on June 9. He was, apparently for the first time since the march to Kilsyth in February, out on horseback to conduct the review. He had a formidable force assembled: fourteen regiments of horse, six troops of dragoons, and twelve regiments of foot, perhaps a somewhat larger force than the 16,000 which originally invaded. At the same time, Major-General Harrison's force at Carlisle now amounted to about 6,000 soldiers, a third of Cromwell's army. Adding to these the casualties and the deserters, the campaign had so far required at least 30,000 Englishmen.[1]

King Charles's forces were now largely concentrated at Stirling, in case this English concentration presaged a full-scale attack. The Scots numbers are uncertain, most estimates coming from English sources, which may well have relied on deliberate Scots misinformation. It seems unlikely, for example, that their numbers reached the 29,000 which Whitelocke quoted, but they do seem to have been much larger than Cromwell's forces. It is quite certain that they were much less well equipped than the English, and less well organised, though the arrival of the growing season did at last permit the stockpiling of a magazine of supplies.[2]

In addition, there was the force of Major-General Montgomery which was active in the south-west. He had camped near Dumbarton in the third week in May – presumably at his family home there – and on the 18th the word had spread through the south-west from the pulpits of the churches that all men between the ages of 16 and 60 should be ready to turn out. Montgomery moved to Kilmarnock and was there by 24 May. This was what had originally been intended by his father, Lord Eglinton, before his untimely capture in Captain Crook's raid. Now the plan was implemented, if without the lord. The English resistance to Montgomery's movements was minimal. He concentrated on beating up small and isolated garrisons – at Carnwath on the 31st, and at Douglas soon after, both held by no more than a troop of dragoons – and on seizing their horses. By June 1 the Hamilton garrison was withdrawn and Colonel Alured was pulling out of Dumfries. These withdrawals strengthened the main English forces, at Edinburgh and Carlisle respectively, but they also permitted Montgomery to raise forces in his homeland in relative peace. From then on Montgomery was quiescent, perhaps preoccupied with organising his new men. Another raid netted him more English horses, and Montgomery was in command of three cavalry regiments – one commanded by the intrepid Captain Augustine Hoffmann – near Dumfries on June 9. There were undoubtedly others under his command: he must be credited with 5,000 or 6,000 men, to add to the main army at Stirling.[3]

The main concentrations at Edinburgh and Stirling pointed to rival strategies. These were well known and had been discussed widely. The king wanted to use his army to conquer England, and Montgomery's removal of the English detachments from the south-west now opened the way there. Cromwell knew this full well, as did the Council of State in London. He urged them to build up another reserve force at Chester, as a backstop to that at Carlisle.[4] The Chester force could be used to block the Mersey crossings, and to dominate the Royalists of North Wales and Lancashire, just as the Carlisle force, now under Major-General Harrison, could block the Solway crossings and the narrow route through the Cumberland mountains. Cromwell's intention was to use these garrisons to halt or slow down the Royalists, and then to bring his own force down upon the invaders from the north.

All this was perfectly clear to the Royalists, of course, who had to find a way, first, of escaping Cromwell's army, then of evading the blocking garrisons, and finally, of avoiding Cromwell's nutcrackers. The Royalist assumption was still that the concentrated Scots army would march south united, and that once in England it would be welcomed as a liberator and would be joined by many disgruntled English Royalists. But with Cromwell's army concentrated at Edinburgh, it was impossible to escape him, and this was the essential first step. To be caught by Cromwell's army in open country and forced to a battle in Scotland would spell the doom of the whole enterprise before it began. It is quite clear that the Scots and the Royalists were determined to avoid such a fight for as long as possible.

So the Royalists in effect relied on Cromwell to leave the way to England open for them. He had already tempted them by withdrawing his western garrisons. It was his aim, and had been from the very beginning of the war, to get the Scots army out of its fortifications and into battle, for he knew, and had proved, that the English forces were much superior to the Scots in an open fight. But, having been bitten once at Dunbar, the Scots were now thoroughly shy. It was, therefore, up to Cromwell once more, as before Dunbar, to hazard his forces so dangerously that the Scots would once more be tempted out.

The English alternatives were clear, just as those of the Scots were. One was a frontal attack on the Scots position at Stirling. Cromwell had shown his great distaste for this often enough. One of his most remarkable characteristics as a general was his unusual care to avoid a large butcher's bill in battle. The manoeuvres around Edinburgh had been a case in point. He could have made an assault on the Scots army more than once, if he had been prepared to accept the normal casualty rate. The Leith-Edinburgh lines, the Corstorphine and Gogar positions, and afterward Stirling, were all places where an assault could have been legitimately mounted, and he declined every time. His battle casualties were accordingly few. (This consideration did not extend to his enemies, of course.) He even understated his own casualties, so it seems, so sensitive was he on this point.

Why he should be so concerned about this is partly due to the recognition that any army is a finite resource. The Scots climate and the local and army diseases were wasting it away quite efficiently enough without the assistance of the enemy. The other reason was that this English army was the main army of the republican regime. To lose it would be to so weaken the republic that it might fall. But, beyond this, there was also something personal in it as well. A little later, the prospect of a fight is said to have set him to riding about agitatedly, muttering, 'O God, spare Christian blood'. The story may be apocryphal, but it represents his normal attitude well enough. He was one of those soldiers who hated bloodshed. His soldiers knew this. It was one of the bases of his popularity with them. He also kept winning, of course, which helped. The effect of all this was to promote intelligent and devious generalship, and this, coupled with the fact that he never explained either what he did or why he did it, and rarely what his plans were, makes his military career difficult to explain.[5]

So, to return to the immediate issue, Cromwell's rejection of a frontal assault on Stirling was rooted deep within him, and was unlikely to change. But this did not mean that he was willing to let the fortress dominate him, like some Scottish Monte Cassino. There were other possibilities. Alternatives to a direct assault included the English crossing the barrier of the river Forth at fords either above or below Stirling, though neither of these possibilities had been seriously explored so far. Then there was a move reminiscent of the reverse march to Dunbar, a withdrawal from the positions gained so far, even from Edinburgh, aimed at bringing the Scots army out to reoccupy the city; this was scarcely a viable option, however, since abandonment of conquests was unlikely to do more than let the Scots move forward to yet another powerfully fortified line – such as the Leith-Edinburgh lines once more. And abandonment of the port of Leith was not to be contemplated.

The third possibility was to invade Fife. The English had made several attempts already to seize a town there, but without making a serious effort to invade. At the end of May there had been another of these small raids. Colonel Lidcott had taken a force across from Blackness Castle to seize Rosyth Castle, but found that he could not land. The castle was, in fact, on a small island accessible from the mainland only at low tide – the land was later drained, and became part of the naval dockyard – so even if Lidcott had landed and seized the castle, it is doubtful that it would have been much use as a base. The whole enterprise seems to have been an unfortunate piece of private initiative. The Scots had kept ten regiments of horse strung along the Fife coast until then; Lidcott was probably fortunate that he failed to get ashore.[6]

But now the fifty flat-bottomed boats had arrived, with their crews 'of approved fidelity to the commonwealth', and this enlarged the options. Now a landing could be made away from a regular port, and in much greater strength: the boats made real invasion a serious possibility. It was still a difficult enterprise, but the boats, and the opening of the Firth above Inchgarvie, made it less difficult than before. Yet a landing directly into the face of the alert Scots regiments of horse was not to be contemplated, and a failed landing on a large scale would be a first-class disaster.

So the Fife option depended on the Scots withdrawing their guards along the coast for long enough to allow the English to get a force ashore large enough to defend itself. But, even if they were withdrawn, any subsequent threat to Fife would bring those Scots forces back, and it was a nice point whether the distance the Scots would need to march would counter the inevitable slowness of the English landings. This is where the flatboats were important, for they permitted a much larger English force to cross and get ashore. And so long as the Scots army was concentrated near Stirling, any threat to a landing in Fife would be even more credible. So the initial requirement on the English side was to force a concentration of the whole Scots army at Stirling. This, of course, was exactly what the Royalists wanted so that they could escape into England. But many of the Scots had no wish to invade England if that meant losing Scotland in the process, and the English conquest of Fife, the richest part of Scotland still unconquered, would guarantee a loss of all their homeland. So it was in Cromwell's interest both to have the Royalist army divided, to prevent the invasion of England, and to have it united, to permit the invasion of Fife.

On the other hand, if he sent a substantial force across the Firth to invade Fife, which was obviously necessary if the peninsula was to be conquered, this would mean dividing his own army, which would in turn endanger a substantial fraction of that army in Fife, while at the

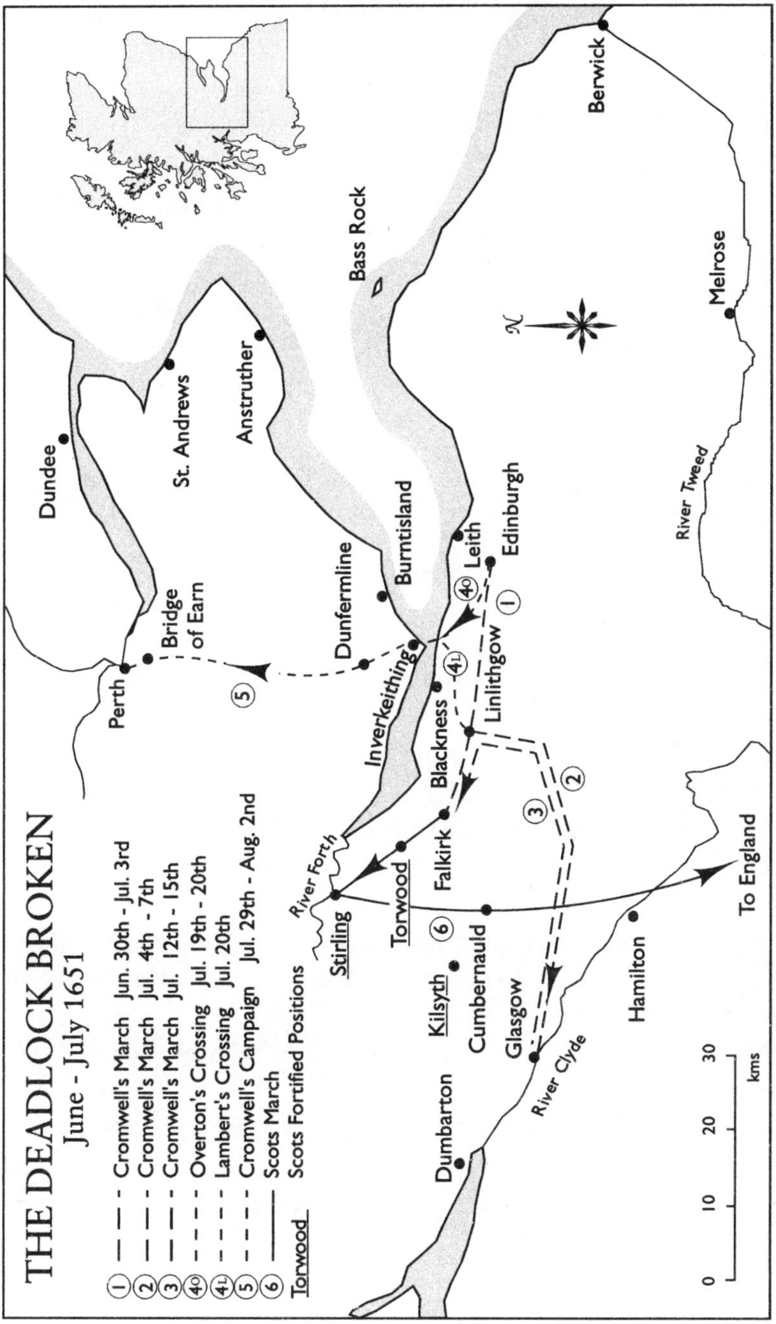
THE DEADLOCK BROKEN
June - July 1651
1 Cromwell's March Jun. 30th - Jul. 3rd
2 Cromwell's March Jul. 4th - 7th
3 Cromwell's March Jul. 12th - 15th
4O Overton's Crossing Jul. 19th - 20th
4L Lambert's Crossing Jul. 20th
5 Cromwell's Campaign Jul. 29th - Aug. 2nd
6 Scots March
Torwood Scots Fortified Positions
Perth
Bridge of Earn
Dundee
St. Andrews
Anstruther
Bass Rock
Dunfermline
Burntisland
Inverkeithing
Leith
Edinburgh
Blackness
Linlithgow
Falkirk
Torwood
Stirling
River Forth
Kilsyth
Cumbernauld
Glasgow
River Clyde
Dumbarton
Hamilton
To England
River Tweed
Melrose
Berwick
0 10 20 30
kms

same time it would permit the Scots to march south without hindrance, since the English force south of the Forth would not be strong enough to prevent the march. In the face of this intricate dilemma it is no surprise that the English army held a fast on June 16. Guidance would certainly help. Three days later the whole army was camped, ready, in the Pentland Hills south of Edinburgh, and there it remained for another fortnight.[7]

Cromwell could afford to wait. The first move had to be made by the Scots. Having gathered their army and concentrated it at Stirling, and collected there what the English estimated to be six weeks' worth of supplies, they had to do something. And it was necessary to do it in that summer of 1651, because it was most unlikely that the whole process could be repeated, or that their remaining lands could support the army for another winter. On the other hand, the English had a well-established supply line in place, and a substantial magazine of supplies had been built up. Cromwell's preparations recognised this. And, at last, on June 28 the Scots moved out, marching six miles out of Stirling to take up a powerful defensive position at Torwood.[8]

Cromwell's response was cautious. The Scots' advance might be the first move towards England, or it might be a move against Edinburgh. Cromwell's position on the Pentland Hills was chosen to cover both options, just as the Scots position at Torwood was chosen to imply both. So Cromwell's first march, only halfway towards Linlithgow, camping at Newbridge on the 30th, was designed to keep the options open. From there he could still move either towards Linlithgow, or along the well-tramped route towards Hamilton. Two marches would bring the English to Bothwell Brig, a likely staging point for the Scots marching south from Torwood towards England. This would place the English army across the line of march of the Scots south along Clydesdale.

By next day, however, it was clear that the Scots were not yet moving from Torwood. The English moved forward to Linlithgow, stayed a day, and on July 2 marched to Falkirk. There they contacted the Scots cavalry screen, which retired towards the trenches at Torwood. Next day the English marched to the Scots position and drew up their line a mile in front of the enemy. The Scots had occupied a hill, which they had fortified both on the summit and at its base, and which was protected by boggy ground in front. It was all very familiar to the veterans of the Gogar and Corstorphine confrontations, down to the skirmishing and a mild mutual cannonade. The position, like those earlier ones, was too strong to attack directly; the only hope of a battle, as before, was to entice the Scots off their hill. 'We marched up to their very teeth,' said a correspondent. The English stood battle-ready from noon till dusk, drawn up for a fight, but the Scots stuck fast, only their guns firing. There was a house nearby held by the Scots, like Red Hall near Corstorphine. This was Callander House, which Cromwell had summoned once before without result. Next morning Cromwell received reports from spies sent into the Scots camp, held a council of war, then tried once more. He drew the army back as far as Callander House, clearly threatening it. No result. The Scots did not move.

So Cromwell pulled back still further, to Linlithgow, closer to his supplies, which were now being brought by water as far as Blackness before being landed. Still the Scots stayed in their trenches. Reprovisioned, Cromwell took his army due south from Linlithgow, by way of Torphichen, a route he had not used before, and then west along the old road through Shotts to Shettleston. By July 7 the army was once more at Glasgow, having trailed its coat right across the Scots front. A Scots detachment under Major-General Massey raided as far as Linlithgow while he marched. They savaged the English tents, left standing there, thus reputedly annoying Cromwell.[9]

One of the purposes of this march was to interrupt the recruiting which the Scots were conducting in the west. Two hundred muskets were seized in Glasgow, though the recruits themselves had vanished. Major-General Montgomery might be induced to attempt something, as his predecessor in the area, Colonel Ker, had done at Hamilton. There is also a suggestion that Cromwell was intending something more permanent in the west than before. From Glasgow he sent out patrols along both banks of the Clyde estuary. One of a hundred foot and some horse and dragoons under Captain Badger reached and took Newark Castle at Port Glasgow; the other, under the enterprising Captain Crook, reached to within two miles of Dumbarton, but

Dumbarton Castle itself was scarcely to be attempted by a patrol. Cromwell wrote to Sir Harry Vane in London asking that supplies should be sent to the Clyde from the western ports of Liverpool, Chester, and Bristol.

These supplies would be needed if the result of a third patrol, by Lieutenant-General Lambert, were more favourable. This was a much larger patrol, made up of three regiments of horse. It had gone north, sent off on July 8 while the main army marched through Shotts. Lambert went through west Stirlingshire to the fords across the upper Forth. He penetrated into Perthshire, perhaps to Aberfoyle or to the Port of Menteith, or further towards the town of Callander. When he came back he reported that the fords were practicable for horse and foot, and that the way was not blocked by forts as had been assumed, but that moving cannon that way was out of the question. Put together with the request for supplies from the western ports and the capture of posts along both sides of the Clyde estuary, this was yet another of Cromwell's attempts to tackle the problem of the Scots defensive tactics. Like many others, it was unsuccessful.

Under the threat of all this activity in the west, the Scots moved their army west from Torwood to Kilsyth. There Leslie took up another of his powerfully defensive positions, with 'ragged crags and mountains' on one side and marshes on the other. In this position, he blocked the northern route from Glasgow to Edinburgh and Stirling, and protected the fords Lambert had located, but it was a much less likely starting place for a march south.[10]

Next day, July 12, Cromwell began the return march, first to Monkland, a march of eight miles, where they were only four miles from a cavalry patrol of Scots, possibly part of Montgomery's regiments, the threat of which kept the English horse alert and saddled all night. Next day's march, returning by the Torphichen road again, took them to a camp halfway between Falkirk and Linlithgow. Simultaneously the Scots moved back from Kilsyth to Torwood, and by the time Cromwell's force was camped again, the Scots cavalry were patrolling beyond Falkirk, and next day Cromwell and Lambert were fired on during their regular patrol.[11]

Cromwell, after a further council of war that day, made yet another attempt to bring the Scots out, for his main aim was still to bring about a battle. An attack was mounted, at last, on Callander House. A bombardment lasting all day produced a practicable breach by the evening, and a summons went in. The commander, Lieutenant Galbraith, asked for a night to see if relief would come. Cromwell refused, and the house was stormed, with 61 Scots being killed. The whole Scots army stood and watched. It was Red Hall all over again, with as little result.[12]

It seems highly unlikely that Cromwell expected anything else. All these exertions leave a strong impression of futility. Leslie was firmly in command of the Royalist army, even though the king was to be seen riding conspicuously about at Torwood. And Leslie had learned his lesson at Dunbar. He was not to be tempted out again. So the patrols taking Newark, reconnoitring the upper Forth, conspicuously seen near Dumbarton, the march to Glasgow, fully observed by the Scots cavalry, and the prolonged, slow, day-long battering and storming of Callander House – all these cannot have been expected to bring on the battle Cromwell needed and looked for. He knew, surely, that Leslie would not fight, and he knew, certainly, that Charles wanted to march on England. So the march to the west was designed to fix the Royalist staff's attention on his army. Lambert was conspicuous too, at the fords of the upper Forth, on patrol near Falkirk. Of course, if Leslie *did* emerge, perhaps under the pressure of more foolhardy and reckless spirits in the Scots-Royalist camp such as the duke of Buckingham, then Cromwell had his field army ready and waiting. But it seems obvious enough that he expected no battle.

On the other hand, what he *had* done in the past weeks had successfully achieved one objective. All Scots eyes were on his army, and all Scots forces were concentrated at Stirling and Torwood, just in case Cromwell began an assault. This was one of Cromwell's main objectives, surely. He was a general who could simultaneously pursue several aims, ready to shift from one to another as circumstances developed. He had even tried this approach before, at Hamilton, where his first and conspicuous march can be seen as a cover for Lambert's move.[13] So now, having hypnotised Scots attention, he was ready for the concealed move.

Two days after the battering of Callander House, a detachment of Daniel's regiment of foot marched out of Leith, where it had been part of Colonel Overton's garrison, and was ferried across the Forth to land at North Queensferry. Four more companies of foot and four troops of horse followed swiftly, under the command of Colonel Overton himself. That night, two more full regiments of foot and two of horse were ordered across, and Lambert went to take over the command. These later troops were from the main army at Linlithgow, while the first two forces had come from Overton's brigade at Edinburgh and Leith. The reinforcements crossed on Saturday and Sunday, July 19 and 20.[14]

This was a very different affair from the earlier attempts to land in Fife. The landing was at a small inconvenient port, not before threatened, using the specially built flatboats, and it was much larger in numbers. Monck had had no more than 1,500 men at the earlier attempts, but Lambert had nearly 5,000. There are also clear indications of a carefully laid plan. Overton's move was clearly not spontaneous. The crossing took place at a point closer to Cromwell's headquarters than to Overton's, and the march of Daniel's troops would have looked like a reinforcement moving towards the main army until the moment they reached the ferry crossing. Cromwell's army was under constant Scots observation, and any move by any of his troops would be noted at once. So it was Overton's troops which were used in the initial landing, and only when surprise was no longer important were troops sent from the main camp.

Two days later Major-General Harrison arrived at Edinburgh with reinforcements of two full regiments of horse, and twelve extra troops, 4,000 men.[15] Overton had thus been able to use his garrison troops without any danger to his city garrisons. The approach of Harrison was known well in advance. It was mentioned in a letter dated from Linlithgow on the 14th, and so it was well known in the English camp, and therefore also in the Scots camp, for there were few secrets. The Scots would have been expecting something to happen as a result – but they would have expected it *after* the arrival of Harrison's party, scarcely before. Here is another example, like the attack before dawn at Dunbar, of Cromwell using the enemy's expectations to spring a surprise. In addition the landing took place at a point never attempted before, which was certainly at the narrowest point of the Firth, the ferry crossing, but also close to the guns of Inchgarvie Castle on its little island. The landing took place close to a small fort at North Queensferry, and below a new fortification on the hills of the peninsula which the English called the Great Sconce. This had seventeen guns in it, so it was by no means negligible. The whole operation, with its careful timing, fresh troops, use of deception and choice of landing place, was a masterstroke. Typical Cromwell.

The landing seems to have taken place at the neck of the small peninsula, either on the east or west side (or perhaps both). The Great Sconce, and the small fort at the village of North Queensferry, were both overrun quickly, and four small ships in Inverkeithing Bay, loaded with coal and salt, were captured. These were armed, more evidence of the continual naval struggle waged in the Firth of Forth since the beginning of the war.

The Scots were compelled to react. Cromwell's main force at Linlithgow was still twenty-two regiments strong, and was still close enough to Torwood to be threatening, and this effectively immobilised the main Scots army. Lambert's force, though small, was strong enough to dominate all Fife if left unchallenged, and if it did so would cut off Stirling from the rest of the country. It was therefore necessary for the Scots to remove it. Major-General Holborne was sent with a force of 4,000 men, horse and foot. Despatched from Stirling on the news of the first landing, he reached Inverkeithing, a mile or so north of the landing place, before Lambert's regiments had finished their disembarkation, on the 20th. Holborne discovered a much stronger force there than he had expected, and naturally hesitated. His best course would probably have been to entrench, prevent the English from getting out of their bridgehead, then call for reinforcements. But the heterogeneous nature of his force – Highlanders, local militia from Dunfermline and Inverkeithing, archers from Perth, regular cavalry – was scarcely an encouragement to static warfare. In the event, Lambert did not give him the chance. The English could not afford to be locked into a narrow peninsula, dependent on ships for supplies. Nor could they afford to delay in case the Scots did entrench.

Lambert immediately decided to attack. It was for just such an eventuality that Cromwell had sent Lambert as commander of the landing force; no other English commander had the swift decisiveness and tactical flair of this master of war.

Holborne pulled back to find a good position to hold. He deployed his forces on some hills north of the hollow which separated the peninsula from the mainland. His aim seems to have been defensive, to hold on until the reinforcements he had sent for came up. He was outnumbered, and faced a professional, experienced force, while his own forces formed a mixed and unsteady array. He did his best, placing part of the cavalry under Major-General Sir John Browne of Fordell on his left, and taking command himself on the right. The narrow passage of Castlandhill was lined with musketeers, and the rest of the infantry filled the centre.

Lambert was more subtle. He placed his foot on the reverse slope of the Ferryhills, and used his cavalry to tease the Scots into attacking him. This they did, only to come up against the solid rock of the English infantry, while the retreating cavalry turned on them at the decisive moment. The preliminary skirmishing took some time, but the final fight, at very close quarters, lasted only a quarter of an hour. Holborne fled first, taking some of the Scots horse with him; Browne was quickly overwhelmed with the rest of the cavalry; the infantry, particularly 800 men of the Clan Maclean and 700 Buchanans, were destroyed where they stood, unable to escape without the protection of their cavalry comrades. The Macleans, under their chief Sir Hector Maclean, died where they stood, eight of the clansmen successively killed protecting their chief, by their clan account shouting 'Another for Hector' as each man threw himself between him and the English. The other highland regiment, the 700 Buchanans, similarly stood and died, but without such a memorable war cry. These two joined the regiment of Campbell of Lawers at Dunbar, eliminated by their stubbornness.

Lambert began one of his ferocious pursuits, following the Scots for at least six miles. Two thousand of the Scots force were killed, and 1400 were taken prisoner; only a thousand men escaped back to Stirling. Browne was wounded, captured, and died soon after; five regimental commanders also died. Holborne got away, and, not unreasonably, got the blame as well. A court-martial exonerated him, but he resigned his command.[16]

George Downing, the Scoutmaster General, remarked in his account of these operations which he sent to the Speaker, that the Scots cry at the battle was 'Scotland', and that 'it seems they were sensible that Scotland lay at this bout much at the stake'.[17] So the full consequences of the defeat were clear to both sides very quickly. Fife was about to be lost to Lambert's force. If Leslie brought the main army into Fife to deal with him, Cromwell would be able to take Stirling, or at least cross the Forth to either side of the city-fortress. Leslie's army would then be out of its trenches once more and in danger of destruction. The loss of either Stirling or Fife meant defeat. Still quite unable to risk fighting Cromwell's own main force, the Scots now had nowhere to go but England as the king had always wanted. But still the Scots army could not move south while Cromwell was at Linlithgow. So Leslie pulled his force back from Torwood into Stirling, leaving his camp standing, the wounded untended, the dead unburied, and abandoning quantities of food and ammunition in his haste. From Stirling he began marching the army across the narrow Stirling Bridge to deal with Lambert's army in Fife. Cromwell followed them as far as Bannockburn, no more than a mile from Stirling, and watched the Scots movements through 'prospective glasses'. There were fords below Stirling which he could use to cross over to take the Scots in the rear if they moved fully into Fife.

It would have been clear that Lambert was now in great danger. Leslie could leave a relatively small force to hold Stirling, which would certainly prevent Cromwell from taking the town, and the ford-crossing would be slow. So Leslie could move the great bulk of his army against the invaders of Fife, and eliminate them before Cromwell's main force could arrive. Lambert's force of 4,000 or 5,000 could not seriously expect to defeat an army of perhaps three times that size, no matter how skilful Lambert was. Once Cromwell was convinced that the bulk of the Scots army was marching towards Dunfermline, where Lambert was on the 21st, he turned his army about, and marched it back to the ferry crossing and to Leith and Edinburgh.

There he stayed for a week, supervising the transport of most of his army across to Fife. Cromwell was staying at Dundas Castle, close to South Queensferry, and Lambert ensured the safety of the crossing by compelling the surrender of Inchgarvie, where the castle was found to hold sixteen pieces of ordnance. Cromwell left eight regiments on the Edinburgh side, under Harrison. Most of his forces, 14,000 men, were moved across, largely by the use of every boat and ship he could find, and every port, large and small, he controlled.[18]

But if Cromwell could deceive the enemy, so could David Leslie. Once Cromwell had been seen to turn away from Stirling, the Scots army marching into Fife had turned back. It seems clear that their object had been to get Cromwell into Fife. Of course, if Cromwell did not take the bait and follow Lambert, Leslie could still go on to deal with the invader. Either must happen. The Scots army stopped moving into Fife when Cromwell was seen to have left Bannockburn. Once Cromwell, by moving his forces across the Firth, showed that he was definitely moving into Fife in strength, the Scots had plenty of time. They were still intent on avoiding a battle with the English main force, but now that that force was marooned in Fife, with the usual quantity of castles and towns to delay it (including Perth and Stirling), the Scots could hope to steal several marches on their enemy and reach England without a fight. They had to wait a while, to gather up all their forces, collect their provisions, mount their men, and to see just what Cromwell did. Cromwell must have known what was going on, but he continued transporting his army northwards. He was deliberately inviting the Scots to march for England. In fact, whatever Cromwell did, the king now had a clear run south.

As it happened, Cromwell did as they would have hoped. He moved his army due north to attack Perth, with the intention of cutting off the main Scots army at Stirling.[19] Had he moved against Stirling itself, the Scots could have retreated into the fortifications again, but Cromwell would have been able to cross the river and march after the Scots army, no more than a day or two behind them. By moving against Perth, Cromwell was carefully leaving the Scots army free to cut loose from Stirling. In fact, one can go further. By taking Perth, Cromwell would in effect *force* the Scots army to march south. Their other alternatives were to starve inside Stirling, or to fight the English main army in the open field. By taking Perth, he could block that retreat. With Fife lost, Perth about to be lost, and only a few weeks' supplies stockpiled, the only real option which gave the Scots any hope of winning the war was to march south and invade England. It would appear that the decision had been made before July 24, for it was then that the duke of Buckingham wrote to the earl of Derby that what he called 'our late misfortune in Fife' was not going 'to hinder our march . . . towards England', and he hoped to see Derby there 'very shortly'.[20] Thus an English Royalist exile in his optimism. But the Scots were not so keen to abandon their own homes to the invader. They may have hoped that by doing so they would draw all the English forces after them, and so free Scotland, or they may have hoped that those forces would stay in Scotland, and that all England would rise and sweep away the republican regime, and then they could all march back to deal with Cromwell, still marooned in the north. Cromwell knew full well all these nuances, of course, for he had had a year to think them out. Harrison at Edinburgh had contingency orders in case of an invasion of England.

While the English forces were being ferried across, the Fife bridgehead was expanded. Inchgarvie fell on the 24th, and Burntisland, with its good harbour, on the 29th. Cromwell then crossed over himself, using that newly gained harbour, and began his move northwards. Commissary-General Whalley was sent to march along the Fife coast with a contingent of horse, paced by ships, from Burntisland through the small fishing ports and burghs there. Already on July 29 Cromwell reported that he had captured artillery and ships.[21]

Camp for the main army on the 30th was near Kinross, and on the next day the army marched to Bridge of Earn, three miles south of Perth. There were coincidences and ironies to relish along this march. The army passed along the banks of Loch Leven, from which the Scots nominal commander-in-chief took his title; they cut off King Charles from his first royal home in Scotland at Falkland in the Lomond Hills; the General Assembly of the Kirk had been meeting, disputatiously and futilely, at St Andrews, and the ministers scattered as the English advanced; the army marched past Fordell, from which Sir John Browne took his title; in Dumfermline the soldiers had the pleasure of ransacking the home of Johnston of Wariston, and any who had come into contact with him no doubt enjoyed it – Cromwell did execute two men for plundering, but no-one seems to have been punished for drinking Wariston's wine.[22]

Another victim was Sir Robert Douglas of Blaikerstons, who lost 'a great quantity of silver plate, arras, hangings, carpets, and other household plenishing' to the English looters, at least according to his later claim. The heavy contributions required of the county do not seem to have affected such men overmuch. But the historian Balfour compiled a detailed account of Fife's payments in men, supplies, and money. He found that almost 8,000 men were levied in 1650 – 51, out of a total population of less than 100,000 – perhaps 10% of the whole – and in cash 137,000 pounds sterling was contributed, perhaps a third of the rental value of the county. In addition, he noted requisitions and contributions of horses, tents, dishes and axes, meal, cheese, oats, and 'provisions', as well as providing quarters for ten regiments of horse before the concentration at Stirling. And there was still considerable private wealth for the English plunderers even after all that. The rich seem to have passed the greater part of the burden on to the poor very successfully. But equally there can be no doubt that the land could not go on contributing at this rate much longer. And if Fife was almost exhausted, the condition of the lands which had been fought over and conquered was much worse. Scotland was close to economic collapse.[23]

Once Cromwell's direction of march became known at Stirling, the Scots army marched out of the city southwards. That this was the signal is shown by the timing: Cromwell's march north from Inverkeithing began on the 30th, and the Scots move south began on the 31st.[24] Until then the Scots could not be sure that the whole Fife affair was not a bluff. After all, it had been largely a bluff *by* the Scots which had persuaded Cromwell to cross over in the first place – or, at least, that could be a reasonable interpretation. That this seems to have been what Cromwell wanted them to do anyway does not mean that the Scots danced to his tune. They made their own choice.

It had not been easy. The king, so the English thought, had

advocated an immediate march south after Inverkeithing. It may be true, but only for a moment. It was clearly necessary to get clear of Cromwell's army first. Numbers of the Scots had already been caught by Cromwell and Lambert in a march into England, in the doomed invasion of the Engagers in 1648, and they would have had no wish to repeat the experience. Nor was it a unanimous decision. As soon as the march south began, some of the Scots soldiers deserted. Some of the English Royalists argued that it was a mistake for the king to lead an invasion of his own kingdom at the head of a foreign army. Several men refused to march with him. Further, Charles could not afford to leave Scotland entirely defenceless, so garrisons had to be left, particularly at Stirling. Then, also, the essential elements of a Scottish government had to remain in place under Loudoun, and some of the Scottish nobles agreed with those who had deserted, that it was nothing to do with Scotland whether Charles ruled in England, and they refused to join the expedition. Four earls – Crawford-Lindsay, Glencairn, Balcarres, and Marischal – remained to raise yet more troops from the exhausted land. There had been plenty to talk about in Stirling between Cromwell's march back from Bannockburn and the beginning of his march on Perth.[25]

But at last the king had got what he had wanted ever since he had landed a year before at Garmouth. He was at long last on the march into England. He had been warned often enough that it was a mistake, and many of the Scots who did march were clearly reluctant. But the king was trapped. If he marched at the head of a foreign army, he would be branded an invader; if he did not march, he would be told that his Royalist supporters in England were being betrayed. Why should anyone else risk his life for the king, if the king would not risk his own life? Sir Edward Hyde, the architect of the Restoration along with General Monck, clearly recognised this later on. He had opposed the Scots adventure all along, but realised that it had to be tried, even if its failure was certain, before Charles II gained any credibility.

So the king and his Scots army marched south to their doom. As in all true tragedies, they knew they were going to their doom, but could do nothing to avoid it. Most of them died in the process.

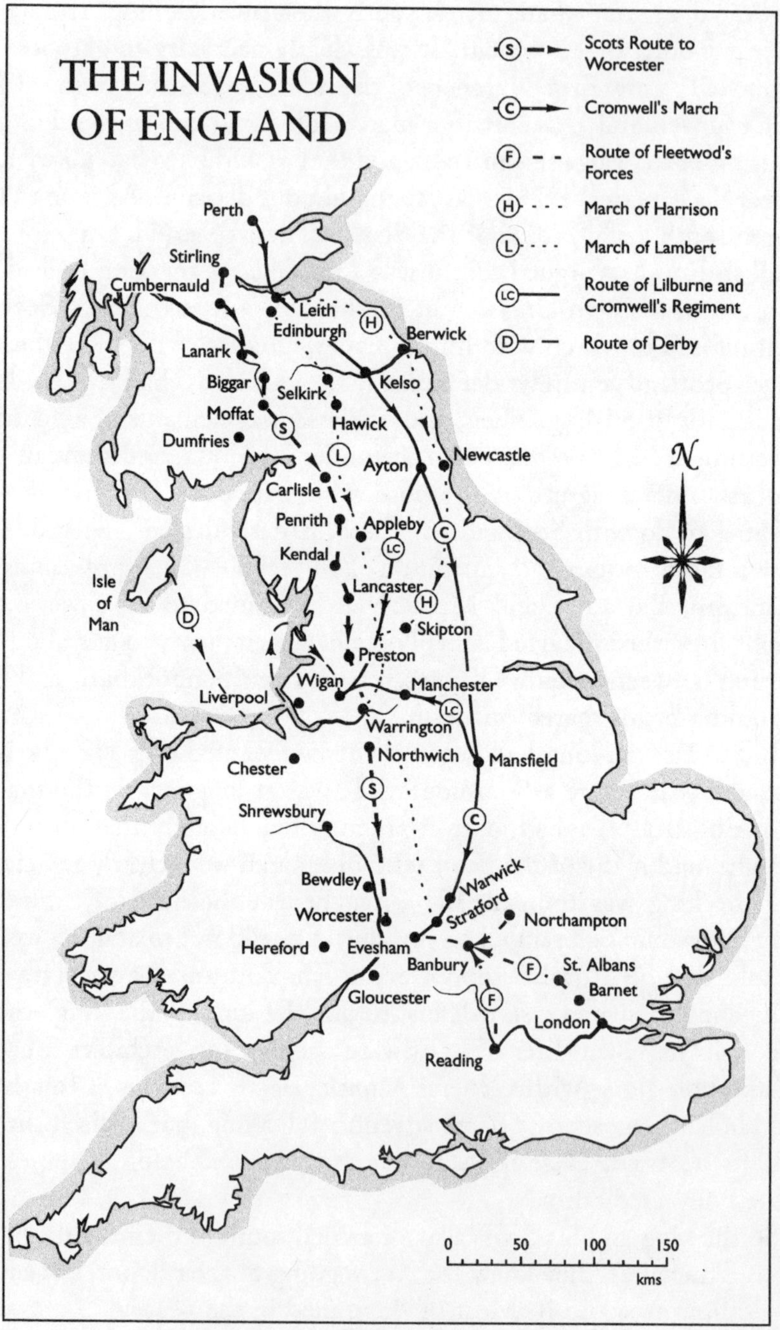
THE INVASION OF ENGLAND
Scots Route to Worcester
Cromwell's March
Route of Fleetwod's Forces
March of Harrison
March of Lambert
Route of Lilburne and Cromwell's Regiment
Route of Derby
Perth
Stirling
Cumbernauld
Leith
Edinburgh
Berwick
Lanark
Kelso
Biggar
Selkirk
Moffat
Hawick
Dumfries
Newcastle
Ayton
Carlisle
Penrith
Appleby
Kendal
Isle of Man
Lancaster
Skipton
Preston
Wigan
Manchester
Liverpool
Warrington
Northwich
Chester
Mansfield
Shrewsbury
Warwick
Bewdley
Stratford
Worcester
Northampton
Hereford
Evesham
Banbury
St. Albans
Barnet
Gloucester
London
Reading
N
0 50 100 150
kms

CHAPTER SEVEN

THE INVASION OF ENGLAND

July 31 – August 25, 1651

THE Scots army marched out of Stirling on the southward road on July 31, to camp that night twelve miles along their way at Cumbernauld. That same day Cromwell resumed his march on the northward road through Fife towards Perth. He camped at Bridge of Earn, where he had heard that Major-General Montgomery was preparing the defences three miles south of Perth. But Montgomery had gone, and most of his horse with him, to join the march south. A few Scots troops supervised some press-ganged local people in destroying the Earn bridge. They all fled as the English arrived. It seemed that Perth lay open to capture.[1]

Next morning Cromwell's force moved on the city, having found boats to carry them across the river. Assuming the city was ungarrisoned, he sent in a trumpeter to demand immediate surrender. But a garrison, 1,300 Highlanders, mainly Gordons, commanded by the earl of Sutherland, had arrived just a couple of hours before Cromwell's own arrival. So the trumpeter was refused admission, and told that any communications must be addressed to the governor of the city. So another summons went in, correctly addressed, and received no answer.[2] The whole business was clearly a time-gaining ploy by Sutherland, whose task was to delay Cromwell as long as possible to let the main army get a good long lead.

He did gain a day or two. Cromwell brought up his guns and bombarded the city through the night of August 1/2. The English also set about breaking the sluices on the river, lowering the water level in readiness for an assault. The prospect was sufficient. Sutherland, perhaps pressured by the unenthusiastic citizens, agreed to surrender. He was given the usual generous terms, allowing his soldiers to march out with their arms and possessions to their homes. The people of the city were to be protected against plundering, and the possessions of others could be removed without interference. Similarly there would be no interference with personal religion, an item designed by the Scots to protect the Kirk, but which fitted in well with Cromwell's own Independent opinions.[3]

It was during that day, in the morning, that Cromwell heard of the king's march. Whereas the Scots had taken at least a week to organise themselves for the march, Cromwell was on the move at once. In fact he had anticipated the need. Harrison, at Leith, already knew of the Scots' move, and had at once set off, on the morning of the 2nd, before he could have contacted Cromwell. He, with Colonels Fenwick and Twisleton, wrote to Cromwell reporting their dispositions. Harrison himself marched off along the main east-coast road with the cavalry forces which he had brought north only a fortnight before. By the end of August 3 he was at Berwick: fifty miles in two days, excellent marching. There he would be joined by the regiments of Colonels Rich and Sanders, and would stimulate Sir Arthur Haselrig and Lord Fairfax, the governors respectively of Newcastle and Hull, to recruit forces to defend northern England, 'so the enemy might receive a considerable opposition without withdrawing much of the forces . . . now marching with you'. He notes also a half-regiment already at Teviotdale to suppress recruiting for the Scots there.

This has all the air of a previously planned reaction, and the letter is careful and correctly composed. But there is a postscript, quite different in tone to the main body of the letter, which reveals greater agitation in Leith, and suggests some of the difficulties the English faced. It seems that Harrison and the others relied on the 'foot post', the official messenger, a Scot, for their information. He was unwilling to say much, clearly a Scot who wanted the Scots army to get away clean and clear. 'He is very hardly drawn to confess anything', Harrison wrote, mercifully not revealing his interrogation techniques. The man had eventually confirmed that the Scots army was marching towards England. It was only confirmation – it *was* a postscript to the letter – but the man, 'who is a subtle old knave', had perhaps delayed the

English response in Leith by half an hour or so. All grist to the mill, of course.[4]

Meanwhile Cromwell had swiftly disposed of his own forces. He had with him only part of his main army, 13,000 or 14,000 men, he said. He decided to leave half in Perth and Fife, and to take the rest back with him. So he had to move 6,000 or 7,000 horse and foot back to Burntisland and across the Firth. This movement was started on the 2nd, as soon as Perth's surrender was confirmed; and the whole move was completed within two days, for they were in Leith on the 4th. It is often claimed that Cromwell delayed to capture Perth, and then moved only slowly on the march south. On the contrary, what had taken the Scots a week to organise, took Cromwell a mere two days.

He had left a substantial force behind. Colonel Overton with two regiments and some dragoons was left to garrison Perth, and from there to supervise Fife, which had not been completely conquered by any means. Major-General Monck, with 5,000 or 6,000 of the newer recruits, was left in general command in Scotland, with the first task of attacking Stirling. At Perth orders were given, either by Cromwell or in his name, to tear down some of the suburban buildings on the western side, facing the still-hostile part of Scotland, to leave the garrison in the citadel with a better field of fire. Two English troopers were hanged for plundering in the town.[5]

By the time Cromwell had taken Perth, the Royalist army had been on the march for three days, and was making excellent time. Most of the troops were cavalry, and the foot had been mounted for the march as well, so, after the relatively short march to Cumbernauld the first day, they covered nearly sixty miles through the Southern Uplands to Moffat in the next two days. The route was by way of Lanark, their camp on the night of August 1, and a detachment threatened an English force at Boghall, by Biggar, without success. It may have been this group who upset the inhabitants of the upper Tweed valley. Their animals were seized, and the people of Drummelzier had to spend the sabbath defending their homes, or feeding the passing troops, or chasing after their disappearing goods, according to temperament. Upstream the session clerk at Tweedsmuir was quite certain that these Scots soldiers were 'the enemy'.[6]

The march of the rejoined force from Moffat along Annandale brought the whole army to the border by August 5. There had been no real opposition, and the whole force was mounted, but this was still excellent marching, through hills and along steep valleys in the August heat, and with an army in which a 'purple fever' had been reported for some time. The border region was clear also. In London there was a report on August 4 – and so several days old by then, and referring to the end of July – that a string of 'forts and places' had already been taken by the Scots. The names are mostly mangled beyond recognition, but Dumfries and Annan are there. In fact, these had been abandoned for some weeks, but patrols no doubt operated in and out of the area. The Scots forces would have been those recruited by Montgomery and left to control the borderlands. At 'Langton' (presumably Longtown) the Scots 'did seize upon a whole regiment of Harrison's horse'. Harrison was the official commander in the area. It was clearly a substantial Scots force which was at work, for it then went on to Brampton and beat off another force of English cavalry, reputedly killing 200 and capturing 200 more. They then retired with loot. Even if the number of English casualties is exaggerated, this certainly implies that the Scots were in full control of the borders and could raid with impunity. But they stayed clear of Carlisle.[7]

Carlisle was the main defence bastion. The Royalist army came up to it on August 6, having had Charles proclaimed king of England by a man appointed king-at-arms for the occasion. He also promised a pardon to any man – meaning enemy soldiers – who joined him, with the exception of four named individuals – Cromwell, Ireton, Bradshaw, and John Cook – but he can scarcely have expected them to join him. All this cut no ice in Carlisle. A summons in the name of the king was ignored. The king rode with eighty horse towards the bridge, which was guarded by a patrol of the garrison. Perhaps he hoped that the magic of his presence would open the gates and bring the soldiers over to his side. The patrol simply retired: the gates remained shut.[8]

The army the king had with him had been winnowed by this time, by desertion, by exhaustion, by sickness. What may have been 20,000 or even more at Stirling was now no more than 12,000 or 13,000. Some, of course, had been left to garrison Stirling, but others would have been collected in southern Scotland on the march south, especially those recruited by Major-General Montgomery. So there were some thousands missing now. Some had no doubt dropped out on the march, for the march had been very hard. But that still leaves a good third of the original army unaccounted for. The English had commented even at Perth that many of the Scots were deserting, and it is surely this which caused the reduction in numbers. This, in fact, might not have been too worrying, for the deserters probably left because they were unwilling to invade England. But they would have been much more ready to fight to defend their homes. The several thousands of deserters might therefore in many cases enlist again to fight the much smaller English army under Monck.[9]

And then, of course, the desertions were not so worrying because the Royalists were convinced that they would be replaced by thousands of English Royalists as they marched south into England. Hence the king's testing of the determination of the Carlisle garrison. This failure could, just about, be shrugged off, for such an important garrison had to be ideologically compatible with the republican government in London, but as the army went further into England a much livelier response was expected. The day after Carlisle the army reached Penrith, and the king declared a day's rest for the footsore horses. There, the son of Lord Howard of Escrick joined with a troop of horse from his estates. His arrival was mentioned in so many letters written during that rest day that it only emphasises that there were so few other recruits.[10]

The swift Scots march was matched by even more impressive marching by the English forces. Harrison reached Newcastle from Leith by August 5. This was the day the Scots reached the border, so Harrison had already made up two days on the invaders. From there, in his capacity as commander of the forces in England, he wrote to the Militia Committees of the northern, north Midlands, and north Welsh counties, warning them of the invasion, and telling them to remove food supplies and animals out of the way of the Scots army. The selection of counties indicates clearly that Harrison (and so presumably also Cromwell and Lambert, who had surely discussed the possibilities involved) expected the Scots to march through

Lancashire. The warning to North Wales was connected with the expected activities of the earl of Derby, who could be assumed to be intending to join the king from the Isle of Man. But just in case the Scots tried a march into Yorkshire a strong guard was put into Barnard Castle to block the route down Teesdale.[11] On that same day, the 5th, Lambert was just setting off from Leith, for he wrote to Harrison that day, telling him to use his horse and dragoons to locate the Scots flank. This had been done by the next day, when it was known in Newcastle that the enemy were at Carlisle.[12]

Lambert himself, with the horse which had been shipped over the Firth, rode due south from Edinburgh, along the road through Selkirk, Hawick, and Liddesdale, and so came upon the Scots from the rear. He rode so well that he reached their Penrith camp on the 9th the day after the Royalists' rest day there. He was by then just one day behind, having made up five days' leeway in five days' march.[13]

Cromwell meanwhile was bringing on the foot. His was the only force not horse-borne, and the only way to march without exhausting his men was in careful, even stages. Cromwell had written to warn, and reassure, the Council of State,[14] and he could be confident that the armed forces of England, the regular troops and the militia, would be mobilised by the Council. But he knew also that the Scots were seasoned troops, and, if Leslie retained influence, under experienced and canny command. And there was always anxiety as to the reaction of the English Royalists. The destruction of their organisations after the revelations of Birkenhead and Coke might be enough to prevent a Royalist rising, but no-one in England could be certain until the test came. Only when the king and his army actually arrived in England and proclaimed themselves and their purposes would the answer be known. And even if no immediate rising took place, a Royalist victory in England could still spark one. It behoved the whole republican regime to be very careful. The battle, when it came, had to be a victory.

It was, therefore, essential that the troops Cromwell commanded, the tough, outspoken, infinitely loyal soldiers who had been fighting the Scots in Scotland for more than a year, had to be in at the final battle. Only they would have the skill to destroy the Scots army comprehensively. Cromwell had deliberately weeded out the less experienced men, who had been left behind with Monck in Scotland. He now led the best army in all three kingdoms.

Cromwell's force left Leith on August 6, the day after Lambert's horse. In two days they were forty miles on at Kelso, and four days later, on August 13, he gave them a day's rest at the Tyne at Ryton, where they were refreshed by food and drink presented by the magistrates of Newcastle. They had marched over a hundred miles in six days, and deserved their day off. By this time it seems clear that Cromwell had had reports of the Royalists' march, and of the responses of Lambert and Harrison. Harrison had sent one of his regiments, nine troops of horse under Colonel Sanders, across to the west to join with Lambert. They clashed with some of the Scots near Appleby. It was thought that this was responsible for the delay in the Scots march, but there are better explanations.[15]

The king was now entering rather more promising territory. The people of Cumberland and Westmorland might draw themselves aside, but the land was thinly populated anyway, and relatively few supporters can have been expected. But Lancashire was dotted with sympathetic lords and communities, Catholic, Royalist, Presbyterian, and it was here that the earl of Derby was expected to join. Attempts were made to drum up support by exercises of authority. Colonel Wogan, an old enemy of Cromwell from Ireland, levied contribution at Kendal, and Colonel Boynton, a victim of confiscation after the 1648 war, did the same at Lancaster, where the prisoners in the castle were released. When the king arrived he was welcomed at a series of houses, first of all at Aston Hall near Lancaster, the house of Colonel Wainman. He had been host to Hamilton during the invasion of the Engagers. Charles stayed there for two days, and then moved only to Myerscough, ten miles to the south.[16]

That was the day Cromwell rested at Ryton. By then he had received an intercepted letter written at Penrith by the duke of Buckingham, discovered by Lambert's scouts on a captured Royalist major, showing clearly that the Scots were in a gloomy mood. Lambert and Harrison joined their forces together that day as well, Harrison having moved across to Lancashire by way of Skipton and the Craven Gap. They met at Hazelmoor, but found that they had just missed blocking the king's further advance southwards. They had about 6,000 or 7,000 men between them, and clearly did not feel themselves strong enough to tackle the Scots army. It may also be that they had instructions not to do so, unless sure of victory. It was the old problem: a republican defeat on English soil might be the start of an accumulating snowball of defection. Harrison's report shows that they hoped to block the Royalists' advance at Warrington. From Ryton on that day, the 13th, Cromwell sent on Colonel Lilburne's regiment of horse to catch up with Lambert and Harrison in Lancashire. So Cromwell was clear that they were not strong enough.[17]

By this time the machinery of resistance to invasion under the control of the Council of State was operating smoothly. The Council knew of the Scots invasion by August 7, and reacted with a most impressive and detailed series of measures, coordinating the movements of troops all over England, warning the counties in the path of the invader, calling up militia forces in every part of the country. Lieutenant-General Fleetwood was put in command of the army which gathered in the south midlands to block any advance by the Scots on London. Troops in the north Midlands were to join with Harrison, with Newark in Nottinghamshire as the rendezvous. The militia committees of the same counties as Harrison had written to two days before were also addressed. Colonel Birch at Liverpool was warned to look out for trouble in Lancashire, a warning somewhat superfluous by then.[18]

More information over the next few days allowed the Council to make clearer plans. The militia committees of counties in the south and the south Midlands were told that 'the Scots army have given up their own country for lost, which they had not the courage to defend' – scarcely true statements in any respect, but good propaganda – and were reported to be marching south with 11,000 men. Harrison's reinforcements were now to rendezvous at Northampton, and were to receive part of Colonel Berkstead's regiment, a double-strength foot unit usually stationed at Windsor. Major-General Philip Skippon was put in command of the London forces, and the usual regular guard for the city was to be replaced by London volunteer units. Two days later, on the 13th, the day that Cromwell's marching army rested at Ryton, a rendezvous for 8,000 foot and 2,000 horse to defend London was appointed at Barnet. Half the force were regulars, the rest militia from London and the home counties.[19]

Meanwhile, the Earl of Derby had landed from the Isle of Man. He had been one of the king's great hopes, for his influence in Lancashire was reputed very great. He had gone first to north Wales, another Royalist area, it was hoped. He had landed at Castle Ruthin on the 11th, but had brought no more than 300 men from Man with him, and they needing arms. On the 13th Derby was still in north Wales, and the king was in effect waiting for him, going slowly through Lancashire, expecting recruits, but hampered also, no doubt, by exceptionally heavy rain.[20]

By that date, therefore, the republican garrisons in the southern half of England had received warning of the invasion from London, and those in the north from Newcastle. The king's army was moving fairly slowly southwards through Lancashire, waiting to join up with the earl of Derby, who was in north Wales. Lambert and Harrison had joined forces and were shadowing the Scots army on a parallel course through eastern Lancashire. Cromwell's battle-hardened infantry force was resting at Ryton, with Lilburne's regiment riding to reinforce Lambert. Throughout southern and midland England militia forces were gathering, with rendezvous appointed for Northampton, Barnet, Reading, and Gloucester. The Scots were already surrounded. The more time elapsed before they met the English defenders, the greater that defensive force would be, and the more certain their defeat.

For the present, however, the Scots army was the most powerful force in its immediate area. It was a few miles short of Warrington on the 15th. The king stayed at Bryn Hall, the home of Sir William Gerrard, described by the republicans as 'a subtle jesuited papist'.[21] Here was undoubtedly one of the main reasons for the lack of enthusiasm in Lancashire, for the king stayed in more than one Catholic house; this annoyed the Protestant groups, above all the Presbyterians of the small towns, who, in other circumstances, would be Royalists. It cannot have pleased the Scots either, marching with their Covenanted king, but Charles had by now shown often enough that he would not accept Scots dictation in matters of religion or personal conduct.

Warrington was the place where the English forces hoped to block the Scots advance, by holding the bridge over the Mersey there. A force of 3,000 militia and regulars from Cheshire and Staffordshire had been heading there for some days, and Lambert and Harrison were able to march on the 16th to join them. But the fight was an infantry contest, and the cavalry were unable to deploy properly in the enclosed land close to the bridge. The militia foot did block the bridge for a time but the Scots attack was too swift and close to give them time to get the bridge down. The Scots held the town on the north side of the crossing, and could shelter there, while the English were more exposed in the open land to the south. Lambert and Harrison decided not to make a fight of it, but to withdraw before they could be accused of being defeated. The Scots pursued closely, the hedges and lanes slowing the English forces, until Lambert was able to turn and drive them off. Casualties were few, but greatest among the infantry on the bridge. Once away from the Mersey, Lambert and Harrison, outnumbered, resumed their shadowing role, carefully pacing the Scots on a parallel route to the east.[22]

The Scots had therefore passed the last major geographical barrier on their road into England. They camped at Northwich on the night of the 16th, and next day the earl of Derby at last appeared. His force was small and unarmed. He clearly relied above all on raising forces in Lancashire. He insisted that this was still possible, and was sent back there to prove his contention. It may also be that the Scots had news of the approach of Lilburne's regiment, for Major-General Massey was also detached. Derby returned to his ships and sailed north to land in the estuary of the Wyre, near Fleetwood, while Massey returned north over the Warrington bridge. Lilburne was approaching from the north-east. It looks like a plan to crush him between them.[23]

Massey would certainly need troops if that was the intention. He had a regiment of horse with him, probably under strength. He and Derby rode towards each other through Lancashire, recruiting. Massey went towards Manchester. His efforts were directed at the Presbyterians, who were concentrated in the towns. He carried a letter from the

Presbytery of the Scots army, addressed to the Lancashire ministers, but this included a comment on earlier 'malignancy' which would certainly set Presbyterians against Old Royalists. The king wrote to stop the letter being released, but it was intercepted by a patrol from Chester. The effect of the letter would be to discourage the Presbyterians, which perhaps explains why Derby had rather more success in recruiting than did Massey. Massey himself intercepted a letter at Eccles, near Manchester, on the 19th, by which he learnt of the approach of Lilburne's regiment, and in turn he wrote to warn Derby. Derby had gone north again, where his ships were based, and where many Old Royalists like the men the king had stayed with had nothing more to lose.

Lilburne was north of Manchester on the 9th, but then marched across the county towards Liverpool, where Colonel John Birch had a garrison from which Lilburne could get the foot soldiers he needed to form a balanced force. Derby came south, and on the 21st he and Lilburne were only seven miles apart, at Ormskirk and Prescott respectively. Lilburne was clearly worried. His regiment was weary, and he had lost numbers of men on the march, so he was unwilling to risk a fight. This implies also that Derby had many more men than his original 300 by this time. Next day, clearly in response to Lilburne's situation, reinforcements were sent to him: Cromwell detached his own regiment of foot, recruited mainly in Lancashire, from Mansfield, Colonel Birch sent all the infantry he could spare from Liverpool, and 300 foot were sent from Chester. It also seems that Lilburne withdrew the garrison from Manchester. Birch sent ships to prevent the escape of Derby's vessels from the Wyre. The Royalist position in Lancashire, surrounded by converging enemy forces, was a microcosm of that of the king's army.

Massey was recruiting in Manchester, and managed to gather about 500 men. Derby retreated north to Preston, followed by Lilburne, now reinforced. Having drawn him north, Derby then turned back, passed Lilburne and headed for Manchester to join the foot there. Lilburne again followed, closing on him. Near Wigan, Derby turned to fight. He had, presumably, now heard of the approach of Cromwell's foot regiment, which reached Manchester that day (the 25th) and he was thus intent on destroying Lilburne's force before the two enemy forces could join together. Lilburne certainly knew of their approach, for he ordered them towards Wigan, with a warning to take care. Derby seems to have outnumbered Lilburne, having 1,400 or 1,500 men, according to Lilburne. He had thus recruited well over a thousand men in Lancashire, not counting the 500 in Manchester, who never joined him. Lilburne had his own depleted regiment of horse, plus three foot companies and some extra cavalry. Derby clearly had a good chance of victory, and the fighting lasted an hour. Lilburne's account is vague as to the reason for his victory, but the casualties were relatively light, ten of Lilburne's men and sixty of Derby's being killed, though many more were wounded. Derby escaped, wounded, and most of his soldiers were scattered. Some were rounded up by Cromwell's regiment, newly arrived. Lilburne had about 400 prisoners. Most of Derby's force clearly escaped back to their homes.[24]

This little campaign, with no force much above a regiment or so in strength, was more important than the numbers involved suggest. Derby's task was to recruit reinforcements for the king, and he was clearly fairly successful in this. Starting with his own 300 and Massey's under-strength regiment, his forces totalled over 2,000 within a week. He gave it out, according to Lilburne, that there were no republican troops in the area, which reassured the recruits. Given another week, and no interference (scarcely likely, of course), he could well have had a respectable force of several thousands, especially if Massey could persuade the Presbyterians to rise. A victory over Lilburne – and then perhaps one over Cromwell's own regiment! – might have encouraged other waverers. It would certainly have encouraged the main Scots army. Equally, Derby's failure discouraged other potential Royalist supporters, while giving heart to the republicans.

While all this was going on, the various English forces steadily closed in on the king's army. The Scots army marched southwards, with Lambert and Harrison pacing them to the east. Disputes developed as to where the Scots should go. North Wales was suggested, London was Buckingham's choice, the West Country held out some hopes. But the governor of Shrewsbury defied a summons, rudely nailing his colours to the mast by addressing his reply to 'the commander-in-chief of the Scottish army'. Some recruits in southern Shropshire came in. Ahead was Worcester, the last city to be surrendered to the Parliamentary forces in 1646, which would be a useful base from which all the West and Wales could be roused. On August 22, the Scots reached the city. And there they stuck.[25]

The English forces closed in. Cromwell's marching army came steadily south. He met Fairfax at Ferrybridge on the 19th, when Massey was at Manchester; when the Scots threw themselves into Worcester he was at Mansfield, and sent his own regiment to help Lilburne; when Lilburne was winning his little battle near Wigan, on the 25th, he was at Warwick, where at last he met with the commanders of the forces gathering in the south.[26]

The Council of State had co-ordinated all these southern forces. On the 18th Lieutenant-General Fleetwood was appointed commander-in-chief of the army at the Barnet rendezvous. The Scots were then reported to be in Lancashire, and, with a certain sense of relief, the Council commented that 'the country flees from them and carries and drives away all they can'. If that was happening in notoriously Malignant Lancashire, then the rest of the country, as the Council noted, was rising 'very cheerfully'. The rendezvous for the East Anglian and south-east Midlands militias was appointed to be St Albans, and for the east Midlands at Daventry. With the Barnet force there were thus three militia armies gathering in a line in front of the Scots advance. The London militia was appointed to take over the regular army's duties in the city, to release the better troops for the fight.[27]

Fleetwood combined the forces within his reach and moved them forward to Banbury. Lord Grey of Groby had 1,100 horse raised in Northamptonshire and thereabouts. Cromwell's brother-in-law, Major-General John Desborough, came up from Reading. All these men met at Warwick on the 24th, and prepared to bring their forces together under Cromwell's overall command. When his foot and artillery arrived the next day, Cromwell and the Council of State had succeeded in placing their forces, in twice the numbers of the invaders, in front of them. All the English could now slow down and recover their breath in preparation for the battle.[28]

The sheer deliberation, and absence of any sign of panic, are tributes to the nerves of these tough republican soldiers. But there is another aspect to all this which must be addressed. Cromwell's strategy in Scotland had deliberately left the way to the south open to the Royalists. This may well have been the only method he could devise to prise the enemy army out of its prepared defences. But he had shown precious little anxiety about the invasion of England. The Council of State's reaction had also been suspiciously swift and comprehensive, almost as though the danger had long been anticipated. This is surely very likely, and there had certainly been scares before, but Cromwell's strategy had almost *invited* the invasion. It was, when it came, universally denounced, not as an invasion by the Royalists but by the Scots, a foreign invasion of English soil. There is also no doubt that very many people in England did see it that way, so the Council of State's propaganda was working with the grain. In other words, this was doing wonders for the authority and popularity of the new republican government. Some of its leaders were certainly machiavellian enough to perceive the uses to which an invasion could be put, and while it might perhaps be too simplistic to accuse Cromwell of deliberately inviting the invasion, it is certain that he could have done a good deal more to discourage it. But he must always have remembered the argument he had with Fairfax before taking up the Scottish command: Fairfax had said that the invasion of Scotland was an unjust war; so the invasion of England by the Scots, on the other hand, gave him a just cause to fight for. It is significant that Fairfax rallied to the cause in Yorkshire, and that Cromwell had a long talk with his old commander as he rode south. The invasion of the Scots healed lots of English wounds.

Not all Englishmen saw it that way, of course. Some at least were not persuaded by the Council of State's propaganda. There were, in fact, several thousands of Englishmen who rallied to the Royalist cause as they marched south. The Council of State reckoned the Royalist numbers at about 11,000, and the Scots accepted a figure of about 13,000 as they crossed the border. But at the final battle at Worcester, the Royalists numbered, according to Cromwell, about 16,000. Assuming that the Scots army would have lost some men on the march south, and so taking the Council's estimate of 11,000 as the minimum figure of Scots at Worcester, that implies that at least 5,000 Englishmen had joined between Lancashire and Worcester. Then there were those in Lancashire who were raised so briefly by Derby and Massey, another 2,000 perhaps. Some were undoubtedly citizens of Worcester, pressed to serve, and others came in during the ten days the army was camped at the city, but others joined on the march south. It was not safe to admit it after the battle, and by the time Charles became king in 1660 it was a long-lost episode, a defeat not to be too well remembered, hazed over by the memory of the king's heroic escape. But several thousand Lancastrians, men of Cheshire, Salopians, Welshmen, and Worcester men had joined him by the time of the battle.

After the crisis was over, the Council of State pointed out to the Militia Committees of the English counties that 'many persons . . . withdrew from their houses' during the invasion. Some of these had succeeded in joining the king, others were only on their way.[29] It would seem, therefore, that the long delay at Worcester was working in the king's favour, and that his army was growing.

The fact remains, however, that this was not nearly enough. Charles did not only need troops at Worcester or on the way there, he needed actual risings elsewhere in order to pin down the republican troops who menaced him. Yet there were none. Not even in Wales, where one hoped-for recruit, Sir Thomas Middleton, in Montgomeryshire,[30] simply arrested the king's messenger and sent him to the Council of State in London. Yet the numbers which did come in are yet another indication of the attraction of the king's name. Even facing certain defeat he could bring out thousands.

CHAPTER EIGHT

WORCESTER

August 22 – September 3, 1651

THE use of Worcester by the Scots had been anticipated by either Lambert or the Council of State, and a garrison of 500 men had been pushed into the city, horse and dragoons. They were not popular. The townsmen, from the Mayor and the Common Council down, could see a body of 500 men proposing to fight an army of 15,000 in the midst of their city. It was a big enough force to make a fight, but too small to hold the city for long. The citizens could only look forward to violence, destruction, and sack. The assumption had been that the citizens would make up the numbers to a defensible force, but this was mistaken. Worcester had suffered quite enough in the civil wars, and the great majority of men took neither side. When the new garrison shut the gates on the approaching royal army, they were threatened by the Common Council. When the garrison persisted, and sallied out to discomfit the approach of the forlorn Royalists, the townsmen rose against them, and harried them out of the city and over the Severn bridge.[1]

This was not the prelude to a lavish welcome for the king, however. The mayor, Thomas Lysons, and the Sheriff, James Brydges, did turn out, knelt, ceremonially gave up the keys and so on, and this may have dazzled the king for a time. But not for long. The citizens' resistance to the activities of the republican garrison had not been the result of Royalist enthusiasm, but rather of a wish to be left alone. The opening of the North Gate to let the king and the Scots into the city was accompanied no doubt by a similar opening of the Sidbury Gate, at least symbolically, and the lowering of the drawbridge, inviting them to keep on going.

But they didn't. The English thought the Scots were sick, footsore, and mutinous, and that Charles had taken refuge in the city to rest his army. He was there by the 23rd, when he met, and knighted, the mayor, and by next day the decision had been made to stay in the city, and convert it to a defensive bastion.[2] So much for the citizens' hopes.

This is clearly a change of plan by the king. Since entering England, a fortnight before, the army's southward march had been continuous, and Worcester was a good place from which to strike in any one of several directions. Continuing with this plan would imply a resumption of the march on the 24th or 25th. The king clearly changed his mind, and two considerations were presumably uppermost. One was the continuing expectation that a rally to his banner was imminent. The response in Lancashire had been slow, but Derby had perhaps reported a steady growth of support. Massey arrived at Worcester about this time, with forty men, and could report that Derby had recruited up to 2,000 men, outnumbering Lilburne's detachment. Wales should have the chance to contribute, and perhaps the Western Association was expected to rise. Worcester was a good centre upon which all these forces could rally. Certainly it was expected that the local gentry and people would come in.

The second consideration perhaps owed its force to the successful defensive strategies of Leslie in Scotland. Based at Edinburgh and then Stirling, the Scots had, after all, held up Cromwell's conquest for a full year. Worcester was in a strategic position similar to Stirling's, backed by loyal territory to the west, and controlling a vital bridge. Cromwell had shown a marked reluctance to attack well-defended cities. Here was another chance to use the same method. The effect on the reluctant Royalists in England of a Royalist army encamped in a famous city in the centre of England, perhaps for months, could only be encouraging. In Scotland the effect had been to bring all parties into the Royalist camp. Perhaps the same would happen in England. The authority of the republican government was by no means powerful enough to withstand the strain of such a situation. The response to the king's arrival had certainly been lukewarm, but he had only been in England a fortnight. There was plenty of evidence of loyal feelings – rebellions in Norfolk and Cardigan in the past year, the passive resistance to the republican regime by Presbyterians, the continued existence of the conspiratorial Royalist associations – all of which could be exploited over the long term.

This, of course, was the crucial point. The republic could see this as well, and its response had been to emphasise the foreign invasion, its weakness, and to aim to contain it and destroy it quickly and thoroughly. The Scots experience of Cromwell's methods in the north was not therefore relevant. For now, for the first time, he had superiority in numbers. For the first time he could squander lives in an assault on defended positions. By locking themselves into Worcester, the Scots and the king were ensuring their own defeat. Yet it is difficult to see what else they could have done. The impossibility of a Scots conquest of England was evident, just as the maintenance of Scots independence of England relied on English forebearance.

It seems unlikely that the king and his generals had accurate information about the movements and strengths of their enemies, but something could be conjectured on the basis of minimal knowledge. The presence of Lambert and Harrison on their left was well known, and presumbly by this time the march of Cromwell's force to the south was known to them in outline. The gathering of forces in the south of England could be presumed, if details were unclear. The militia of the counties the Scots had marched through had been called out by the Council of State, so the various rendezvous in the Midlands were known. The sense of having advanced into hostile territory would have been growing; the sense of being enclosed and surrounded at Worcester undoubtedly affected them.

But, having been ceremonially welcomed, the king set about the necessary measures for rendering the city defensible, and drumming up the required forces. A proclamation went out on the 23rd, summoning all men of Worcestershire between the ages of 16 and 60 to a parade at Pitchcroft, a level area north of the city (now the racecourse) for the 26th.[3] The constables of the parishes around the city were ordered to send in contingents of men to repair the fortifications, and to dig and build new ones.

There followed a pause until these orders could be received and responded to. On Sunday the 24th the basic difficulty the king faced was illuminated when the notables attended a service in the cathedral. The differences between the Scots and the English were emphasised when the sermon at the Cathedral, attended by the king and his commanders, was preached by a man called Crosby in purely Royalist terms. The Covenanters were not at all pleased, and Crosby had to be reprimanded, perhaps not too severely.[4]

Next morning, the 25th, parties were sent out to break the bridges over the Severn at Upton and Bewdley.[5] This would leave Worcester bridge the only one intact over the river south of Bridgnorth, 30 miles away to the north. The west would thus be largely isolated. And if Derby won in Lancashire, the king would control all the west and half the north. In addition the army in Worcester would not be taken in the flank, and would therefore be able to fight behind the city's fortifications with a secure escape route over the bridge behind it.

The muster on Pitchcroft next day was not so convincing, however. A number of the local gentry later claimed to have appeared at the muster, but the list is probably a later compilation. Sir John Pakington of Westwood Park claimed that he was taken forcibly to Worcester, and avoided any incriminating actions; Sir Rowland Berkeley of Spetchley proved that he was not there at all; Lord Talbot of Grafton Manor stood to lose heavily if the republicans won. What is singular about the list, however, is that it comprises men whose seats were mainly in the northern half of the county, the part through which the Scots army had already marched. Whatever the truth of the list, these men were implicated, and the lack of republican vindictiveness after the battle ensured their escape. The later list of their names is thus perhaps based on more than a wish to gain royal favour after the Restoration.[6]

The main problem for the king was that these men were distressingly few. The muster on Pitchcroft meadow on the 26th produced, so it is said, 2,000 men: a not inconsiderable number to appear in two days, but it is probable that few of them were either trained soldiers or were equipped as such. Nor did they evince much enthusiasm for the royal cause.[7] Yet they did boost the Royalists' numbers to 16,000 or so, of whom several thousand were now Englishmen who had joined on the march since Carlisle – perhaps one third of the total. And this was the product of a foreign invasion, and in the absence of a royal victory on English soil. It was no mean number, and provided a certain degree of encouragement for the king and the Scots.

Major-General Massey had commanded for Parliament in Gloucester during the civil war, and he knew this whole area. Now he rode south, past the broken bridge at Upton, leaving a garrison there, and another at Hanley Castle, the home of the republican lawyer Sir Nicholas Lechmere. Massey's arrival with forty men, from Lancashire, had brought good news of Derby's progress there. Now he was aiming to renew old acquaintance in Gloucestershire, but he could not raise much support. He ferried across the Severn between Tewkesbury and Gloucester, but could only locate a group of women, who were uninformative. He returned to Hanley Castle and its garrison of 130 Scots horse.[8]

The fortification of Worcester went on apace. No doubt the unarmed men who arrived at Pitchcroft found themselves employed in digging, along with any men of Worcester who were too slow to avoid being drafted, and others from the countryside were dragooned in to help. The walls were protected with earthen banks, the star-shaped fort out along the London road was refurbished and connected to the walls by earthworks, and the north gate was blocked. The fort was ceremonially named Fort Royal. There were not enough men to hold all the walls, but it was probably never the intention to sit behind them and fight a siege. If the Scots *were* besieged, they had lost. More serious was the shortage of artillery. The Scots had been short of guns at home, and very few had been brought south with the army, nor were many to be found on the march. What there were went into Fort Royal.[9] The king meanwhile had issued yet another proclamation on the day of the muster at Pitchcroft, more or less in the same terms as that issued at Carlisle. He offered a Covenanted religion, and amnesty and pay for all deserters from the Commonwealth armies, except for the regicides.[10] That is, he was still fully in the grip of the Scots. The proclamation had no discernible effect. The presence of the Scots army was the argument most of the English took note of; no assurances of liberty counterbalanced that.

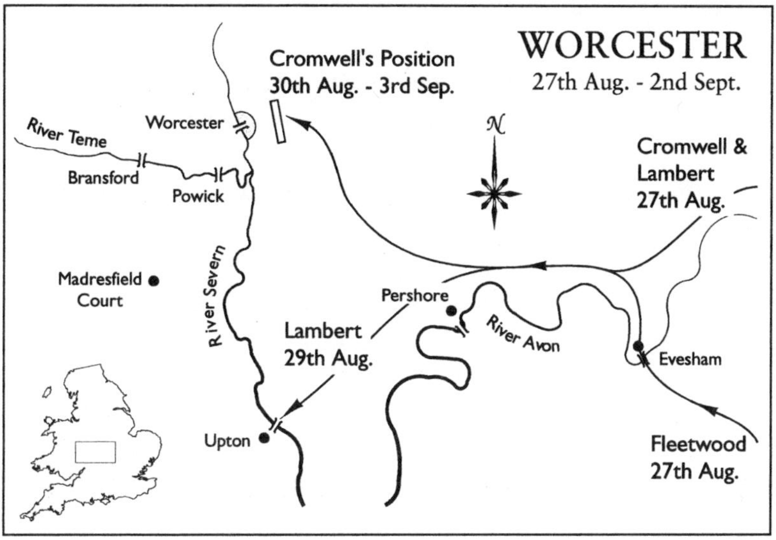
WORCESTER
27th Aug. - 2nd Sept.
Cromwell's Position
30th Aug. - 3rd Sep.
Worcester
River Teme
Bransford
Powick
River Severn
Madresfield Court
Pershore
Lambert
29th Aug.
River Avon
Evesham
Cromwell &
Lambert
27th Aug.
Upton
Fleetwood
27th Aug.
N

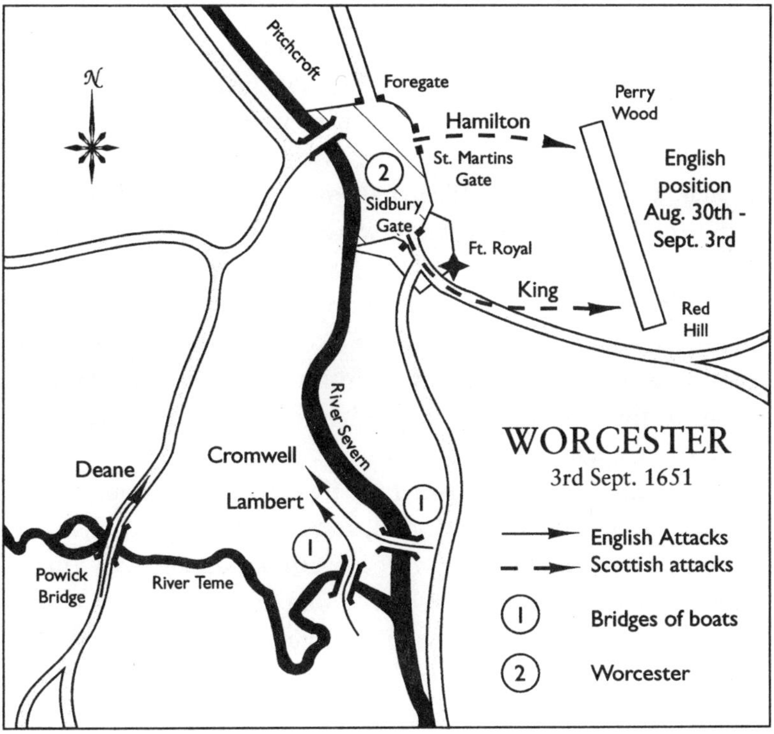
Pitchcroft
Foregate
Perry
Wood
Hamilton
St. Martins
Gate
English
position
Aug. 30th -
Sept. 3rd
Sidbury
Gate
Ft. Royal
King
Red
Hill
River Severn
WORCESTER
3rd Sept. 1651
Deane
Cromwell
Lambert
Powick
Bridge
River Teme
English Attacks
Scottish attacks
Bridges of boats
Worcester
N

The armies of the English republic were meanwhile steadily closing in on the city of Worcester. After his conference at Warwick on the 24th with Fleetwood, Groby, and Desborough, Cromwell brought his forces on slowly. They were at Stratford-on-Avon by the 26th, and marched on to Evesham next day, where they were joined by Fleetwood's army. There were still several other contingents in other places, but even now the main English army was 28,000 strong, much larger than that of Charles.[11]

And now the news from Lancashire began to affect the situation. Lilburne's messengers reached Cromwell by the 27th, at Stratford, and he sent back an order for Lilburne to come south to Worcester, then countermanded that order and sent him to Shrewsbury instead. Thus Lilburne would both block the route into Wales, and be available to move south towards Worcester if needed. And indeed soon afterwards Lilburne was ordered further south to hold Bewdley, and the bridge over the Severn there.[12]

Everything slowed down. Cromwell now knew exactly where the king's army was, saw that it was not moving, and was indeed entrenching, and he could see clearly that the chance had at last arrived to enclose that army and crush it utterly. Next day, the 25th, Lambert and Harrison reached him, with perhaps another 7,000 or more men, tough cavalry. His army was now over double that of the king and the Scots, and still more were approaching. Gloucester was strongly held, and the miners of the Forest of Dean had come out for the republic. The militia of Hereford, where there were very unpleasant memories of the behaviour of the Scots army during their siege of the city in 1645, had taken guard against a repetition, despite the basic Royalism of the citizens. Bewdley, Hereford, Gloucester, Evesham – the king's army was surrounded.[13]

For the main army, there was now no hurry, the troops could rest and recover from their long marches, and careful preparations could be made to ensure that none of the Royalists escaped. On the 28th, Cromwell advanced from Evesham along the Worcester road, and marched his huge army to camping grounds along the ridge overlooking Worcester from the east. The army was deployed along a line of low hills, about a mile from the city, which they overlooked. The key was Red Hill where the London road began to dip down in its approach to the city. This was the centre of the Commonwealth line, with forces spread along the hills for a mile or more, troops towards the north as far as Perry Wood, and more placed on the low ground between Red Hill and the river. The main position was from Red Hill to Perry Wood. Cromwell took up his quarters at the ruined house of Sir Rowland Berkeley at Spetchley.[14]

He had already contemplated a siege, and had asked the Council of State for 5,000 shovels, spades, and pickaxes, just in case.[15] He had also identified, as the Royalists had, the absolute necessity of getting a force across the river onto the western side, so as to block the Royalist retreat. On the 28th, as his main force began moving directly on Worcester, Lambert was sent with some horse and dragoons down to Upton. Whether Cromwell knew the bridge was broken is unclear; it is likely he was simply exploring all possible options. If Lambert could get across the bridge, he should do so.

Lambert was just the daredevil to accomplish this. Keeping his men out of sight on the night of the 28th, at dawn next day he sent a small group of dragoons to the bridge to cross by the single plank which the Scots had left over the gap they had broken in the bridge. Other men were sent to cross the river by the ford downstream. There was no guard on or near the bridge, and the men were able to get right across in single file, and to form into a body before they were noticed. They went into the church, and resisted the counter-attack by the now awakened Scots. Meanwhile the other party, also undetected, had crossed the river by the ford below the bridge, and they now tackled the Scots at the church from behind. The fighting was fierce for a time, and Massey himself came to supervise, only to be badly wounded in the hand and arm. The Scots were driven off and out of the village.

There had been some hundreds of Scots soldiers in the village, and so Lambert's men had won a notable, if small, victory. He sent word to Fleetwood, his immediate superior, for infantry to repair the bridge, while his horse and dragoons moved out to secure the village and its surrounding lands. The Scots withdrew northwards, across the river Teme at Powick. Lambert and Fleetwood now occupied Upton, and repaired the bridge, but did nothing more for the present. The achievement was clearly seen as a welcome but minor one, since the bridge at Upton did not give access to the western side of Worcester. There was still the river Teme to cross, flowing from west to east between Worcester and Upton. Possession of Upton, however, did tighten the ring about Worcester, and prevented Massey from operating southwards again.

Next day Cromwell came to see what his men had achieved. He was greeted uproariously by the soldiers, as so often when he roamed a battlefield before a fight, looking for openings and stratagems. The seizure of the Upton bridge was useful, but in itself it was by no means decisive. It seems that it was Cromwell, or perhaps the three generals together, who now saw the opportunity which the position presented. Lambert was set to collect all the boats he could find along the river, to make new bridges out of them.[16]

The Scots in Worcester launched two probing attacks that night. One was directed due south along the Kempsey road, where Cromwell's forces were spread rather thinly, little more than a dense picquet line, from the low hills to the river; the other was directed at Red Hill, the southernmost post on those hills, along the line of the London road. Surprise was lost before the attacks began, because a man called Guise, a Puritan tailor in the town, somehow warned the English army in advance. So neither attack achieved anything except to confirm that the republican forces were tough and well placed. Guise was caught and hanged in the morning.[17]

Guise was not the only anti-Royalist in the city, and not the only one to risk his life to pass information to Cromwell's forces. After the battle Parliament made a point of ordering the Council of State to 'give reasonable gratuities to such persons as gave intelligence to our forces in the transactions at Worcester', and Cromwell had already asked that Guise's family should be compensated for his death. But Parliament's lugubrious prose went on to single out 'the little maid' who had been mentioned to the Members.[18] There is no other detail, no record of the girl's name, no sign that she was actually rewarded. Who was she? It is provoking not to know.

Cromwell faced a dilemma, as so often in military affairs. His reluctance to assault a well-prepared and fortified position was well known. It was one of the reasons his soldiers were so pleased to see him in command. It provoked his enemies into taking up such positions, but then they were hypnotised into watching what he would do to avoid that assault. They could be reasonably sure that the one thing he would not do was to mount an attack on the walls and the fort at Worcester. Beyond that, he had gained the initiative, as his enemies waited for his move. And now, having control of a bridge, Cromwell could develop an attack along the western bank.

But this only provided another dilemma. His problem now was the river. If he transported a substantial section of his army across to the western side, using Upton bridge, the river would then divide his army, and this would cancel his superiority in numbers, giving the Royalists the chance to destroy his army piecemeal. Any force on the western side might well reach the western end of Worcester bridge, if it could get across the Teme, but Worcester bridge was a drawbridge, easy to defend, and so using it to invade the city itself was out of the question. He therefore needed yet another bridge, across the Severn, one that was closer to the city than the one at Upton, so that he could bring his troops back to the eastern side quickly. Hence Lambert's collecting of the boats, which were to be made into a bridge to cross the river. By Monday the Royalists realised what he was preparing, and a force came out of the city to break down the two bridges over the Teme, at Powick and Bransford. A party of horse covered the bridge-breakers, and clashed briefly with one of Fleetwood's patrols.[19] Once those bridges were broken, the river Teme became as formidable an obstacle as the Severn had been. It thus became necessary to prepare *two* bridges of boats, one for the Severn and one for the Teme.

All this inevitably took time: to collect the boats, tow them to the assembly points, gather nails and planks, construct the bridges, test them. Only then could any serious assault on the Royalists be mounted. Lambert meanwhile patrolled the lands to the north of Upton, taking control of Madresfield Court, a place the Council of State had been worried about even before the invasion, remembering its role in the earlier siege of Worcester in 1646. On the Sunday night (the 31st), Lambert also led a patrol right up to the city, where most of the suburbs had been burned to provide a clear field of fire. However, he had omitted to warn his own side what he was doing. When the Scots discovered him and fired, the whole English army sprang to arms. There were rumours in the English camp that the Scots were preparing to flee, or that they were quarrelling with each other, or that duels were being arranged between commanders, or that the foot had mutinied, and so on. None of it, except the disputes among the commanders, is likely to have been true. Nor was Lambert blamed.[20]

On the Royalist side, however, there were certainly discussions among the commanders about what to do. Which is only to be expected. The Royalist options were four: attack, stand on the defensive in the city, or retreat either north or west. None of these held any serious attraction. To attack a well-posted enemy twice their size was to invite defeat, and those defences had already been tested and had held. The defensive was just as unattractive, for an army which simply defends itself always loses. The openings for retreat were getting fewer as time went on, as the routes were successively blocked. Hereford was now held by the Monmouth and Hereford militias; Ludlow with its formidable castle was now held strongly; Lilburne was at Shrewsbury, and was moving south towards Bewdley, and on the Tuesday another detachment of a regiment of horse under Colonel Barton was despatched from the main army to hold Bewdley. So none of these alternatives was a serious proposition. Still more serious, it had become clear that these blocked routes now prevented any further reinforcements getting through. (The fact that there were none on the way is irrelevant.) The prospect of holding Worcester as a Stirling behind which to bring up the Welsh and the westerners no longer existed. No wonder there were disputes among the commanders.

And steadily, like water dripping on a stone, the Scots' and the king's resolution was being worn down by bad news. The capture of Stirling by the English under General Monck had been disbelieved at first, but none could gainsay Derby's defeat when he arrived at Worcester, wounded and with only eighty men.[21] Cromwell's artillery began to bombard the city from the hills, probably doing little damage, but the Royalists could not reply. All the Royalists' options were vanishing. Now there was only one: to fight it out against Cromwell's superior army – superior in every way. In particular that army was unassailable in its positions. So the Scots and the king had to wait to see what Cromwell was doing, and then profit from any mistakes he made. Not an inviting prospect.

The Royalists, however, did enjoy a number of advantages, and these were by no means negligible. They held a central, fortified position, their army was tough and experienced, with good, experienced commanders, and they could see, almost predict, the moves Cromwell was making. The Cathedral tower, with the use of 'prospective glasses', allowed a clear view of most of Cromwell's positions, and the Royalists could gain a warning of any movements. It became clear that the force under Fleetwood at Upton was increasing, and that meant that it would be used in the attack. Leslie could point out Cromwell's reluctance to mount an attack on a well-defended position – 'the Leith-Edinburgh lines', he could say, or 'Stirling' – and so they could assume that a direct assault on the city was most unlikely. Leslie could also point out the basic similarity of Cromwell's problem at Worcester to that he had faced on a much larger scale in Scotland, where Stirling took the place of Worcester and the Forth estuary that of the Severn. Lambert's boat-collecting forays, and the bridge-building activity, were surely known in the city. The bridges would have been built as close to the points at which they were to be used as possible, just south of the confluence of the Teme and the Severn, and the activity could scarcely have been hidden. Indeed, Cromwell probably would not want it to be hidden, for it might keep the Royalists guessing, and so it would provide options for him.

It is these bridges which account for the long delay in mounting the attack. Cromwell may have been gratified to know that the battle took place on the anniversary of Dunbar, but he would scarcely wait several days for the anniversary to arrive. Generals do not think or act that way. It was not until the Wednesday, September 3, that he was able to mount the attack, because it was only then that he was ready.

The battle began in the morning of the 3rd, with the movement of Fleetwood's and Deane's brigades north out of Upton towards the Teme crossings. They took their time, and problems are said to have arisen, but they did have seven miles to go, and neither commander would want to hurry; it would not be sensible to arrive at the battlefield out of breath, so to say. But the main cause of delay, surely, was the problem of getting the bridges of boats into position. There were two, one to cross the Severn, to be placed just north of the confluence with the Teme, and the other to cross the Teme, just upstream from that confluence; the two were 'within pistol shot' of one another, not more than, say, fifty yards apart. But these could not have been positioned earlier, for they would not be left exposed to the enemy. As soon as they were in position, troops had to cross to guard the dual bridgehead.

Here was where the choice of position paid dividends. The bridges led to what is in effect a peninsula between the two rivers, an area which could be easily held, at least for a short time, by a fairly small force, a 'forlorn', and which could be protected by fire from the southern and eastern banks of the rivers. So, as the two bridges were positioned, a forlorn of Fleetwood's brigade ran across the Teme bridge, and one of Cromwell's, led by Oliver in person, crossed that over the Severn. Meanwhile, another attack, noisy and attention-grabbing, was mounted by Deane's brigade on the Powick bridge, which, though broken, was not irreparable, and where a ford also existed – the lesson of Upton was that broken bridges could be crossed, and that they needed to be defended by a close guard.

The distraction caused by Deane at Powick was sufficiently effective to seem to the Scots to be the more threatening attack, and in fact Deane's forces did get across in the end. But the main English effort was at the bridges of boats. As the fighting began, King Charles came to investigate in person. Major-General Montgomery's horse was supporting Colonel Sir William Keith's highland foot at Powick. At the bridges of boats were the Highlanders of Major-General Pitscottie. These bore the brunt of the English attack. Over the bridge behind Cromwell came Colonel Hacker's regiment of horse, then the foot regiments of Ingoldsby and Fairfax, then part of Cromwell's own regiment of horse and his life guards; from the south, across the Teme bridge, came Major-General Deane's and Colonel Goffe's regiments of foot, a total of six regiments, perhaps 5,000 or 6,000 men. As their numbers increased, so the narrow peninsula must have been very crowded and they could push outwards. The land was hedged fields, and the Highlanders of Pitscottie's brigade made good use of the protection of the hedges to delay the English advance.

Only delay, however. It was in the Royalist interest to draw as much English strength across to the western bank as possible, so the Highlanders fought stubbornly, but they also steadily retreated. Three more regiments were drawn north across the Teme bridge, and three others were being employed at the Powick bridge, before the Scots were driven back to Worcester. The withdrawal was evidently orderly and well conducted, and few of the Scots seem to have been captured. Keith's brigade only gave up the fight at Powick when Pitscottie's men had been driven back, so threatening to expose Keith's flank. Both forces were able to withdraw slowly enough for their reserve troops under Montgomery and Dalziel to pull back into the city across Worcester bridge first. These latter two had scarcely been engaged, and the two defeated brigades were much smaller in number than their English attackers.

This fight had lasted an hour or more, and it was now mid-afternoon. At once, with a large proportion, perhaps a third, of Cromwell's strength now uselessly on the western bank, the Royalists in the city mounted a powerful attack on the main enemy position on the ridge of low hills to the east. Two assaults were made, one led by the Duke of Hamilton out of St Martin's Gate, aimed at the northern end of the Commonwealth line at Perry Wood, the other led by King Charles himself out of Sidbury Gate, past Fort Royal, and against the southern end of the main Commonwealth line at Red Hill.

Both attacks achieved momentary success, and the Commonwealth forces were pushed back a short distance. The noise told Cromwell what he must have surely been expecting, that the main attack had begun. He immediately moved some of the troops on the west bank back across the bridge of boats over the Severn, and used them to bolster his line. In fact, they would have acted mainly upon the king's right flank, extending the line at Red Hill back towards the river. Precisely which regiments were used in this move is not clear, but two are implied in one of the accounts: Desborough's and Cobbet's regiments were both involved in Fleetwood's attack and in the fighting on the hills. Cromwell's own regiment of horse may have been a third. Cromwell was prominent here, 'riding up and down in the midst of the horse', surely once more showing the exaltation in battle which had been visible at Dunbar.

The fight at the hills is said to have lasted three hours, but this is likelier to have been the total time of the fighting, from the opening shots at the bridges to the storming of Worcester. The failure of the Royalist assault would have become evident once the Commonwealth line solidified, and the Royalist defeat would have become clear to all once Cromwell brought his reinforcements back across the river and into position. All this cannot have taken more than an hour, perhaps less.

The king had not committed all his forces, for Leslie, with a body of horse stationed at Pitchcroft meadow, was not used. Needless to say, Leslie was blamed, even to the extent that he was said to have refused the king's order to cross over to the west side of the river. He was also described as 'amazed or seeking to fly'. But the land around Worcester was no more suitable for cavalry than the closes at Warrington. Leslie's horse could not make any difference to the fight on the hills, since the roads – the only way forward for horses – were blocked by the rest of the Scots. His designated role was, surely, to pursue the defeated English, an eventuality which did not occur. Those who criticised him, did so in profound ignorance of the intentions of the various commanders, and in particular of the king. If Leslie did refuse to charge, it would have been at the end, when he would be refusing to waste the lives of his men in a manifestly lost cause.

On the hills, once the Royalists were stopped they were beaten. As they retreated, they were followed by their enemies, so closely that the two armies became intermixed. The Essex militia stormed Fort Royal, cleared it in some bitter fighting, and then turned its guns on the city, and on its walls, and on the increasing confusion inside. Hamilton's attack was also driven back, apparently not directly to St Martin's Gate. Cromwell was present at the assault on the Sidbury Gate. These two events signalled the final act, the confused fighting in the city, along the streets and in some of the houses. Charles got back to the city, and was nearly caught in the fighting, but he and those Royalists with horses got away, to the north, carrying with them Leslie's brigade of horse.

The Commonwealth army admitted to no more than 200 dead, including two officers – one was Quartermaster-General Moseley, the other Captain Jones of Cobbet's regiment, one of the busiest regiments of that day, while Captain Howard of Cromwell's life guard was badly wounded. Major-General Lambert had yet another horse shot from under him. The Royalists had several thousand dead, perhaps 2,000, though no-one ever counted accurately. The streets of Worcester were strewn with the dead. The vast majority, as at Dunbar, became prisoners, 10,000 of them (another very round figure), many of whom were wounded. Some 4,000 were thought to have escaped.[22]

During the following days many of these escapees were captured. The English who got away had the advantage, and little is heard of them, for they could often get home, or at least pretend to republicanism. The Scots betrayed themselves as soon as they spoke. The king, with Derby, Leslie, Middleton, and the mass of the horse rode northwards. At the Worcestershire border the king wisely separated from the rest, going on his travels by way of the Royalist resistance network, but sensibly steering clear of the great lords whose loyalty had been heavily compromised by the system of fines and forfeitures imposed by Parliament.

The rest, perhaps designedly drawing attention to themselves, went on northwards. Cromwell's precautions at Bewdley availed little, and by the afternoon of the 5th, a body estimated at 1,000 of the Scots was reported riding north through Sandbach in Cheshire. They were pelted by the townsmen with clubs and stones and sticks, though when the fugitives turned and threatened to fire, opposition instantly ceased. Perhaps it was this same group which reached Congleton, and lost some more of their men there. The hostility to the Scots had risen with their deepening distress. The king was able to agree most heartily with the Bromsgrove blacksmith who blamed him for bringing in the Scots to Worcestershire. The experience of flight was part of his essential education.

Gradually the fugitives were thinned out, and as despair and hunger took them they were captured. Derby and Lauderdale and fifteen other men surrendered voluntarily to a single startled captain of Cromwell's regiment of foot. Colonel Barton at Bewdley took some hundreds, and then rode north after the main body. Major-General Harrison captured 700 at Market Drayton, and more in the pursuit. Over 300 were taken in Lancashire by Yorkshire militiamen brought across the Pennines. The main body split up in Cheshire: some tried to go back the way they had come, by way of Warrington; others used the Pennine tracks over Blackstone Edge; still others tried to get away northwards through Yorkshire. Leslie, Middleton, and van Druschke were taken at Rochdale, the Earl of Kenmure near Lancaster, Montgomery between Halifax and Bradford. And each of these had soldiers with him. As is repeatedly said in contemporary accounts, 'the country rose against them', and 'all have stuck in the hands of the countrypeople by hundreds and fifties'. Some certainly escaped all the way to Scotland, but they were numbered in tens.[23]

For the second time in a year the Scots' main army had been destroyed, most of its men having become prisoners, and for the second time in a year the English state had to cope with them. This time, however, the matter was complicated by the mixed nature of the prisoners. Most were Scots, but there were significant numbers of Englishmen as well. The first attempt to deal with the problem concerned those men taken by Colonel Lilburne in Lancashire. These were Englishmen, and could be treated as Royalists taken in the civil wars. The officers were to be held and tried as rebels, the men mainly released to go home, though every tenth man was to be held at Liverpool or Lancaster, for what purpose was not stated.[24]

But the problem of the prisoners taken at Worcester was altogether different. As early as September 6, the Council of State wrote to Cromwell that, although the prisoners were to be sent to London, they should not be hurried onward, since the Council needed time to prepare for them. At the same time, the Council had to take note of an Order-in-Parliament that the prisoners being taken by Monck in Scotland – meaning the nobles in particular – should also be brought to London.[25]

When they began arriving in London, the prisoners were held at three main centres: at Tothill Fields, upstream from Westminster, at the Tiltyard at Greenwich, and at the East India House and yard at Blackwall. As problems arose they were tackled: accommodation for the guards at Tothill, an allowance for feeding them, the appointment of guards for the march. The high officers were to be tried. As it became clear that those who had escaped from the battlefield were being rounded up all over the North and the Midlands, lists of prisoners were required. And then how to 'dispose' of the prisoners was considered.[26]

The language is instructive. They were to be 'disposed' of. The word is a constant. They were to be 'provisioned' and 'convoyed'. They were, in short, to be considered as goods and treated accordingly. The word 'slave' is never actually used, but the concept is clearly present, and it became almost explicit when it was decided to get rid of the Scots ministers who had been captured, by sending them off to the colonies. Unlike the ordinary Scots they were to accompany, they were not to be 'under servitude'.[27]

By September 16 the Council had decided that its prisoners Committee could send all prisoners below the rank of captain to the 'plantations'. The wounded were to be attended and sheltered, but the priority was clearly to get rid of as many of them as possible as soon as possible. Those at Chester, Worcester, Liverpool, and Shrewsbury were sent to Bristol to be shipped off, and Virginia and Bermuda were specified. Three hundred were sent to New England, of whom about thirty died on the voyage; the survivors went first to the Saugus Iron Works where they joined their compatriots captured at Dunbar, and were mostly then sold on in smaller groups to farmers and millowners all over New England. A thousand others were contracted to work at draining the Fens, with heavy penalties on the contractors for escapees. Those at Newcastle and Durham – captured at Dunbar a year earlier in most cases – were to be shipped to Lynn for employment in the Fens.[28]

Once again the conclusion is inescapable, that the great majority of Scots prisoners never returned home. Only those who avoided capture on the way home, and those who got away from the prisoners' march to London, and *then* got to Scotland, saw their homes again. The rest died, of wounds, sickness, or overwork, or were transported to the English colonies in America. The Council of State might exhort the contractors to give assurance of 'Christian usage', but by using contractors at all it was abdicating all responsibility, just as Cromwell did after Dumbar.[29]

For England the loss of a few thousand men (at the maximum) was bad enough, but for Scotland the loss of twenty thousand men was close to being a demographic disaster. The total population of Scotland was less than a million people, of whom perhaps 200,000 would be adult males. The removal of ten per cent of the male population, predominantly of the younger and most vigorous group, weakened the kingdom for a generation. This was on top of fourteen previous years of war, revolution, and disturbance. It is a casualty rate vastly in excess of that of any European state in either the First or Second World Wars. No state can easily cope with such losses, and Scotland necessarily required a generation and more to recover. It is not surprising that it was a quiet country for that time, and that its union with England and its rule by Monck passed so relatively peacefully. It was the peace of exhaustion.

CHAPTER NINE

STIRLING AND DUNDEE

August 2 – September 9, 1651

EVEN while he was preoccupied by the march of his army back into England, Cromwell more than once reminded the Council of State of the problems likely to be faced by Lieutenant-General Monck. He had left Monck in charge in Scotland, but with an army which he could only assume was inadequate for the various tasks it faced. After all, although the Royalist army invading England was the larger part of the Scots forces, the remaining garrisons and forces still outnumbered Monck's army if taken all together. They were defending their homes, and held well-fortified positions, of which Stirling had defied Cromwell himself for a year, though they were, because of these obligations, scattered. Cromwell certainly had reservations about Monck's strength. As early as August 4, he added a final comment in a letter to the Speaker in London: 'I hope I have left a commanding force under Lieutenant-General Monck in Scotland', a sentence which has scarcely the ring of a confident commander-in-chief. The Council was thinking similarly, and on August 7 wrote to Haselrig at Newcastle that he should raise 1,200 men for service in Scotland.[1]

Monck's forces were, in truth, small enough, but not so small as is sometimes assumed. He had been left with four regiments of horse, under Colonels Hacker, Okey, Alured, and Grosvenor, and three of foot, his own and those of Ashfield and Rede. But he lost Hacker's regiment at once, for it was ordered south with Cromwell on August 5 – the day after Cromwell's misgivings were committed to paper. He also had two companies of firelockmen, and five troops of dragoons under Colonel Morgan. Most important, however, the greater part of the artillery train had also been left with him. To replace Hacker's regiment Monck was allocated Haselrig's former regiment, which had been in garrison, principally at Linlithgow, and was now placed under the newly promoted Colonel James Berry.[2]

This force was under Monck's direct command, the 5,000 or 6,000 men Cromwell referred to. But there were other English forces elsewhere in Scotland. Colonel Overton had been left at Perth as governor, with two regiments,[3] and there were other troops left in garrisons in southern Scotland, in particular in Leith and Edinburgh under Colonel Fenwick, who were perhaps the same strength as Overton's forces. Then there were scattered garrisons in the lands and houses south of Edinburgh, mainly guarding the road to Berwick and England. So the actual English force in Scotland was nearer 10,000 men.

Even so, this was a small enough force, in all conscience, with which to hold southern Scotland, *and* to conquer the land from Stirling northwards. Monck could not seriously expect much in the way of reinforcement for many weeks, and perhaps not for the rest of the year, depending on the conduct of affairs in England. Further, with the king out of the way, the complexity of Scottish politics might be expected to be somewhat easier; in particular, he might find that the Scots would rally round to expel the invader, especially now that the invasion force was so much weaker, just as England was rallying to the unpopular republican government at the same time in the face of foreign attack. There was still a considerable reservoir of military manpower left in Scotland. The Highlands had not been very successfully levied by any of the Scots parties, and the West of Scotland had been abandoned by both Royalists and English until Montgomery's brief levying activities just before the move into England. The Covenanting sentiment there was strong, and could be tapped by any authority willing to appeal to it. Then there were the Campbell lands, where Argyll had sat out the various disputes for months, and where he could raise an army of some thousands, if he wanted to. Many of the men who deserted from the king's army on its way south did so because they did not want to fight in England, but that did not mean they would not fight the English in Scotland. Above all, many of the men remaining in Scotland had had some military experience, and there were plenty of arms and armaments about in the country after the long years of warfare. The potential for a strong Scottish resistance was considerable, if it could be organised.

The king had, in fact, left a functioning government behind him in Scotland. The Chancellor, the earl of Loudoun, was its head, and the earl of Leven was still the nominal commander-in-chief of the army. The Committee of Estates continued to exist, as did the Parliament, though this was not in session. This was the theory, but Charles had also left one final vial of poison behind when he marched south, effectively paralysing the government which should have co-ordinated resistance to Monck: the king had appointed the Earl of Crawford-Lindsay as commander-in-chief of the Scots army.[4] David Leslie having marched off to England with the king, and Leven having been an inactive commander-in-chief for years, the king could argue that a new one was clearly needed. His choice, however, was more political than military. Crawford-Lindsay had been an unsuccessful Covenanting commander against Montrose, then an Engager, and he had only just been re-admitted into military and political affairs by the repeal of the Act of Classes. He was now a thoroughgoing Royalist.

The purpose of this appointment was to block the Kirk party, whom the king rightly expected to seize the opportunity provided by his absence to try to regain the power which they had lost to him during the summer.[5] Crawford-Lindsay's other task, which was apparently secondary, was to recruit a new army and use it to drive out the English. The result was, of course, confusion, many disputes, a rapid collapse of Scots morale, and the fragmentation of the remaining powers of resistance in the kingdom.

The forces in Scotland were therefore more evenly matched than any numerical calculation might suggest. The Scots certainly had more troops, both immediately available and in arms, than the English, but both had to leave much of their strength in garrisons. The Scots' political divisions more than cancelled out that numerical advantage. However, this Scottish political condition was very obvious to both sides, and it would not have taken much to rectify the Scots divisions. Monck's only hope of survival, with a small force in a hostile land, was to keep the Scots off-balance and disunited. And the very hostility of the land loosened quarrels among English – which were just as virulent, given the chance, as the Scots varieties. Monck therefore adopted a continually aggressive stance. He appears to have decided at once, as soon as he was placed in command (or was it by Oliver's canny advice?) to make an attempt to complete the conquest already begun. The Scots had clearly expected all the English to march away, so surprise, of a deeper and more shocking sort than an attack before dawn, was on his side.

Monck began the process by moving at once, as soon as Cromwell left him in command, against Stirling. The Scots Committee of Estates were present in the town, but they moved out smartly, going off to the unconquered and as yet unthreatened area north of Perth. After some problems with transporting his guns over the bad roads and over a steep and narrow pass, Monck reached Stirling on August 6, the day that Cromwell was marching south from Edinburgh. The extent of the loss of Scots nerve was shown when he summoned both the town and the Castle. There was no answer from the Castle, but from the burgh the town clerk, as the English called him, came dashing out. He tried to insist on conditions for the surrender; Monck replied by threatening to storm the town. Their respective positions thus made clear, the subsequent discussion about terms lasted into the night. The garrison was not strong enough to defend both the Castle and the town walls, and so the negotiations were essentially designed on the Scots side to allow the Scots troops to move themselves and their supplies into the Castle. At last the English accepted the town's surrender and occupied it not long after midnight. The Scots troops had moved into the Castle, where they remained defiant.[6]

Monck's success was heartening, but its partial nature might well be his undoing. It was all very well to be vigorous and aggressive, with the aim of keeping the Scots off-balance, but it was also even more necessary to be continually successful. A defeat or a siege would hearten the enemy, and either could entirely destroy his small force. The capture of the burgh of Stirling was a good start, but the failure of the Castle to surrender might well condemn him to a long siege. This would provide the Scots with the time they needed to reorganise, recruit, re-equip, and unify. This was the role Stirling had already played in the war since Dunbar. The destruction of the Scots army in that battle had been made good behind the shelter provided by the defiance of Stirling. And the length and difficulty of the siege of Edinburgh Castle showed that these old fortifications were by no means easy targets.

This was where Cromwell's keen judgement of his subordinate commanders told. He had promoted Monck over the past year from a colonel without a regiment to lieutenant-general in charge of the whole Scots campaign. His official second-in-command all that time had been John Lambert, the victor of Inverkeithing and Hamilton. When Cromwell allocated the commands in the crisis caused by the invasion of England, he had, it seems, never hesitated: Lambert, the dashing cavalryman, went after the king; Monck, the stolid Devonian infantryman, stayed in Scotland. But the slow, deliberate care needed in the north was not Lambert's style, and Monck's deliberation would be out of place in a campaign which needed flair and dash. Further, Monck was now an artilleryman, and had plenty of experience of using his guns against Scottish fortifications – Tantallon, Blackness, and so on. Then there was the matter of political judgement. Nearly ten years later, Lambert and Monck were again rivals, for the political leadership of the English republic after Cromwell's death. And it was Monck's careful deliberation and proper preparedness which overcame Lambert's impulsiveness. This difference was clearly obvious even in 1651. Certainly Monck's political canniness was more useful in Scotland, with its confusing politics. And it turned out that Cromwell's choice was spot-on. Monck had captured Stirling Castle two days before Lambert faced the Scots at Warrington. Monck had moved thirty-three miles while Lambert was riding over three hundred. Neither could have accomplished what the other had done.

The dangers Monck's small force faced were already being made clear, only a week after Cromwell's departure. The victories at Inverkeithing and Perth, and even Stirling, had not extended English control in Scotland by very much. The withdrawal of English forces from the west had never been made good, and the easy march of the Scots army through Clydesdale had shown the people there just how

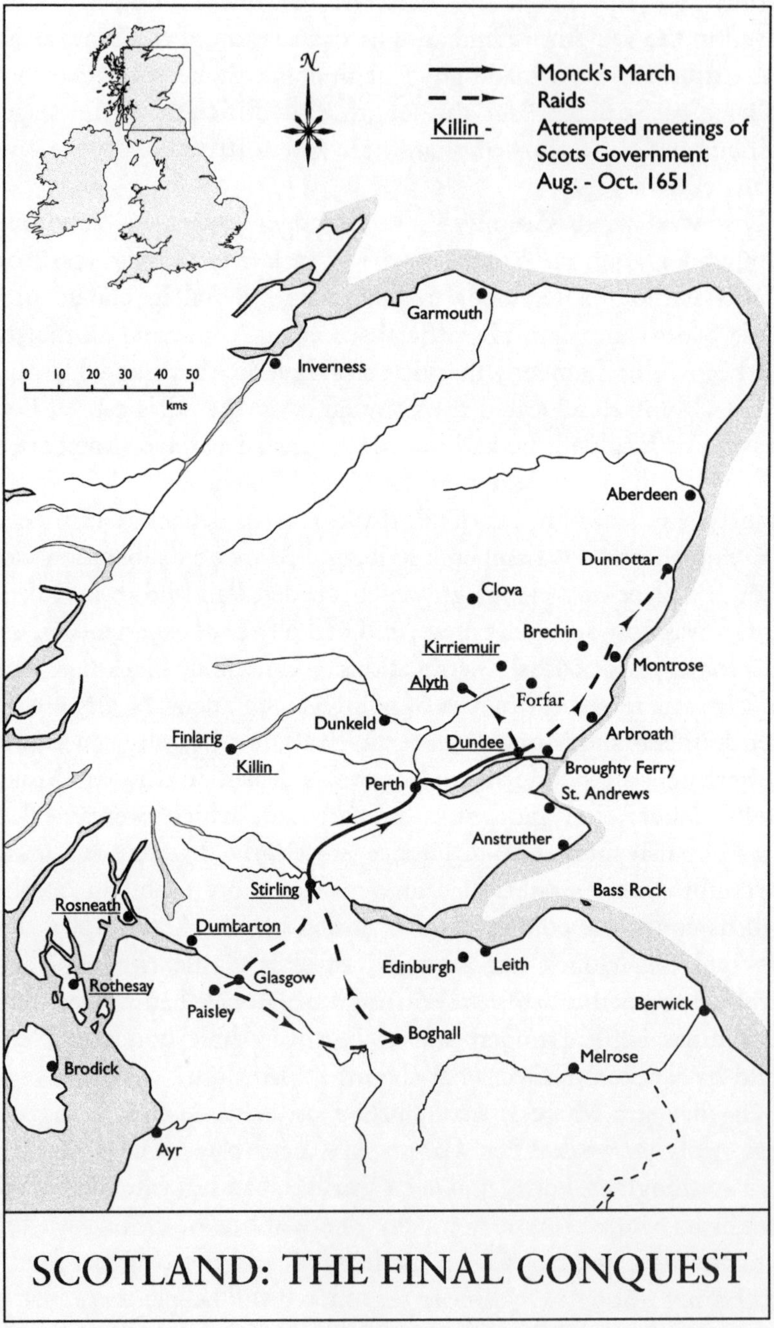

SCOTLAND: THE FINAL CONQUEST

empty the land was. Similarly, Commissary-General Whalley's sweep along the Fife coastline had been cut short, and had had no more permanent effect than the original superficial conquest of the west.

Monck set about attacking Stirling Castle. He had with him most of the artillery train which Cromwell had accumulated over the past year. In particular, he was, it seems, the only English commander to appreciate the uses which could be made of mortars in sieges. Cromwell, for example, had used 'great guns' at Edinburgh, and had only employed his mortars briefly, and without much success. Mortars were heavy and awkward to move, expensive in powder, dangerous, difficult to fire with any accuracy, and needed well-prepared ground for their foundations. They also had a short range, which meant that the gunners were exposed to retaliation by the besieged. Definitely an expert's game.

As soon as the town was occupied, Monck set his gunners to work, preparing a firing platform for both mortars and great guns. Meanwhile the guns themselves were coming by ship, presumably from Leith. The guns – four 'battering' guns and two mortars – arrived on August 10, but the platforms for the cannon were not ready until the 12th, and that for the mortars until the next day. Meanwhile the garrison hindered the work as much as possible by its own fire, and the English used the steeple of a church (probably Holy Rood, but which church is not specified) to fire back at the Scots gunners. The Scots shot right through the steeple, and killed one of the English gunners, but did not noticeably hinder the preparations.[7]

Meanwhile Monck had been receiving disquieting news out of the Western Association's old territories. The king, before leaving Scotland, had appointed commissioners to recruit more troops in the west, and the number mentioned was 6,000 horse and foot. Perhaps by no coincidence, this was just the force Monck had with him. His intelligence was good, as Cromwell's had been, and he was able to move quickly to nip the Royalist recruitment efforts in the bud. He sent two regiments out of Stirling, those of Okey and Berry, both horse regiments, with two extra troops of horse and two of dragoons. This was a powerful and mobile force, 1,400 strong, whose soldiers could be used much better in the open country than in the enclosed and unhealthy town, and whose absence would not weaken the English siege.[8]

The situation to the east, in Fife, was no better. There had been 'some risings' according to the report to a newspaper in London. This was the responsibility of Colonel Overton at Perth. He sent out Alured's regiment of horse to quell the trouble. Anstruther at the eastern end of the peninsula was the focus of the problem. The town had submitted, presumably to Whalley, but had then decided that Cromwell's evacuation of Fife had changed the situation. When English sailors arrived to take control of the guns and ships which the town was required to give up by the terms of its surrender agreement, the town resisted. Three of the sailors were killed and fifteen taken prisoner. Colonel Alured replied to this defiance vigorously before it could spread. His regiment stormed the town, killing twenty of the resisters, and capturing two hundred, and Alured then let his soldiers loose to plunder and burn. As a result, most of the other 'risings' subsided, but the situation was clearly unstable. There was still the problem of St Andrews, which had not yet surrendered to anyone, and there were numerous members of the local gentry of Fife who had not yet submitted. The whole area was obviously in a very uncertain state of mind, and it was exactly these people who had to be persuaded by a constant string of English victories that it was useless to resist.[9]

The problem in the west was dealt with equally expeditiously. Okey, the senior of the two colonels, spent no more than a week on the task, and in that time the west was quietened and no more was heard of recruits for the king. He rode to Glasgow and then to Paisley, at both of which the king's commissioners were actively gathering men together. There were some hundreds of men already gathered there, but the sudden arrival of the English troopers scattered the recruits and made some of the commissioners prisoners. The chief commissioner was Lord Osbaston, according to Okey, and he captured three more as well, though two other men escaped across the Clyde northwards. The English force went on to reach the sea at Irvine, and patrols were sent out in all directions. Okey claimed that all was now calm and that patrols of a hundred horsemen would suffice to keep things that way.

He had also imposed substantial fines on Glasgow and Paisley, and a smaller one on Lord Rosse, to deter any further recruitments. One prisoner who readily surrendered, apparently at Glasgow, was Colonel Pinchebanke, a Royalist commander who had recently been forced to surrender the Scilly Isles to republican forces. He had come to Scotland to serve the king, but could not stomach the invasion of his own country by the Scots. Here, for Monck, was a powerful indication of how many Englishmen would react to the invasion, and his political sense was sufficiently attuned for him to realise that, if he wanted to build a reputation in Scotland, he must move fast. The war in England would not take long.

Okey had come up with another strong political hint as well. His men had ranged widely over the land south of Glasgow, and had captured a group of ministers meeting in a barn at Boghall, near Biggar. He let them go when it became clear that they were hostile to the political and religious pretensions of the General Assembly, and that at large they would be a usefully divisive influence. By August 17 Okey was back in Stirling writing his report.[10]

By that time Monck had been equally successful at Stirling in his siege of the Castle. The great guns began battering at the thick walls the day after Okey's force went off, though they had little effect on the solid masonry. Next day, however, August 13, the chief gunner, a German called Joachim Hane (Hein?), brought the mortars into play. His second shot fell right into the centre of the Castle, causing damage and inflicting considerable casualties. The lesson having thus been administered, Monck offered the governor, Colonel William Cunningham, talks about the exchange of prisoners, clearly intending that such talks should lead on to something more. Cunningham refused, so next day, August 14, the two sets of guns resumed their bombardment. The great guns battered at the walls, the mortars lobbed their explosive shells over the top, where they began the destruction of the more thin-skinned buildings inside, and, more to the point, of the even more thin-skinned and vulnerable soldiers.

The Castle's garrison was composed mainly of Highlanders, and this long-distance and unnerving war was not to their taste and more than they could accept. They took things into their own hands, and one of them beat a drum to call for a parley. Cunningham was still not ready to give in, but he could not control his men any more, and had to yield to their demands. Monck sensibly offered generous terms, and the governor, perforce, agreed. By noon it was all over, Cunningham and the 300-man garrison had marched out, with arms and belongings, having looted the goods left in the Castle for safekeeping by the local people; the thirty-six English prisoners had been released, and Colonel Rede was appointed the new governor. The spoil taken by the English was considerable, and included the Records of Scotland, yet again. They found that there were provisions which were reckoned at a year's supply for the garrison. The mortars were judged to have 'deformed the castle in divers places', and that was after only two days' bombardment.[11]

Okey returned next day with the news of the calming of the west, and, with Alured's exploits in Fife also accomplished, Monck could now rest safe. His orders had been to attack Stirling, and he had captured the place much more quickly than anyone could have expected. He gave orders to prepare to march, carrying ten days' provisions, but then called a council to discuss the next move. Colonel Fenwick came up from Edinburgh and Colonel Hubbold as well. No doubt the colonels already present – Okey, Rede, Berry, Grosvenor – were included, and it would make sense to consult the rather touchy Overton as well, who, like Fenwick, held a separate appointment directly from Cromwell.

Over the next days, intelligence flowed in. Remnants of the Scots forces which had survived the recent defeats had withdrawn to the Dundee area, including the former garrison of Stirling, but the exact strength concentrated there was not known. The Highlands were also busy. A cattle raid was reported to have reached to within a few miles of Overton's post at Perth, and the Marquis of Huntly, long an ogre figure for the English, and said to have a considerable force at his command, was also reported in the Perth area at the head of a thousand men. It could be assumed that the Scots could gather a substantial force still, and the total area of the country which was still unconquered was huge. Further, the Royalist government of Scotland was still in being, and would be the natural centre of resistance. It was also somewhere in the Dundee area, or further north. Monck's colonels agreed to continue the campaign.

The English left a garrison in Stirling and marched north out of the town on August 21, camping that night at Dunblane, then at Blackford, and then just short of Perth. (The king's army had just thrown itself into Worcester.) Monck had with him five regiments, three of horse, two of foot, and one mortar and three great guns in the artillery train. At Perth more intelligence was collected. Lord Leven had been offended by Crawford-Lindsay's appointment, and had effectively gone on strike; Huntly also wanted the chief command and refused to provide troops unless he got it. Other Royalists, of whom the earls of Errol, Atholl, and Tullibardine were mentioned, were busy raising troops, but had not been very successful so far.[12]

The Committee of Estates was thus a government without much authority over its most powerful subjects. Above all, Argyll was sulking in Inveraray. His wife had been at Stirling when the siege began, and Monck had carefully let her leave, on a pretence of illness. Argyll was to be given no excuse to rejoin the Estates. The Committee had issued an appeal from Dundee on August 20 requiring all Scots to join in fighting the invader, and the Chancellor Loudoun made a personal appeal to Argyll on the 24th, but by then Monck was approaching Dundee. The members of the Committee showed no more willingness to stand and do some actual fighting at Dundee than they had at Stirling, and they diligently removed themselves from the line of fire once again. By this time the Committee itself had begun to dissolve, not surprisingly. At a meeting at Kirriemuir, fifteen miles north of Dundee, on the 24th, there were no members of the Burgess estate present, so technically there was no quorum.[13]

Monck's organisation had been excellent. He was met at Perth by ships bringing supplies for his army, and by news from Major Browne, the captain of the frigate *Speaker*, that he had been fired on from Dundee as he ran up the Firth of Tay. A new summons was sent to St Andrews, reinforcing an earlier one from Overton, and those in Fife who were still not convinced were given until September 1 to submit. A reply came from St Andrews, arguing about the conditions. Clearly this time-wasting would continue until definite news came from

England, or until direct force was exerted. The ministers at Perth demanded the right to pray for the king and the Scots army in England; Overton required them to preach the gospel only, 'but', Monck remarked, in the pure tones of English disdain, 'it seems *that* is not their business'.

The next move began on the 25th, with simultaneous attempts on both Dundee and St Andrews. The army began to march along the road through the Carse of Gowrie towards Dundee, and a new summons was issued to St Andrews by Major Browne in the *Speaker*. Monck and Overton sailed to summon Dundee, while in Perth ladders were built for a possible assault. An attempt to send the guns by water only partly succeeded, for the mortar proved to be too heavy for the shallop in which it was loaded, which broke. Captain Augustine Hoffmann, still active on the Scots side, but under no control by now, raided as far as Scone on the 27th; next day the garrison left at Perth began to dig a moat to cover the western approach to the town.

It must have been that day, the 27th, that Monck, with the army approaching Dundee, heard of the precise whereabouts of the Committee of Estates. They had moved east to Alyth, still only fifteen miles from Dundee. At once Colonel Alured, with a cavalry force of about 800 men, marched through a dark and wet night over the Sidlaw Hills and descended on Alyth early in the morning. Surprise was total, the defending troops – about 4,000 of them, so Alured estimated – were driven off in all directions, and most of the Committee were captured. Monck listed the prisoners as the earl Marischal, the earl of Leven and the earl of Crawford-Lindsay (the two rival commanders-in-chief), five other lords, three knights, eight gentlemen and ten country gentlemen, nine ministers, and seventy others. It was not quite the whole of the Scots government, but there were now very few of them left at liberty. As a further bonus the gathered Scots forces were dispersed, and thus would be unable to intervene in the siege of Dundee which was about to begin.[14]

As if that blow were not enough, Monck was simultaneously making systematic and rapid preparations for the assault on Dundee, displaying an efficiency and speed which implied plenty of confidence of early success. Colonel Robert Lumsdaine, the town's governor, replied to

Monck's summons with a bravura counter-summons of his own, calling on the English to submit to their rightful king. Perhaps he had been buoyed up by the false news of a Scots victory in England, which had been celebrated two nights earlier, but the gentlemen of St Andrews were not so sanguine. They finally submitted on August 30, being fined for their tardiness and reluctance.

Monck sent out Colonel Okey with his regiment north to scour the land to ensure that there was no interference from the scattered forces which had survived Alured's raid. Another English reconnaissance force discovered that Broughty Castle, on the coast a mile or two north of Dundee, had been abandoned and promptly occupied it. When Okey returned, therefore, having found no force larger than 400 strong – which rode away rapidly at his approach – Monck had the city surrounded. His guns had arrived, including the errant mortar, and were in place by August 30, when the bombardment commenced. Rain the next day suspended the bombardment, and a second summons went in, to be rejected again. The delay also allowed the collection of information about the condition of the city, such as that provided by a boy 'who frequently used to get over the works in the sight of their own sentinels . . . without notice taken of them (sic)'.[15] The final assault began on September 1.

The great guns began firing at 4 a.m., and breaches were soon made in the wall. The mortar was also used, though its effect on the more spacious town would be less than within the narrow confines of Stirling Castle. The garrison replied with shots and insults, though 'dogs' seems to have been the worst name thrown at the English: always guaranteed to annoy them, of course. By 11 a.m. the breaches in two forts, at east and west sides of the town, were judged to be practicable. An assault force of foot, horse, dragoons, and seamen, in all a thousand strong, with 400 horse as a reinforcement, had been ready since dawn. Now they went in. The fighting at the walls and at the forts lasted half an hour before the Scots were driven in. Some took refuge in the church, even climbing the steeple. Several hundred had been killed, including Lumsdaine, and including some women and children, and it was not until the market place was reached that the English invaders gave quarter.

Then, since the town had been taken by assault, having been given the chance to surrender more than once, it was plundered by the conquerors. There was plenty for them to seize, since Dundee had been the repository of many wealthy people in the other, more threatened towns. The value of the spoil was said to be 200,000 pounds sterling, with individual soldiers enriched to the tune of 500 pounds each. Monck's report to Parliament claimed that enquiries suggested the townspeople were determined to refuse a surrender, which may be true, but it looks much more like a shame-faced excuse. He also claimed that there were no Scottish casualties in the sack, which is hard to believe. Monck certainly found it difficult to bring his army back to full discipline afterwards.

The number of civilians killed is not known; certainly some fifty or so women and children are mentioned; Nicoll, the Scots diarist, claimed 1,000 men and 140 women and children, perhaps as exaggerated as the English account is underestimated. These were, no doubt, mainly victims of the bombardment and the initial assault. There were also 500 soldiers taken prisoner, including Colonel Cunningham, last seen at Stirling, and numbers of his old soldiers with him. Nearly 200 ships were taken in the harbour, to be argued over later by the English officers as to their prize status. Monck admitted to about twenty of his men killed, but again this is a suspiciously low figure, one which occurs all too often, for it tends to crop up in English accounts of other fights. It is not to be trusted, in particular because it does not account for the many wounded who died later in those days of primitive medicine.[16]

The effect of the capture and sack of Dundee was immediate. Within two days Overton was despatched to Montrose to see that the town was not fortified, and next day Colonel Okey with more cavalry and Colonel Morgan with the dragoons were sent to secure Aberdeen. That city had already been frightened into sending timorously to enquire as to the situation. On the way north Okey's force met the deputation from the city, led by Alexander Jaffray, the former provost of the city whom some of the soldiers would remember as a prisoner of war after Dunbar. He was a clever choice, having become friendly with Cromwell during his captivity. Okey promised no greater punishment for the city than free quarter if they gave in peacefully. Once in the city, however, he managed to find enough excuses to impose a fine of a thousand pounds sterling on the city.[17]

By this time Monck had fallen ill, and the English forces, without the central direction he provided, and stretched thinly from Berwick to Glasgow to Aberdeen, might have faced more resistance. Indeed early in September they became stretched even further. A small Scots force of horse and foot had been in occupation of Dumfries since the English withdrawal in June. A raid by about 500 English horse under Major Scott was mounted from Edinburgh by way of Boghall. He sent in a hundred of his men to beat up the suburbs and then withdraw, and this induced a counter-attack by the Scots, deceived by the small number. They discovered that the hundred had grown during the night to a much greater force. The Scots were defeated, many of the local lairds were taken, and the English, as they tended to say, 'scoured' the countryside. This unpleasant process went on through September. It prevented a Scots rally at Ayr, and so, from the English point of view, it was very successful.[18]

By then, of course, the correct news from Worcester was known. It was initially disbelieved by the Scots, but as fugitives trickled back to Scotland, the truth slowly sank in. Some recalcitrant gentlemen of Fife submitted on the day the English in Dundee fired a salute to celebrate the English victory. The complete disappearance of the second Scottish army in a year, either dead or prisoners, the capture of most of the country's government, the disappearance of its king, the conquest of all its main cities, all combined to make further resistance seem hopeless. Scotland had been beaten into the ground.

CHAPTER TEN

THE FINAL CONQUEST

September 10, 1651 – May 24, 1652

Many of the Scots fought on after Alyth and Dundee and Aberdeen, despite the blows they had received. It is worth appreciating the weight of these blows. At the end of July the Scots were an independent state, with their own king, their own government, and their own army. A month later all their cities were under enemy occupation, their army was destroyed, their king a fugitive in a foreign land, and their government decapitated. The physical blows were bad enough – Stirling, defiant for a year, was captured in less than a week – but the psychological effect was even greater, and all the worse for being the result of a sequence of successively heavier blows. In the circumstances, the Scots' reactions were either despair, or futile resistance.

Centres of resistance, however, were few and scattered. Dumbarton Castle, high on its rock, and overlooking the Clyde estuary, held out under the command of Sir Charles Erskine, though the garrison had already gained an evil reputation for requisitioning food from the surrounding lands. It remained a potentially aggressive base for forces from Argyll, and that meant the marquis of Argyll, based at Inveraray. The Bass Castle, on its island-rock in the mouth of the Firth of Forth, ignored any and all summonses. Colonel Fenwick threatened confiscation of property and court martial if the governor and his garrison did not surrender in the aftermath of Dundee, but this had no effect. The continued resistance of the castle, almost within sight of the Scots capital, was an inspiration to the resisters, and a base for maritime raids as well.

Further up the east coast, Dunnottar Castle, on its rock south of

Aberdeen, was described by one Englishman as the strongest place in Scotland. It had been otherwise ignored by them, and refused to submit: its very strength made it a problem. Monck was talking of making an attempt on it in September, but he could not afford to tie up any substantial part of his force in a siege, nor could he afford serious losses, nor could he allow himself to be defeated.[1] It was Cromwell's old problem in miniature. An English defeat would stimulate a Scottish revival, revealing just how vulnerable the English were; but the odds were that the Scots would continue to weaken, until the accumulation of blows, captures, surrenders and defections brought the final collapse.

The one remaining source of strength for the Scots was now the people of the Highlands. For beyond the line from Aberdeen to Stirling, more than half the Scottish kingdom in area, no-one had yet submitted. This was the ultimate redoubt which had held out against all previous conquerors, from the Romans onwards, and any imaginative English military man would have quailed at the prospect of having to campaign there, amid the bleak mountains, through narrow passes, cold, hungry, and wet, and amid a people even more alien than the Lowland Scots, who often did not even speak English. And Monck had that sort of imagination.

There were still a number of members of the Scottish government free of restraint, and if they could combine they would be formidable. Some of those who had escaped from the disaster at Alyth had met briefly at Aberdeen, but had then left as the news of Dundee spread and the English cavalry under Colonel Okey approached the city. Their withdrawal was not hindered by Aberdeen's quaking council, which, having given itself up to the English, then found that the English soon withdrew. In the Gordon lands, Huntly had men under command, and he was joined by Alexander Lindsay, earl of Balcarres. Together their forces would have been sizeable, and, once again, had they combined, they could have formed a rallying point for other resisters.

But even in this extremity the Scots could not resolve their differences. Huntly was an out-and-out Royalist, whose father had repeatedly rebelled against Covenanter rule, and had been executed for it. Balcarres was an old Covenanter who had frequently been at odds with the rest of his colleagues, and too often proved right for those colleagues' comfort. He had been a member of the Parliament which had condemned Huntly's father to execution, though characteristically he had voted against it (along with all the nobles). The party differences between these two were formidable. Loudoun, on the other hand, the legal head of what remained of the government, was a thorough Kirkman, and had been all his career. It is likely that he had rarely agreed with Balcarres, and never with Huntly, about any aspect of government, war, or religion. And these three men were not about to let down their political defences at this moment of mutual danger.

Loudoun, as Chancellor of the kingdom, had summoned a meeting of the rump Committee of Estates to meet at Killin on September 5. Killin was deep in the Highlands, at the western end of Loch Tay, well protected from attack by the English cavalry whose approach, along one of only two possible routes, could be easily signalled. It lay, as a report pointed out, 'amongst mountains, locks (*sic*), woods, and strait passes'.[2] Killin was also as central a position as could be devised, given the political geography of the resistance, and Argyll reached it from Inveraray. He was the fourth of the chieftains whose combination was essential for the war to continue. But his ambition had long been too obvious, and by now he was thoroughly distrusted by all the rest. His personal armed following, if not so large as the English had thought, was still twice what Huntly and Balcarres could raise between them. Yet he showed no willingness to contribute in any way, either to the war or to the political proceedings. Monck's gesture of releasing his wife from the Stirling siege may well have helped Argyll to his posture of busy neutrality, but it was perhaps by now his habitual attitude anyway.

His presence at Killin had no result. Balcarres refused to attend. He wanted the meeting to be held further north, in territory more deeply Royalist, and where he had local power. And, of course, Huntly, not being a member of the Committee, was not there either. The notice Loudoun had given for the meeting was too short, and it was not until September 10 that he had a serviceable group on hand, with representatives of all three estates providing a quorum, if only a paper-thin one. The members tried to exert some control over the Royalist forces, ordering a rendezvous at Dunkeld, ten miles north of Perth, for September 24.[3]

Dunkeld was a well-chosen rendezvous. It lay at the mouth of Strathtay, which the Highland contingents could reach without passing through English-held lands. A strong force there would provide a direct threat to Perth, now the centre of the English position. It might compel Monck to withdraw from Dundee and Aberdeen – though it was more likely to provoke an attack. If so, Strathtay could provide a means of retreat into the Highlands. Balcarres and Huntly were ordered to attend, and the levies of Perthshire and Angus, such as there were left, were to be called out. But the Committee of Estates also agreed that they should meet on the day after, September 25, at Dumbarton. Balcarres clearly could not attend both, though Dumbarton was very convenient for Argyll. It may have been a nefarious plot to separate Balcarres from his forces, but, if so, it was such a blunt instrument, and so obvious, that it was bound to fail. It is so nonsensical that one must assume it to be the product of a compromise within the Committee. It guaranteed further division.[4]

The English were very conscious of the precariousness of their position. The city of Aberdeen complained to Monck that the fine of a thousand pounds sterling was beyond its resources, which may even have been true, for there had been heavy taxation by the Royalist government during the past year. Okey had withdrawn his troops from the city without collecting any of the fine, and so it found itself in a no-man's-land, between the English to the south and Huntly and Balcarres inland. The English reacted to Aberdeen's complaint by suspending the fine, which left it hanging over the city very neatly. This was the method used to control the English 'malignant' gentry, and it had worked well enough to prevent most of them from joining Charles in his recent invasion. It worked in Scotland just as well. But it was clearly dangerous to push Aberdeen too far, just in case the city joined Huntly or Balcarres. Monck's moderating influence upon the bellicosity of his colonels may well be evident here.[5]

The area of Scotland under direct English control stretched north as far as Montrose. The southern half of the county of Angus was now heavily garrisoned, partly to control it, and partly as a base for further patrolling. The English troops were spread over the lands behind Dundee in garrisons based at Montrose, Forfar, and Brechin, a regiment and some dragoons in each place. It was clearly realised that Aberdeen was beyond reach of a permanent occupation. The various garrisons needed to be sited closely enough to support each other in case of risings. Patrols were sent out regularly towards the Highlands, to gather intelligence, to intimidate, and to break up any gatherings. Having to perform these tasks, the English lacked the numbers to move deeper into the country in any strength, and so they had to wait to see what became of the Scots rendezvous. Moreover, Monck learned after Worcester that his forces were to be increased to about 12,000 men, which presumably did not include the forces under Fenwick or Overton, and so this represented a doubling of his own force. This would allow him to go on the attack once more. It would thus make sense to wait for reinforcements.[6]

The rendezvous at Dunkeld on September 24 did not happen. The men of Angus and Perthshire could scarcely be expected to reach the place except in small numbers, since their towns and their best lands were occupied and thoroughly patrolled by the English. Huntly was reported to be marching towards Loch Tay with 600 horse and 1,000 foot as late as September 22, and Balcarres had agreed to attend, and was reported to have 250 horse under his command. But neither actually turned up. Huntly threatened to burn Aberdeen, which diminished his support there, and frightened the city into relying even further on English protection. This was now much more credible in the absence of any Scots field army. The English could continuously expand. Arbroath was now occupied by the English, a governor was appointed, and orders given to establish a fortified base in the old abbey.[7]

The meeting of the Committee of Estates at Dumbarton on the day after the unsuccessful rendezvous was uncomfortable, partly no doubt because of the failure of that rendezvous, but also because of the proximity of English forces at Glasgow. The Committee moved rapidly to Rosneath on the western shore of the Gareloch, and then further down the Clyde to Rothesay on the island of Bute. All this took time, and decisions could not be reached in the confusion. In particular Loudoun wanted the next scheduled meeting of Parliament to be summoned to a new venue. It had originally been set for Stirling, which was out of the question now, and Loudoun wanted the Committee to decide on the new meeting place. But when the Committee finally got round to making a decision on this, it no longer had a quorum, for at Rothesay only one burgess was present. This was the provost of Ayr, John Kennedy, and his town was about to be occupied by the English forces expanding out of Dumfries. Nevertheless, at last, despite the technical illegality, the Parliament was invited to meet at Finlarig, close by Killin on Loch Tay, on November 12. This proved to be the end of the Committee of Estates, whimpering into oblivion. The Committee did write to the Provost of Stirling, informing him of the change. The letter sent him into a panic, and he made a special note of it in the burgh records, including its date of receipt, two days after the day set for the Parliament's meeting.[8]

All this shifting and dithering had its effect on the rest of Scotland. The English were able to set themselves up as defenders of the law-abiding against the threat to life, limb, and property posed by Highlanders and moss-troopers. Monck's stern discipline kept plundering and destruction by his own troops within bounds, while the disintegration of authority on the Scots side was manifested in increasing anarchy in areas outside the control of the English army. There were very many men who had some experience of war and arms, and weapons were widely dispersed among the population. Brigandage seemed a preferable way of life when the alternative was hard work, whose products vanished under heavy taxation as though into the air.[9]

The failure of the Dunkeld rendezvous and the disintegration of what was left of the Committee of Estates coincided with some deliberate attempts by the English military authorities to restore a semblance of normal peacetime activities. These efforts centred on the south-east, the area longest under English control. At the end of September a meeting of sixty or so ministers was held in Edinburgh. Perhaps it was hoped that they would formulate some instrument of submission and acceptance of English rule, but they could decide nothing, though they did indulge themselves in a week of fasting and prayer. The main point was, of course, that the meeting could be held at all. It also demonstrated English confidence, and it was this indulgent superiority which would be decisive in persuading the Scots to accept English rule, and exclude their moss-trooping champions.[10]

About this time also, Colonel Fenwick, the governor of Edinburgh, gave permission for fishermen from three of the Fife burghs to resume their activities, and one of the towns was sacked Anstruther. Here again the resumption of normal life – despite the continued defiance of the Bass Rock – would persuade people to accept the situation. But there was also the more general problem of food supplies. Not surprisingly the harvest was poor, and much had been taken by the soldiers of both sides out of what had been gathered. There was nothing in reserve from the previous year, and little wealth left in the country to pay for imports. Prices had soared in the scarcities. The resumption of fishing would restore at least one source of food.

Fenwick also began to examine the prisoners who were being held in the Edinburgh Tolbooth. He found that he could release most of them: another restoration of normality. Those who had been in authority, of course, such as the men captured at Alyth, had been quickly shipped to England, where they were out of mind because they were out of sight. More of the gentry of Fife submitted. At Brechin there was, as befitted a place more or less in the front line, a less subtle pressure. Colonel Okey issued a threat of forced free quartering throughout the winter, and this induced the gentry of the area to begin submitting. At a meeting in Brechin cathedral Colonels Okey and Alured then waved an inducement before them. They suggested that the lairds should take over responsibility for security for the area. When they agreed, this allowed Monck to withdraw two regiments and five troops of dragoons in exchange. These, of course, could now be used to extend the area of security further. Thus the expansion of the area of English control went on.[11]

The ministers meeting at Edinburgh were, according to William Clarke, Monck's army secretary, 'much troubled they cannot have power in civil things'. This may well have been something which the rest of the Scots were relieved about. Certainly the rule of the Kirk was much resented, and the decline in its authority provided a fertile compost to generate communities of other denominations. By the spring of the next year, the diarist Lamont decided that 'much hypocrisy and falset formerly hid did now break out', and some became 'papists and atheists' – or ceased to be hypocrites and practiced their real beliefs, perhaps one should say. And he recorded Antinomians, Antitrinitarians, Familists, Seekers, Brownists, Independents, Erastians, and Anabaptists as organised congregations, apparently in Leith and Edinburgh alone.[12]

The Kirk had had control over more than religion, of course, and its loss of civil power now raised the issue of what the future government of Scotland should be. The English Council of State had made some tentative stabs at the problem since December of 1650. Then Cromwell had suggested that the English Parliament should appoint a commission to deal with the issues of finance raised by the prolonged occupation of parts of Scotland. Although he made the suggestion in December, it was only in March that three men were named to the commission, and two months later Samuel Desborough, the brother of Cromwell's brother-in-law, was added. The problem was that there was little to be done in Scotland while the fighting continued. It was hoped to finance the war to some extent out of Scottish revenues, but the army's various requisitions left nothing to collect. There is no sign that the commission achieved anything.[13]

The invasion of England and the progressive conquest of more of Scotland, however, induced the English government to take a larger view. The original aim of the war had been to prevent an invasion from the north, and presumably peace could have been arrived at if the Scots had repudiated Charles and thus ended the invasion threat. The long war, however, brought the English to believe that there could be no peace while there was *any* independent Scottish government. There is no sign that, at first, the Council of State or Parliament intended the annexation of Scotland. It is tempting to assume that the revolutionaries in London always intended to spread their concept of freedom to their benighted neighbours, and the successive conquests of both Ireland and Scotland seem to lend support to this notion.[14] But the two conquests were in reality very different, as different as the two countries, their peoples, and their histories.

Ireland had long been under English rule, either in part or wholly. It had been a rebellion there against the rule of Charles I which had triggered the crisis in England which finally led Royalists and Parliamentarians to fight each other. In a sense the English civil war had been a quarrel over who should control the reconquest of Ireland – and the spoils thereof. Scotland, on the other hand, had been a continuously independent state, like England, since its unification in the eleventh century, not long after England achieved its own unity. Further, its government was revolutionary, like England's, and had been the English Parliament's political and military ally during the English civil wars. A war here was of a much more traditional state-*versus*-state type, and the physical conquest of an independent state was a much more difficult process than the suppression of a rebellion. Cromwell had found this out quickly enough.

Even more difficult, and virtually unprecedented, was the annexation of a state *after* its physical conquest. Conquests did not usually last very long, the invaders going home once a peace treaty had been agreed. But annexation dispensed with a peace treaty, for it presupposed the extinction of the annexed state itself. It was an unpopular move, on both sides, since the annexed remained inevitably hostile, and the conquerors were constantly, and correctly, apprehensive of rebellion. But, once the Scots government had become thoroughly Royalist, a process steadily accelerating after the Start in October of 1650 – or even since Charles's landing at Garmouth in June – the English had no alternative. Peace with a Royalist government with Charles II at its head in Scotland was impossible; therefore the withdrawal of English forces was impossible. The English were driven to annexation as the only possible solution.

The collapse of Scottish resistance in August and early September was the signal for the English government, or rather for its Parliament, to move on from the tentative stab at a policy which had been made so far. In the midst of the celebrations after Worcester – during which news arrived of the capture of Dundee and of the Committee of Estates at Alyth – the House read a bill for the first time for 'asserting the title of England to Scotland'. This implied that the right of conquest was being asserted.[15]

The process from the first resolution for annexation to the presentation for a first reading took three weeks. Parliament was habitually dilatory in such matters, but the fact that the bill got no further suggests that first thoughts had been succeeded by doubts. The impetus for the new policy, which appeared during October, has been ascribed to Cromwell, and it would be natural for him to be consulted, as the conqueror of the Scots army, but he could not have been the only one to have doubts about a policy of crude annexation. The new policy was articulated on October 13, in a Council of State declaration. Oliver had presumably met with like minds in the privacy of the Whitehall drawing rooms. The bill had been referred to the Council of State's Irish and Scotch Committee, and it was presumably from here that the change emanated. The new policy marked a decisive break with the annexationist idea – and took the form of a deliberate attempt to persuade the Scots to accept a union of sovereignties.[16]

The process was supposed to be consultative and persuasive, with the English Parliament appointing commissioners to consult with elected Scottish representatives. Of course, it was closer to *force majeure*. The English army was camped throughout the country, and the commissioners were not prepared to take 'no' for an answer – though the Scots were not backward in plain speaking. But, as so often in Britain, the appearance was as important as the content. The English, despite their military victory and occupation, were effectively saying that a union was insufficient unless it was accomplished voluntarily. Over the next eighteen months that union was certainly accomplished, and Scots representatives participated in the Protectorate's Parliaments, but the acts were scarcely voluntary.[17] Nevertheless we can see here the beginnings of the qualms of conscience which the British displayed throughout their imperial career.

Almost all Scottish military resistance ended before the winter of 1651–1652. In the Highlands, Huntly and Balcarres were finding increasing difficulty in maintaining themselves without resorting to simple robbery. Sir Charles Erskine at Dumbarton was in the same plight. Once it was clear that the Committee of Estates was finished,

Argyll wrote to Monck, on October 15, asking for a meeting. Monck's condition for accepting was that Argyll should exert himself to prevent the Finlarig Parliament meeting from taking place. Whether Argyll had to do anything to accomplish this is not clear, but the fact is that the Finlarig meeting was a complete failure. Only three nobles and no lairds or burgesses met Loudoun there. This was effectively the end of organised Scots resistance. There was now no Committee of Estates, no Parliament, no king. All that was left was for the last men in arms to surrender or be killed.[18]

Huntly and Balcarres were now resisted by their own populations. The approach of winter concentrated all minds on survival. Continued requisitioning by their forces would lead to starvation for all. Huntly laid down his arms on November 6, and Balcarres contacted the English as a preliminary on the 17th. And English reinforcements were arriving. Colonel Fitch's regiment was ordered up from Carlisle, and reached Dundee on November 14. It then marched north, first to Aberdeen – where Huntly signed his surrender on the 21st – and then on towards Inverness. Troops of Ashfield's and Monck's regiments occupied Moray, and Fitch's men rescued Inverness from the threats of Captain Hoffmann, whose moss-trooping was increasingly at the expense of the Scots, not the English. By the end of January English forces had spread north, and there were even two companies in Orkney.[19]

Castles held out longer. Dumbarton, whose situation to some extent protected Argyll from English attention, finally gave in late in December after a siege. There were then only the Bass Rock, Dunnottar, and Brodick on Arran defying the English, and that largely because they had not yet got round to a serious attack on any of them. They fell one by one over the next six months. Dunnottar had been the repository of the 'Honours' of Scotland – the regalia – and these were buried under the floor of the local church to preserve them.[20] Without a king they were symbols only. In the ground, in secret, they were inert symbols. These last remnants of independence were futile.

These final sparks of resistance were extinguished one by one during the period when the English commissioners were organising the presentation of the English plan of union to the Scots, and getting the agreement of the Scots in their various corporate bodies – burghs and shires – to that plan. By the time the castle at Dunnottar had surrendered, and the regalia were buried, all the 'assents' to the plan had been received: after a good deal of discussion, to be sure. Several groups failed to accept the plan, but it was too dangerous to be openly defiant. The exercise quite suitably concluded before Dunnottar's surrender. The symbolism is exact: Scotland had agreed to the union because it had been conquered. The union was therefore temporary, enforced, and unsuccessful.[21] It lasted less than a decade, and Scotland's formal independence was resumed in 1660.

CONCLUSION

HISTORY can be studied for its own sake, as a personal pleasure, and that is satisfying enough, but it is also profoundly useful. It is a tool for understanding our own complex and difficult situation. It has 'lessons' to offer. It is an inspiration in crisis, a guide to conduct, a powerful myth. So Garrett Mattingly was inspired to write on the Armada by Britain's crisis in 1940, and A. J. Toynbee was provoked into his *magnum opus* by the discovery that the modern Greeks took a manifestly selfish view of the great European crisis of 1914. One of the reasons for looking at this previous crisis in the affairs of England and Scotland is because we are in the midst of another.

Recent developments in Scottish politics have raised the issue of the political union of England and Scotland once more. The union of 1707 is seen by many Scots as the product of a confidence trick by the English at a time when the Scots, as a result of the disastrous Darien scheme, were economically prostrate. The Scots magnates who negotiated the union were bribed, the ordinary people ignored or gulled. Hence, so say the nationalists, such a misbegotten union should be dissolved. Then, of course, all will be well in Scotland, rich, independent, with full employment – no doubt even the weather will improve.

It will be evident that I do not accept this interpretation. It is my opinion that the union of these two kingdoms was a political masterstroke of the highest order, whose benefits far outweigh the sordidness of the political machinations which were needed to bring it about. It is almost unique in international affairs for two states to unite in such a voluntary way – and I insist that the 1707 union was essentially voluntary on the Scots part. Protests were few and brief; later Jacobite rebellions were unsuccessful, even though they tended to appeal to separatist notions. I may add that I am also entitled to my opinions, for my parents are both Scots, while I was born and raised in England and have lived there all my life. The Scottish argument has been conducted as though it was a Scottish issue. It is not. It is a *British* issue.

The union of 1707 was achieved only in part because of the consequences of the Darien scheme's failure. In the background, not necessarily mentioned but inevitably in the minds of all participants, was the recollection of recent history. And for the Scots, the most unpleasant event in their recent past was their conquest and rule by the English between 1650 and 1660. Indeed I would argue that this conquest and its undoing in 1660 were an essential prelude to the successful, peaceful, voluntary union of 1707. Without the Scots experience of foreign rule – foreign *military* rule – the alternative to union, independence, would have beckoned much more strongly. Similarly, without the experience of civil war in England the subsequent Glorious Revolution might have been much bloodier. If the union scheme in 1707 had failed, and Scotland had then opted for independence, war between England and Scotland would have been the result. England and Scotland were involved in a war with France and Spain at the time, and if the separation had been resisted by the English, the Scots' only means of defence would have been an alliance with France. And Scotland would have lost. There can be no doubt about that. Regardless of Scottish dreams and myths, Scotland has lost every war it has ever fought against England, and in 1651 the English demonstrated that they had the wealth, the manpower, and the will to subjugate Scotland completely. By 1707 the imbalance between the two states was even greater.

The issue of the union had been on the political agenda ever since the 1570s, when it became clear that James VI of Scotland, if he survived, would become king of England after the death of Elizabeth I. Between then and the political union of 1707, various expedients were tried: a union of the crowns, forced union, effective independence, English rule, none of which had worked for very long. The union of 1707 was yet another attempt to solve the problem. Scotland surrendered its legislative separateness, but kept its distinct identity, legal, religious, educational, even financial. It was, like most political decisions, a compromise: the Scots surrendered the minimum autonomy which would satisfy the stronger English.

After that, of course, the two kingdoms, now united, went off together to plunder the riches of the world in partnership for two and a half centuries. And now that is no longer possible, the issue of the union, dormant for much of that time, has arisen once more, growing from the idea of a fringe party in the 1930s to the second or third largest political group in Scotland in the 1990s, whose preferred policy is now independence.

But independence for Scotland means inevitable conflict with England. The actual grounds for argument do not much matter, though it takes no time at all to conjure them up: the status of Berwick-on-Tweed or of the Northern Isles, or the ownership of the North Sea oilfields, will do for a start. The fact is that neighbouring states quarrel. Always. And some of these quarrels result in wars. It is perhaps fashionable to believe that war in Europe is no longer possible. This is an ahistoric notion and a delusion. Independent national states *always* have the potential for warfare. Look at the Balkans. Or the Falklands.

This is the real problem. The union of 1707 has effectively precluded warfare in Britain while it has lasted. The Jacobite rebellions were not serious matters, nor were they national risings. Before 1707 warfare had been a regular occurrence between the two states, a war breaking out more or less every generation from the time the two kingdoms emerged as single states. And if Scotland became an independent state once more, as a result of the resentment at what the Scottish nationalists ludicrously describe as 'English rule', the stage would have been set for further conflict. And political conflict between states can end, and frequently does end, in war.

This is what is at stake. This is why we need to study the past. This is the real significance of the last war between England and Scotland. For it is only the last war until now. If the countries separate, there will be another.

NOTES

Abbreviations

ABBOTT – W. C. ABBOTT (ed.), *The Letters and Speeches of Oliver Cromwell*, vol 2, 1649–1653, Cambridge, Mass., 1939.

AKERMAN, *Letters* – J. Y. AKERMAN (ed.), *Letters from Roundhead Officers written from Scotland*, Bannatyne Club, 1856.

ANCRAM-LOTHIAN CORR. – D. LAING (ed.), *Correspondence of Sir Robert Ker, first earl of Ancram and his son William, third earl of Lothian*, 2 vols, Edinburgh, 1875.

APS – *Acts of the Parliaments of Scotland.*

BAILLIE – D. LAING (ed.), *The Letters and Journals of Robert Baillie*, 3 vols, Edinburgh, 1842.

BALFOUR – Sir John Balfour, *Historical Works*, 4 vols, Edinburgh, 1824–1825.

CARY, *Memorials* – H. Cary (ed.), *Memorials of the Civil War in England*, London, 1842.

CSP DOM – *Calendar of State Papers, Domestic.*

Ed. Recs. – M. WOOD (ed.), *Extracts from the Records of the Burgh of Edinburgh, 1642–55*, Edinburgh, 1938

FIRTH, *Scotland* – Sir Charles Firth (ed.), *Scotland and the Commonwealth*, SHS, 1900.

GARDINER, *Charles II and Scotland* – S. R. GARDINER (ed.), *Letters and Papers illustrating the Relations between Charles II and Scotland in 1650*, SHS, 1894.

HODGSON – SIR W. SCOTT (ed.), *Original Memoirs . . . of Sir Henry Slingsby and Captain Hodgson*, Edinburgh 1806.

Merc. Pol. – *Mercurius Politicus.*

NICKOLLS – J. Nickolls (ed.), *Original Letters and Papers of State addressed to Oliver Cromwell . . . found among the Political Collection of Mr John Milton*, London, 1743

NICOLL – J. Nicoll, *A Diary of Public Transactions* (ed. D. Laing), Bannatyne Club, Edinburgh 1836.

Perf.Diurn. – *Perfect Diurnal of the Army.*

RCAHM Scot – Royal Commission on the Ancient and Historical Monuments of Scotland.

RCGA – J. Christie (ed.), *Records of the Commissions of the General Assemblies of the Church of Scotland, 1650–2*, SHS, Edinburgh 1909

Sev. Proc. – *Several Proceedings.*

SHS – Scottish History Society publications.

STEVENSON, *R&CR* – D. C. STEVENSON, *Revolution and Counter Revolution, 1644–1651*, London, 1977.

WALKER – Sir Edward Walker, *Historical Discourses*, London, 1705.

WARISTON – D. H. Fleming (ed.), *The Diary of Sir Archibald Johnston of Wariston*, vol 2, 1650–1654, SHS, 1919.

WHITELOCKE – Bulstrode Whitelocke, *Memorials of English Affairs*, 4 vols, Oxford, 1853.

Notes

Chapter 1: Garmouth and Whitehall

1 *APS* VI, 11, 156.
2 Accounts of the negotiations from rival viewpoints are in D. Stevenson, *R&CR*, 149–169, and R. Hutton, *Charles II*, London 1989, 44–48.
3 Walker, 158.
4 W. Mackay (ed.), *Chronicles of the Frasers*, SRS, 1902, 365.
5 Gardiner, *Charles II and Scotland*, 141–2; Walker, 138.
6 Mackay, *Frasers*, 365–6.
7 C. V. Wedgwood, *Montrose*, London, 1952, 133–150; Stephenson, *R&CR*, 158–169; Hutton, *Charles II*, 46–47; there are as many books on Montrose as on Charles II.
8 Abbott, 267–8.
9 Whitelocke III, June 25.
10 Ibid, 460–2; Abbott, 269–71.
11 Abbott, 268.
12 *CSP Dom*, 1650.
13 *APS* VI, ii, 216–9.

Chapter 2: The Invasion of Scotland

1 *CSP Dom* 1650, 214; *Commons Journals* VI, 431 and 433.
2 *CSP Dom* 1650, 207 and 209.
3 *APS* VI, ii, 579.
4 Ibid, 584–5.
5 Akerman, *Letters*, nos 1 and 2.
6 *CSP Dom* 1650, 242–7; Abbott, 283–8.
7 *CSP Dom* 1650, 225 and 230–237.
8 Ibid, 221, 228; Whitelocke III, July 17, 1650.
9 Abbott, 281.
10 H. Stace (ed.), *Cromwelliana*, Westminster 1810, quoting various newspapers; *Merc. Pol.* Jun 29, Jul 13, 23.
11 *CSP Dom* 1650, 22.
12 Hodgson, 126.
13 M. Ashley, *General Monck*, London 1977.
14 *Perf. Diurn.*, Jul 27: Abbott, 290–1.

15 Abbott, 293.
16 Nicoll, 21; Whitelocke III, July 29 and 31.
17 Nickolls, 11–13.
18 *Merc. Pol.*, Jul 30; Hodgson, 130.
19 *Perf. Diurn.*, Aug 6; *A True Relation of the Proceedings of the English Army*; *Sev. Proc.*, Aug 2; Abbott, 299–301.
20 Whitelocke III, Aug 15; Walker, 140.
21 *Ed. Recs.*, Jun 24–Jul 31.
22 *A True Relation* and *A Large Relation of the Fight at Leith*, both printed with Hodgson.
23 Abbott, 301.
24 Hodgson, 135; Nicoll, 22; *Perf. Diurn.*, Aug 17.
25 *RCGA*, Jul 24 – Aug 1 1650; Wariston, Jul 28.
26 *APS* VI ii, 601 – 2 and 607.
27 Wariston, Jul 29 – Aug 1; *Ed. Recs.*, Jul 31.
28 Wariston, Aug 2, 3; Walker, 163.
29 *CSP Dom* 1650, 268–276.
30 Abbott, 302–3.
31 Ibid, 305.
32 *Merc. Pol.*, Aug 24.
33 Wariston, Aug 10 – 13; *RCGA*, 33 – 40; *Charles II and Scotland*, nos 83 and 85.
34 Abbott, 306 – 8; *Ancram-Lothian Corr.*, II, 280–90; Walker, 97; *RCGA*, 33 – 40; Stevenson, *R&CR*, 176–7.
35 *A True Relation.*
36 Ibid; *APS* vii, 345; *Merc. Pol.*, Aug 29.
37 Nicoll, 24.
38 Wariston, Aug 16 – 20; Nicoll, 25; *RCGA*, 43; *Ed. Recs*, Aug 12–17.
39 Nicoll, 25; Wariston, Aug 18, 19; *A True Relation*; Abbott, 308–9.
40 Nicoll, 25; *Perf. Diurn.*, Sep 6.
41 *Several Letters from Scotland*; Abbott, 311–2.
42 Hodgson, 142; *A Letter from a Collonel in the Army*; *Perf. Diurn.*, Sep 6.

Chapter 3: Dunbar

1 *Perf. Diurn.*, Sep 16; Wariston, Aug 15; Whitelocke III, Aug 19.
2 Hodgson, 143; Major Cadwell's relation in T. Carte (ed.), *A Collection of Original Letters and Papers*, 2 vols, London 1739, 380–4; Abbott, 313 and 321 (Cromwell's account).
3 *Merc. Pol.*, Sep 10.
4 Cadwell; Hodgson, 143; Abbott, 322.
5 C. H. Firth, 'The battle of Dunbar', *Transactions of the Royal Historical Society* 14, 1900, 19–52.
6 Hodgson, 143; J. Rushworth, in *Old Parliamentary History* XIX, 341; Abbott, 323; *Merc. Pol.*, Sep 12.
7 Abbott, 323; Walker, 181; Cadwell; Firth, 'Battle of Dunbar', 23–25.

8 Cadwell; *A True Relation of the Routing of the Scottish Army near Dunbar*, Firth, 'Battle of Dunbar', 29–30; Abbott, 314–5.
9 Firth, 'Battle of Dunbar', 30, note 3; Abbott, 314–5.
10 Cadwell; *A True Relation*; Rushworth, *Old Parliamentary History*, 342; Firth, 'Battle of Dunbar', 33.
11 Cadwell.
12 Ibid; Whitelocke III, Sep 16.
13 Cadwell.
14 Hodgson, 144.
15 Abbott, 323 – 4; Firth, 'Battle of Dunbar', 38–9.
16 *Diary of Ambrose Burnes*, Surtees Society, 1867, 111.
17 Nicoll, 27; *Ancram-Lothian Correspondence*, 27–8; Walker, 180.
18 Abbott, 323–5; Rushworth, *Old Parliamentary History*, 341; Hodgson, 144–7; *A True Relation*; Cadwell; Whitelocke, 236–8; Nicoll, 27–28; J. Aubrey, *Miscellanies*, 113; J. Maidment (ed.), *Collections by a Private Hand at Edinburgh, 1650–61*, Edinburgh 1836, 28; Firth, 'Battle of Dunbar', 39–40, 42–6.
19 Abbott, 324; Cadwell; J. Barclay (ed.), *The Diary of Alexander Jaffray*, 3rd ed., Aberdeen, 1836, 57.

Chapter 4: A Rearrangement of Parties

1 Abbott, 321–30; Firth, 'Battle of Dunbar', Appendix, p. 53; R. Renwick (ed.), *Extracts from the Records of the Royal Burgh of Lanark, 1150–1722*, Glasgow 1893, Sep 5; *CSP Dom* 1650, 331; Whitelocke III, Sep 7; G. F. Warner (ed.), *The Nicholas Papers*, vol 1, Camden Society, 1886, 196.
2 *Ancram-Lothian Corr.*, 297–8; Walker, 183.
3 *Merc. Pol.*, Sep 18.
4 Walker, 183–9; Baillie, iii, 111–14; J. D. Marwick, *Extracts from the Records of the Royal Burgh of Glasgow, 1630–62*, Glasgow 1881, 192; Gardiner, *Charles II and Scotland*, 151 note; D. Stevenson, 'The Western Association, 1648–50', *Ayrshire Collections* 11, 1, 1982, 148–187.
5 *RCGA*, 48–58; J. Evelyn, *Diary and Correspondence*, London 1852, IV, 195–6; Balfour, IV, 107–12; Walker, 188.
6 Hodgson, 339; *Merc. Pol.*, Sep 20; Abbott, 331.
7 Abbott, 336.
8 *CSP Dom* 1650, 334; Hodgson, letter of Haselrig of 31 Oct.
9 *CSP Dom* 1650, 334, 340, 346, 375, 402, 418–9, 442; *CSP Colonial* 1574–1660, 360, 363, 428; C. E. Banks, 'Scotch Prisoners Deported to New England by Cromwell 1651–2', *Massachusetts Historical Society Proceedings*, 61, 1928, 4–16.
10 *Ed. Recs.*, Sep 2; *Perf. Diurn.*, Sep 9–16; *Merc. Pol.*, Sep 20; Abbott, 335–41.
11 *Modern Intelligencer*, Sep 21; Abbott, 336.
12 *The Lord General His March to Stirling*; *Modern Intelligencer*, Sep 21; *Ancram-Lothian Corr.*, 301–3 and 305; Abbott, 343; Nickolls, 21; *CSP Dom* 1650.
13 *The Lord General . . . Stirling*; *Merc. Pol.*, Sep 20, Oct 8; *Sev. Proc.*, Oct 8.

14 *Charles II and Scotland*, no 86 (from *Perf. Diurn*); *Merc. Pol.*, Sep 25, 26; *Sev. Proc.*, Oct 2–10; *APS* VII, 345.
15 *CSP Dom* 1650, 333, 350, 352.
16 Walker, 188; Balfour, IV, 109–12.
17 Walker, 196–7.
18 Ibid, 197–9; Evelyn, *Diary* IV, 197; Balfour, IV, 112–16; *Ancram-Lothian Corr.* II, 306–7; Stevenson, *R&CR*, 183–4.
19 Abbott, 349–50.
20 Ibid, 352–4; *Perf. Diurn.*, Oct 31.
21 *Merc. Pol.* Oct 29.
22 *Perf. Diurn.*, Oct 31; Abbott, 355–7; Stevenson, 'Western Association', 159.
23 *Merc. Pol.*, Oct 30.
24 *RCGA* iii, 557–62; Stevenson, 'Western Association', 159–160.
25 Balfour iv, 123–8; Walker, 203; *Ancram-Lothian Corr.*, ii, 317–8.
26 *RCGA* iii, 94–5, 106–8; Baillie, iii, 122–3; Balfour, iv, 136–9; Stevenson, *R&CR*, 189.
27 Balfour, iv, 132–5.
28 *Merc. Pol.*, Oct 9, Nov 5; Nickolls, 24; Nicoll, 34,
29 R. Chambers, *Domestic Annals of Scotland* ii, Edinburgh 1858, 203–5; Wariston, Nov 18.
30 Abbott, 359–60.
31 Ibid, 355; *Merc. Pol.*, Nov 5.
32 Whitelocke III, Oct 22; RCAHM Scot, *East Lothian*, Edinburgh 1924, no. 27.
33 *Perf. Diurn.*, Nov 18, 28; Abbott, 361–2; RCAHM Scot, *Midlothian and West Lothian*, Edinburgh 1929, no. 140.
34 RCAHM Scot, *Midlothian*, no. 3; *Ancram-Lothian Corr.*, 319.
35 *Ancram-Lothian Corr.*, 319; Stevenson, 'Western Association', 166–7.
36 *APS*, IV, ii, 609, 613.
37 Abbott, 359–63; Balfour, 165–6; *Merc. Pol.*, Nov 28; W. Chambers, *History of Peeblesshire*, Edinburgh, 1864, 163; R. Renwick, *Extracts from the Records of the Royal Burgh of Lanark*, Glasgow 1893, 28 Nov; Stevenson, 'Western Association', 167–170.
38 *Merc. Pol.*, Dec 10; Nicoll, 36–7; Abbott, 366; Baillie, III, 125; Stevenson, 'Western Association', 171.
39 Abbott, 366–71; K. C. Corsar, 'The surrender of Edinburgh Castle', *Scottish Historical Review*, 1949, 43–54.
40 Balfour, 209.
41 Abbott, 371–3; Corsar, 'Surrender'.
42 *APS* VI, 648–650; *RCGA*, 214–5.

Chapter 5: The Scottish Recovery

1 *Coronation of Charles the Second king of Scotland, England, France, and Ireland as it was acted and done at Scone*, Aberdeen 1651; Baillie, 118; *Merc. Pol.*, Dec 30; R. I. Stuart, Marquis of Bute, *Scottish Coronations*, Paisley 1912, 141–217.

2 *RCGA*, iii, 85.
3 Ibid, 267–71; *APS* VI, ii, 620 and 623.
4 D. Underdown, *Royalist Conspiracy in England, 1649–1660*, New Haven, Conn., 1960, ch. 2.
5 Nickolls, 33–9; *CSP Dom* 1650, 465, 472, 481; 1651, 48; Underdown, *Royalist Conspiracy*, 42–5.
6 *Merc. Pol.*, Jan 1, 6, 13; Nickolls, 48–9; *Letter from Carlisle*, in Hodgson; Abbott, 378; Nicoll, 42.
7 *Perf. Diurn.*, Jan 17; *Merc. Pol.*, Jan 22.
8 Nickolls, 47–8, 58; M. Ashley, *General Monck*, London 1977; Akerman, *Letters*, no. 8.
9 *CSP Dom* 1651, 40–41.
10 Akerman, *Letters*, 8, 11; Abbott, 383; Balfour, 266–7; D. Stevenson, 'The English and the Public Records of Scotland, 1650–1660', *Miscellany One*, Stair Society 1971, 156–70.
11 Balfour, 222, 248, 250; *Merc. Pol.*, Feb 8; *RCGA* 173–431 *passim*; Stevenson, *R&CR* 194–5.
12 *Perf. Diurn.*, Feb 15, 17; *Merc. Pol.*, Feb 12, 14; Nicoll, 49; Abbott, 393–4, 400, 402–7.
13 *Merc. Pol.*, Feb 13; *Perf. Diurn.*, Feb 7.
14 Chambers, *History of Peeblesshire*, 164; Whitelocke, Feb 14; Akerman, *Letters*, no. 15; *Merc. Pol.*, Feb 19; A. Jeffrey, *History and Antiquities of Roxburghshire and Adjacent Districts*, vol 2, Edinburgh 1857; Nicoll, 46.
15 *Merc. Pol.*, Feb 18, 21, 27, Mar 3; Whitelocke, Feb 17, Mar 1; Akerman, *Letters*, nos 15, 17; RCAHM Scot, *East Lothian* no 106; Ashley, *General Monck*.
16 *Merc. Pol.*, Mar 3; Whitelocke, Mar 1; RCAHM Scot, *Berwickshire*; ibid, *East Lothian*, no 108.
17 *Merc. Pol.*, Mar 7, 11; *Ancram-Lothian Corr.* 344–5.
18 RCAHM Scot, *Midlothian and West Lothian* no. 303.
19 *Merc. Pol.* Apr 3, 7; Akerman, *Letters*, nos 24, 25, 26, 28.
20 Balfour, ii, 266; Wariston, Mar 31.
21 *Merc. Pol.*, Mar 21.
22 Underdown, *Royalist Conspiracy*, 45–6.
23 *CSP Dom* 1651, 83–4, 87, 90.
24 Underdown, *Royalist Conspiracy*, 47–8.
25 D. Stevenson (ed.), 'Committee for Managing the Affairs of the Army', *The Government of Scotland under the Covenanters, 1631–1651*, SHS 1982, 105ff.
26 *Merc. Pol.* Apr 11, 13; Akerman, *Letters* no. 28; *Commons Journals* VII, 39.
27 Nicoll, 51–2; Wariston, Apr 16–17; *Merc. Pol.* Apr 22.
28 *Perf. Diurn.* Apr 26, 28; *Merc. Pol.*, Apr 24; Akerman, *Letters*, nos 31, 32; Abbott, 407–8.
29 *Perf. Diurn.*, Apr 28; Baillie, iii, 165; Akerman, *Letters*, nos 31, 32.
30 Baillie, 161–3.
31 Abbott, 410–1.

32 Wariston, May 2; Akerman, *Letters*, no. 35; Abbott, 411–22.
33 Balfour, iv, 297, 299–301; *APS* VI, ii, 651, 663; Stevenson, *R&CR* 198, 201.
34 *APS* VI, ii, 647, 672–3, 676–7; *RCGA* iii, 356–8, 388; Nicoll, 51; Baillie, 160; Stevenson, *R&CR*, 199–202.
35 Stevenson, 'Managing Committee', May 17; Abbott, 411.
36 Stevenson, 'Managing Committee', passim; *Merc. Pol.* May 23, 26.
37 *Perf. Diurn.*, Jun 11; *Merc. Pol.* May 28, Jun 4, 5, 10, 18, 22.
38 Wariston, May 5; *Perf. Diurn.* Jun 6; Abbott, 419–22.

Chapter 6: Torwood and Inverkeithing

1 *Perf. Diurn.*, Jun 13; *Merc. Pol.*, Jun 18.
2 Whitelocke III, Jun 18; Cary, *Original Letters* ii, 31; *Perf. Diurn.*, Jul 7.
3 *Merc. Pol.*, May 26, Jun 4, 5, 10, 11, 18; Whitelocke, May 26, Jun 9; *Faithful Scout*, Jun 19.
4 *CSP Dom* 1651, 584.
5 Cf. also A. Woolrych, 'Cromwell as a Soldier', in J. Morrill (ed.), *Oliver Cromwell and the English Revolution*, London, 1990, 93–119, for another comment on this.
6 *Merc. Pol.*, Jun 4, 5; RCAHM Scot., *Fife, Kinross and Clackmannan*, Edinburgh, 1933, no. 277.
7 *Merc. Pol.*, Jun 24.
8 Ibid, Jul 8, 9; *Perf. Diurn.*, Jul 9.
9 *Merc. Pol.*, Jul 14, 17; *Perf. Diurn.*, Jul 14, 18; Hodgson, 161; Abbott, 427–8.
10 Nickolls, 84; Abbott, 428 and note 12; *Merc. Pol.*, Jul 17, 21, 23.
11 *Merc. Pol.*, Jul 23; Abbott, 429.
12 *Perf. Diurn.*, Jul 25; Akerman, *Letters*, no. 62; *Merc. Pol.*, Jul 23, 25.
13 Stevenson, 'Western Association', 168.
14 *Perf. Diurn.*, Jul 25; *Merc. Pol.*, Jul 25.
15 Wariston, Jul 16; *Merc. Pol.*, Jul 25.
16 Abbott, 432–3; *Merc. Pol.*, Jul 25, 26, 29; Nicoll, 53–4; Akerman, *Letters*, nos 62, 63; Balfour, iv, 313; Whitelocke, Jul 28; W. Stephens, *A History of Inverkething and Rosyth*, Edinburgh 1925, 360–4.
17 *Merc. Pol.*, Jul 25.
18 Hodgson, 162; *Perf. Diurn.*, Jul 30, Aug 1; *Merc. Pol.*, Jul 30, 31, Aug 1; Abbott, 433–6.
19 *Merc. Pol.*, Aug 5.
20 Cary, *Memorials* ii, 283.
21 *Merc. Pol.*, Aug 1, 2, 5, 6; Akerman, *Letters*, no. 66; *Perf. Diurn.*, Jul 30, Aug 5; Abbott, 438–9.
22 *Perf. Diurn.*, Aug 8, 9.
23 Stephen, *Inverkeithing and Rosyth*, 365; Chambers, *Domestic Annals* II, 206–7; *APS* VII, app, 344.
24 Nicoll, 55.
25 Ibid; HMC 29 *Portland* i, 610–11; 21 *Hamilton* ii, 77–8.

Chapter 7: The Invasion of England

1 *Perf. Diurn.*, Aug 8, 9; *Merc. Pol.*, Aug 9.
2 Abbott, 440; Akerman, *Letters* no. 67.
3 Abbott, 440–2.
4 Nickolls, 61.
5 Abbott, 442–5; *Merc. Pol.*, Aug 9, 12; D. Marshal, 'Notes on the Record Room of the City of Perth, II', *Proceedings of the Society of Antiquaries of Scotland*, 33, 1898–9, 430; Hodgson, 152.
6 *Perf. Diurn.*, Aug 9; *Merc. Pol.*, Aug 14; Whitelocke, Aug 9; Chambers, *History of Peeblesshire*, 164, quoting Kirk Session Records of Drummelzier and Tweedsmuir.
7 *Merc. Pol.*, Aug 4.
8 Cary, *Memorials*, 299–300.
9 Abbott, 445–6; Cary, *Memorials*, 303–5.
10 Cary, *Memorials*, 303–12.
11 Ibid, 296–8; *CSP Dom* 1651, 306; Merc. Pol., Aug 14.
12 Abbott, 445; *Perf. Diurn.*, Aug 9; Cary, *Memorials* 295–6; *Merc. Pol.*, Aug 9.
13 *Merc. Pol.*, Aug 13.
14 Abbott, 443–5.
15 Ibid, 447; *Merc. Pol.*, Aug 12, 13; *Perf. Diurn.*, Aug 16, 18, 20.
16 *Merc. Pol.*, Aug 19.
17 Ibid, Aug 14, 16; Cary, *Memorials*, 303–5.
18 *CSP Dom* 1651, 306–9.
19 Ibid, 317–9, 323–5.
20 Cary, *Memorials*, 324; *Merc. Pol.*, Aug 15.
21 *Merc. Pol.*, Aug 14.
22 Ibid, Aug 20; *Perf. Diurn.*, Aug 20.
23 *A Great Victory by the Blessing of God obtained . . . near Wiggan in Lancashire*; *Two Letters from Col. Robert Lilburne*, Cheetham Society II, 1843, 294–6.
24 *Perf. Diurn.*, Sep 1; *A Great Victory*, 296–307.
25 *Merc. Pol.*, Aug 25, 26; *Perf. Diurn.*, Aug 25.
26 *Merc. Pol.*, Aug 21, 23, 26; *Perf. Diurn.*, Aug 26; Hodgson, 152.
27 *CSP Dom* 1651, 338–341.
28 *Merc. Pol.*, Aug 26.
29 *CSP Dom* 1651, 461; *Merc. Pol.*, Aug 25.

Chapter 8: Worcester

1 Whitelocke III, Aug 25; *Merc. Pol.*, Aug 23, 26; *Perf. Diurn.*, Aug 25.
2 *Merc. Pol.*, Aug 25.
3 C. E. Green, 'Charles II and the Battle of Worcester', *English Historical Review*, 1890, 114–8.
4 J. W. Willis Bund, *The Civil War in Worcestershire, 1642–1646, and the Scotch Invasion of 1651*, repr. Gloucester, 1979, 225.
5 Historical Manuscripts Commission, 5th Report, Lechmere Papers, 299.
6 Willis Bund, 227; Abbott, 466.

7 Willis Bund, 226–7.
8 HMC 5th Report, Lechmere, 299.
9 Willis Bund, 225–6, 230.
10 Green (n.3).
11 Abbott, 453.
12 *CSP Dom* 1651, 398–9.
13 *Perf. Diurn.*, Aug 28; *Merc. Pol.*, Aug 28.
14 *Perf. Diurn.*, Sep 1.
15 Abbott, 452.
16 Ibid, 455; *Merc. Pol.*, Aug 30; Willis Bund, 231–3.
17 Abbott, 457, 467; Willis Bund, 237–8.
18 *CSP Dom* 1651, 41.
19 Whitelocke III, Sep 2; *Perf. Diurn.*, Sep 3; *Merc. Pol.*, Sep 3.
20 *Merc. Pol.*, Sep 2, 3.
21 Ibid, Aug 26, Sep 2, 3; *Perf. Diurn.*, Sep 2, 3; Willis Bund, 237.
22 Abbott, 458–61; Cary, *Memorials* ii, 357–9, 362–4; *Perf. Diurn.*, Sep 4, 8, 29; *Merc. Pol.*, Sep 4, 7; *CSP Dom* 1651, 436–7; *Chronicles of the Frasers*, 386–7.
23 Abbott, 464–5; *Perf. Diurn.*, Sep 6, 15; Hodgson, 163; *CSP Dom* 1651, 470; R. Ollard, *The Escape of Charles II after the Battle of Worcester*, London, 1966; Underdown, *Royalist Conspiracy*, 53–5.
24 *CSP Dom* 1651, 410.
25 Ibid, 412, 413.
26 Ibid, 415, 416, 419, 425, 427–8, 430.
27 Ibid, 453.
28 Ibid, 431, 432, 458, 474; Banks, 'Scotch Prisoners', 17–29.
29 Ibid, 440.

Chapter 9: Stirling and Dundee

1 Abbott, 443–5, 451, 457; *CSP Dom* 1651, 399.
2 Firth, *Scotland*, 1–6.
3 *Perf. Diurn.*, Aug 9; Wariston, 105.
4 Nicoll, 55.
5 *Merc. Pol.*, Aug 20; Stevenson, *R&CR*, 206.
6 Firth, *Scotland*, 1–6; Cary, *Memorials*, ii, 330–1.
7 Firth, *Scotland*, 1–6.
8 Ibid, 316–7.
9 *Merc. Pol.*, Aug 14.
10 Firth, *Scotland*, 316–7; Whitelocke III, Aug 25.
11 Firth, *Scotland*, 1–6; C. H. Firth (ed.), *The Journal of Joachim Hane*, Oxford, 1896.
12 Firth, *Scotland*, 1–6.
13 Ibid, 21–3; D. G. Barron (ed.), *In Defence of the Regalia*, London 1910, 91–4.
14 Firth, *Scotland*, 8–9, 320; Cary, *Memorials*, ii, 345–6; Balfour, iv, 314–5; Nicoll, 56–7; *Perf. Diurn.*, Sep 8, Oct 2; *Merc. Pol.*, Sep 4.
15 T. Gamble, *The Life of General Monck*, London 1671.

16 Firth, *Scotland*, 9–11; Cary, *Memorials*, ii, 351–2; Nicoll, 57–8; *Merc. Pol.*, Sep 8, 10; Dow, *Cromwellian Scotland*, Edinburgh, 1985, 14–16.
17 Firth, *Scotland*, 11–13, 323–7; J. Stuart (ed.), *Extracts from the Records of the Burgh of Aberdeen, 1643–1747*, Edinburgh 1872, Sep 5–10, 1651; J. Barclay (ed.), *The Diary of Alexander Jaffray*, 3rd ed., Aberdeen, 1856.
18 Firth, *Scotland*, 14, 321–2; *Merc. Pol.*, Sep 8.

Chapter 10: The Final Conquest

1 Stevenson, *R&CR*, 210; *Merc Pol.*, 2–9 Oct.
2 J. Stuart (ed.), *Extracts from the Records of the Burgh of Aberdeen, 1643–1747*, Edinburgh, 1872; Firth, *Scotland*, 323, 326.
3 Firth, *Scotland*, 16–17, 22–23; Wariston, Sep 20; Stevenson, *R&CR*, 209; Dow, *Cromwellian Scotland*, 21.
4 Firth, *Scotland*, 22–3.
5 Stuart, *Extracts . . . Aberdeen*, Sep 10, 17, Firth, *Scotland*, 15.
6 Firth, *Scotland*, 16; *Commons Journals* VII, 23: Ashley, *General Monck*, 91.
7 Firth, *Scotland*, 16, 18, 326; *Merc. Pol.*, 16–23 Oct.
8 Firth, *Scotland*, 26 note; Stevenson, *R&CR*, 209; R. Renwick (ed.), *Extracts from the Records of the Royal Burgh of Stirling, 1519–1666*, Glasgow, 1887.
9 Dow, *Cromwellian Scotland*, 19–20.
10 Firth, *Scotland*, 327–8.
11 Ibid, 327–33.
12 Ibid, 356; G. R. Kinloch (ed.), *The Diary of Mr John Lamont, 1649–1671*, Maitland Club, 1830, 47–8.
13 Abbott, 380; *CSP Dom* 1651, 19, 29, 46, 71, 177.
14 C. Hill, *God's Englishman: Oliver Cromwell and the English Revolution*, London, 1970, 155.
15 *Commons Journals* VII, 14, 22.
16 *CSP Dom* 1651, 474; 1651–2, 65; Dow, *Cromwellian Scotland*, 30–31.
17 Dow, *Cromwellian Scotland*, 30–51; C. S. Terry (ed.), *The Cromwellian Union*, SHS, 1902.
18 Firth, *Scotland*, 333, 335; Stevenson, *R&CR*, 210.
19 Firth, *Scotland*, 20–21, 337–8, 339–41; Whitelocke III, Dec 19; Akerman, 38, 39, 45.
20 Firth, *Scotland*, 38–9, 334; *CSP Dom* 1651–2, 6, 82, 86, 230–1; Nicoll, 71, 73, 75; D. Stevenson, 'The English and the Public Records of Scotland, 1650–1660', *Miscellany One*, Stair Society, 171, 159–161; D. G. Barron, *In Defence of the Regalia*, London 1910.
21 Dow, *Cromwellian Scotland*, *passim*; Terry, *Cromwellian Union*, introduction.

GLOSSARY

ACT OF CLASSES – an act of the Scottish Parliament which punished the Engagers, who were variously punished and purged by it.

COMMISSION OF THE KIRK – a permanent committee of the General Assembly of the Church of Scotland which had authority in the intervals between assemblies.

COMMITTEE OF ESTATES – a committee of the Scottish Parliament, consisting of twelve members from each Estate, nobles, lairds and burgesses, with three lords of session; in effect, the Scottish revolutionary government.

COUNCIL OF STATE – a committee of the English Parliament, the effective government of England after the Civil Wars.

COVENANT – or Scottish National Covenant, the foundation document of the Scottish Revolution of 1637–1644, to which Charles II had to assent in order to become king.

ENGAGERS – the name given to a party in Scotland who had negotiated a treaty with Charles I in 1648 (the 'Engagement') which led to the disastrous invasion of England in that year; Presbyterian Royalists.

FIFTH MONARCHIST – a believer in the doctrine that the Fifth Monarchy will be that of God, and that its establishment was imminent, and would take place when the rule of saints was imposed; extremists.

GENERAL ASSEMBLY – the governing body of the Scottish Church.

INDEPENDENT – a term which was used in the English Revolution to describe those in favour of a decree of religious toleration (as opposed to the more dictatorial Presbyterians); the toleration was strictly limited, however, and largely the result of political necessity.

KIRK PARTY, KIRKMEN – the party in Scotland attached most firmly to the Covenant, which in effect delivered the government of the country into the hands of the Church.

LORD GENERAL – the title given to the Commander-in-chief of the English republican army.

MALIGNANTS – the name given by their opponents to Royalists, but often expanded to include any enemy.

PRESBYTERIAN – the term for those, in England, who wished to replace the episcopal Church of England by one without bishops; these were the nearest equivalent in England of the Scottish Covenanters.

PROTESTORS – see Remonstrants.

PRIDE'S PURGE – the expulsion, by a detachment of the army under Colonel Thomas Pride, of English MPs unenthusiastic for the punishment of Charles I, 1648; the purge led directly to the trial and execution of the king.

REMONSTRANTS – an extreme party of Kirkmen who were unwilling to admit any authority in the king; also called Protestors; opposed by Resolutioners.

RESOLUTIONERS – a moderate party of Kirkmen, but whose moderation existed only after defeat by the English; opposed by the Remonstrants.

BIBLIOGRAPHY

Listed here are books which have not been referred to in the notes.

AYLMER, G. E., *The Interregnum: The Quest for Settlement, 1646–1660, London, 1972.*

BEATTIE, J., *History of the Church of Scotland under the commonwealth*, Edinburgh, 1842.

BUCHAN, J. W., *History of Peeblesshire*, 2 vols, Glasgow, 1925.

BURNET, G., *History of my own Times*, ed. O. Airy, 2 vols, Oxford, 1897.

BURNET, G., *The Memoires of the Lives and Actions of James and William Dukes of Hamilton*, London, 1677.

CAPP, B., *Cromwell's Navy*, Oxford, 1989.

CLARENDON, Earl of *History of the Rebellion and Civil Wars in England*, ed. W. D. Macray, Oxford, 1888.

CLARK, G., *War and Society in the Seventeenth Century*, Cambridge, 1958.

CRAIG-BROWN, T., *The History of Selkirkshire, or Chronicles of Ettrick Forest*, 2 vols, Edinburgh, 1886.

DAICHES, D., *Scotland and the Union*, London, 1977.

DAWSON, W. H., *Cromwell's Understudy: the Life and Times of General John Lambert*, London, 1938.

Dictionary of National Biography.

DONALDSON, G., *Scotland: James V to James VII*, Edinburgh and London, 1964.

DONALDSON, G., 'Scotland's Conservative North in the Sixteenth and Seventeenth Centuries', *Transactions of the Royal Historical Society*, 1966, 65–79.

DWYER, J. *et al*, *New Perspectives on the Politics and Culture of Early Modern Scotland*, Edinburgh, 1982.

FIRTH, C. H., *Cromwell's Army*, 4th ed., London, 1962.

FIRTH, Sir C., and DAVIES, G., *The Regimental History of Cromwell's Army*, 2 vols, London, 1940.

FRASER, A., *Cromwell: our Chief of Men*, London, 1973.

FURGOL, E., *A Regimental History of the Covenanting Armies, 1639–1651*, Edinburgh, 1990.

GARDINER, S. R., *History of the Commonwealth and Protectorate*, 3 vols, London 1897–1901.

HARVIE, C., *Scotland and Nationalism: Scottish Society and Politics, 1707–1977*, London, 1977.

HILL C., *The Experience of Defeat: Milton and some Contemporaries*, London, 1984.

HUTTON, R. A., *The British Republic, 1649–1660*, London, 1990.
HUTTON, R. A., 'Charles II's only Battle', *Transactions of the Worcestershire Archaeological Society*, 3rd Series 15, 1996, 219–224.
JEFFREY, A., *History and Antiquities of Roxburghshire and Adjacent Districts*, 3 vols, Edinburgh 1855 (?)–1864.
LAMONT, W. M., *Godly Rule: Politics and Religion, 1603–1660*, London, 1969.
MACKAY, W., *The Church of the Covenant*, Edinburgh, 1979.
MITCHISON, R., *Lordship and Patronage: Scotland 1603–1745*, London, 1983.
MORRILL, J. (ed.), *The Scottish National Covenant in its British Context*, Edinburgh, 1990.
NICOLL, J., *Diary of Alexander Brodie of Brodie*, Spalding Club, Edinburgh, 1863.
PHILIPS, C. E. L., *Cromwell's Captains*, London, 1937.
RAIT, R. S., *The Parliaments of Scotland*, Glasgow, 1924.
REID, S., *Scots Armies of the Civil Wars, 1639–1651*, Edinburgh, 1982.
RILEY, P. W. J., *The Union of England and Scotland*, Manchester, 1978.
RUSSELL, C., 'The British Problem and the English Civil War', *History* 72, 1987, 395–415.
SINCLAIR-STEVENSON, C., *Inglorious Rebellion: the Jacobite Risings of 1708, 1715 and 1719*, London, 1971.
SMOUT, T. C., *A History of the Scottish People*, London, 1969.
SOMERVILLE, Lord J., *Memoirs of the Somervills*, 2 vols, Edinburgh, 1815.
STEVENSON, D. C., 'The Financing of the Cause of the Covenants, 1638–1651', *Scottish Historical Review*, 51, 1972, 95–114.
STEVENSON, D. C., *The Scottish Revolution 1637–1644: the Triumph of the Covenanters*, Newton Abbot, 1973.
STEVENSON, D. C., *King or Covenant? Voices from Civil War*, East Linton, 1996.
TOON, P., *God's Statesman: the Life and Work of John Owen*, Exeter, 1971.
TREVOR-ROPER, H. R., 'Scotland and the Puritan Revolution', in *Religion, the Reformation and Social Change*, London, 1967.
WILCOCK, J., *The Great Marquess: Life and Times of Archibald . . . Marquess of Argyll*, Edinburgh, 1903.
WORDEN, B., *The Rump Parliament, 1648–1653*, Cambridge, 1974.
YOUNG, P., and HOLMES, R., *The English Civil Wars*, London, 1974.

INDEX

Abbey Hill, Edinburgh, 24
Aberdeen, Charles II at, 8; falls to English, 160, 161, 162, 163, 165, 166, 172; Map 8
Aberfoyle, 102
Admiralty Committee (English), 18, 81
Airlie, earl of, 62
Allanton, 89
Alured, Colonel, 147, 168; captures Committee of Estates, 158, 159; evacuates Dumfries, 92, 95; in Fife, 154, 156
Alured's Regiment of Horse, 154
Alyth, 158, 162, 163, 168, 170; Map 8
Anabaptists, 169
Angus, 165, 166
Annan, 116
Annandale, 116
Anstruther, 154, 168; Map 5, 8
Antinomians, 169
Antitrinitarians, 169
Antwerp, 51
Appleby, 119; Map 6
Arbroath, 166; Map 8
Argyll, 54, 162, 172
Argyll, marquis of (Archibald Campbell), 9, 66; and Charles II, 54–55, 61, 76; and English conquest, 157, 162, 164, 165; military strength, 59, 148; submission of, 170–171
army, English, at Dunbar, 42–50; losses, 33, 37, 39, 50, 96, 143, march to Edinburgh, 22–23, 30; reinforcements, 58, 61; size of force, 16, 19, 39–40, 92, 94, 115, 126–127, 134, 147–148; supplies for, 22, 27, 30, 37, 92, 100, 101, 102; at Worcester, 130–143
army, Scots, dispositions, 86, 92, 100; losses, 50, 143, 146; march into England, 113, 115–117; at Dunbar, 42–50; purging of, 17; recruits for, 13, 81, 87; size of, 16, 40, 59, 90, 92, 94, 116–117, 149; supplies for, 33, 86–87, 91, 100; at Worcester, 130–145
Arran, 172
Arthur's Seat, Edinburgh, 24, 35–36; Map 2
artillery, English, 19, 40, 148; at Dunbar, 46–48; at siege of Edinburgh Castle, 68, 74; at Stirling, 152, 155–156; used against Scottish houses, 70, 84
Ashfield's Regiment of Horse, 147, 172
Aston Hall, 119
Atholl, earl of, 62–63, 65–66, 77, 157
Ayr, 73, 80, 85, 161, 167; Map 4, 8
Ayrshire, 52; Map 4
Ayton, 22; Map 1, 6

Badger, Captain, 101
Balcarres, earl of (Alexander Lindsay), raising recruits, 111; resistance of, 163–164, 165, 166, 171; submission of, 172
Balfour, historian, quoted, 110
Banbury, 125; Map 6
Bannockburn, 107, 108, 111
Barber, Major, 22
Barnard Castle, 118
Barnet, 120, 121, 125; Map 6
Barton, Colonel, 138, 143
Bass Rock, 70, 81, 84, 162, 168, 172; Map 1, 4, 5, 8
Baynes, Captain John, 18
Baynes, Cornet John, quoted, 17–18, 81

Berkley, Sir Rowland, 131, 135
Berkstead's Foot Regiment, 120
Bermuda, Scots prisoners sent to, 57, 145
Berry, Colonel James, 148, 156
Berry's Regiment of Horse (ex-Hasilrig's), 148, 153
Berwick, 17, 19, 20, 30, 37, 51, 60, 83, 84, 114, 161, 176; Map 1, 4, 5, 6, 8
Berwick, Maine, 57
Berwickshire, 83
Bewdley, 131, 134, 138, 143; Map 6
Biggar, 92, 115, 155; Map 6
Birch, Colonel John, 123
Birkenhead, Isaac, English Royalist agent, 86, 93, 118
Blackburn, 64, 72, 88
Blackford, 157
Blackford Hill, Edinburgh, 35; Map 2
Blackness Castle, 80, 85, 97, 101, 151; Map 4, 5
Blackstone Edge, 144
Blackwall, Scots prisoners at, 144
Blackwall pest house, London, 57
Bog of Gight, Gordon castle, 7
Boghall Castle, 92, 115, 155, 161; Map 8
Borthwick, 70–71, 72; Map 4
Borthwick, Lord, 70
Bothwell Brig, 72–73, 100
Boyd, Zachary, Scots minister, 63–64, 88
Boynton, Colonel, 119
Bradford, 144
Bradshaw, John, 116
Braid Hills, Edinburgh, 31, 32, 35; Map 2
Brampton, 116
Bransford, 137; Map 7
Brechin, 166, 168; Map 8
Bridge of Earn, 109, 113; Map 5
Bridgnorth, 131
Bright, Colonel, 19–20, 48
Bristol, 102, 145
Brock Burn, Dunbar, 39; Map 3
Brodick, 172; Map 8
Brodie of Brodie, Alexander, 62
Bromsgrove blacksmith, 3–4, 143
Broughty Castle, 159; Map 8
Brown, Major, 38
Browne, Major, captain of frigate *Speaker*, 157, 158
Browne of Fordell, Major-General Sir John, 90, 110; at Dunbar, 42, 65; at Inverkeithing, 106
Brownists, 169
Broxmouth House, Dunbar, 39, 40, 43, 45, 48; Map 3
Brydges, James, 128
Bryn Hall, 121
Buchanans, at Inverkeithing, 106
Buckingham, duke of, 28, 86; and invasion of England, 119, 124; and Start conspiracy, 62; lieutenant-general, 90–91, 103, 109
Burntisland, 80, 81, 109, 115; Map 4, 5
Bute, 54, 167

Callander, 102
Callander House, 59, 101, 103, 104
Calton Hill, Edinburgh, 26, 35
Campbell of Lawers, Colonel James, 26; at Dunbar, 49, 106
Canongate, Edinburgh, 24, 26
Carbisdale, battle of, 8, 26, 42
Cardigan, 129
Carlisle, garrison, 19, 30, 92, 94; as base for invasion of south-west Scotland, 61, 79; reinforcements sent to, 65, 90, 95; and Scots invasion, 116, 117, 118, 132, 172; Map 4, 6
Carnwath, 95
Carrick, 54
Cassillis, earl of, 54
Castlandhill, Inverkeithing, 106
Castlehill Kirk, Edinburgh, 68
Castle Ruthin, 121
Catholics, 119, 121
Channel Islands, 6
Charles I, execution of, 5–6, 14; rule of, 10, 13, 170
Charles II, 3–4, 15, 40, 94, 109; aims, 13, 66, 83–84; coronation, 29, 76; enmity towards Kirk Party, 31–32,

33, 54–55; escape, 143; government of Scotland after invasion, 149, 169; increased power, 77, 90; invasion of England, 79, 111, 116, 117, 119, 121; lands at Garmouth, 5, 9, 13, 170; and marquis of Argyll, 54–55, 61; popularity, 7–8; proclaimed king, 6; reaches Edinburgh, 28–29; reported reaction to Dunbar defeat, 52, 64; signs new declaration, 31–32; and Start conspiracy, 62–63; subjected to Scots Covenant, 6–7; voyage to Scotland, 6–7; at Worcester, 129–132, 140
Charles Edward, Prince ('Bonnie Prince Charlie'), 1
Cheshire, 122, 127, 143, 144
Chester, 86, 95, 102, 123, 145; Map 6
Chiesly, Sir John, 52, 54, 64
Chillingham Castle, 20
Civil War, English, 2, 5, 11
Clarke, Major Samuel, contractor for Scots prisoners, 56
Clarke, William, 168
Classes, Act of, 8, 91, 149
Clova, Charles II's refuge, 62, 72
Clyde, river, 72, 87, 101, 102, 154, 162, 167
Clydesdale, 90, 92, 100, 151
Cobbet's Foot Regiment, 141, 143
Cockburn, James, defeated at Home Castle, 83
Cockburnspath, 22, 38; Map 1
Coke, Thomas, Royalist agent, 86, 93, 118
Coldstream, 19, 83; Map 1
Coldstream Guards, 20
Colinton House, 32, 34, 61
Commission of the Kirk, 9, 67, 77, 91
commissioners, Scots, to bring Charles II to Scotland, 6–7
Committee for Managing the Army (Scots), 86, 92
Committee of Estates (Scots), 8–9, 29, 54, 74, 90; and English conquest, 149, 150, 157; final meetings, 164–167, 170; most members captured, 158, 170; and Start conspiracy, 61, 63, 66; and Western Association, 71–72
Congleton, 143
Cook, John, 116
Cornwall, 78
Corstorphine, 4, 34, 64, 96, 101; Map 2
Cortachy Castle, 62
Council of State, 9, 16, 22, 27, 30, 51, 95; and conquest of Scotland, 147; and government of Scotland, 169, 171; and Royalist conspiracies, 78–79, 86; and Scots invasion, 118, 120, 125–127, 128, 130, 135, 136; and Scots prisoners, 56–57, 59, 144–145
Covenant, Charles II and, 6–7
Covenanters, in 1670s, 1
'Cranford', 61
Craven Gap, 119
Crawford-Lindsay, earl of, 77, 111; commander-in-chief of Scots army, 149, 157, 158
Cromwell, Elizabeth, 51
Cromwell, Oliver, 2, 3, 14, 17, 116; appeals to Kirk Commission, 30; appeals to Leslie, 31–32; baggage captured, 80; campaign about Edinburgh, 31–36; and capture of Edinburgh Castle, 73–75; at Dunbar, 37–51; fired at by Scots soldier, 32; and decision for war with Scotland, 9–12, 14–15; and Fife, 107–108; and government of Scotland, 169, 171; illness, 82, 93; and invasion of England, 108, 115, 118–119, 121–127; and invasion of Scotland, 17–20, 22; Lord General, 12, 16; march to Bothwell Brig, 72; march to Glasgow, 63–64, 87–90, 101–103; march to Kilsyth, 82; march to Stirling, 58–59; and Scots prisoners, 27, 55–56; strategy, 93, 96–100; tries to exploit Scots divisions, 63–64; at Worcester, 130, 134–144
Cromwell's Foot Regiment, at Dunbar, 48; in Lancashire campaign, 123, 143

Cromwell's life guards, at Worcester, 140, 143
Cromwell's Regiment of Horse, 26; at Dunbar, 46; at Worcester, 140, 141
Crook, Captain, 87, 95, 101
Crosby, preacher at Worcester, 131
Cumberland, 95, 119
Cumbernauld, 113, 115; Map 5, 6
Cunningham, Colonel William, 155–156, 160

Dalhousie, 69; Map 2, 4
Dalkeith, 33, 35, 69; Map 2, 4
Dalyell of the Binns, Major-General Thomas, 90
Dalziel, Scots officer at Worcester, 141
Daniel, Colonel, 104
Daniel's Foot Regiment, 104
Darien scheme, 174, 175
Daventry, 125
Deane, Colonel, 18; General-at-Sea, 60; major-general, 93, 139, 140
Deane's Foot Regiment, at Worcester, 140
Derby, earl of, and invasion of England, 109, 118, 143; and Isle of Man, 77, 86; in Lancashire, 119, 122–124, 127, 129, 131, 138; in North Wales, 121
Derbyshire, miners from, 73
Desborough, Major-General John, 125, 134
Desborough, Samuel, 169
Desborough's Foot Regiment, 141
Dirleton House, 70; Map 4
Doon Hill, Dunbar, Scots camp, 38–39, 43, 46, 49; Map 3
Douglas, 95
Douglas, Colonel, 19
Douglas of Blaikerstons, Sir Robert, 110
Douglas, Robert, preacher at Charles II's coronation, 76
Douglas, W. S., 2
Dow, F. D., 2
Downing, George, Scoutmaster-General, 107
Drummelzier, 115
Druschke, Johan van, Dutch mercenary soldier, 65–66, 91, 144
Dublin, 51
Duddingston Loch, 36; Map 2
Dudhope, Lord, and Start conspiracy, 62
Dumbarton, 87, 94, 101, 103, 165, 166; Map 5, 8
Dumbarton Castle, 102, 162, 171, 172
Dumfries, 64, 65, 79, 92, 95, 116, 161, 167
Dunbar, 22, 71, 84; battle of, 40–50, 81, 96, 104, 139, 142, 145;
English retreat to, 27, 29, 31, 37, 97; reactions to battle, 51–55, 66, 103
Dunbartonshire, 54
Dunblane, 157
Dundas Castle, 108; Map 4
Dundas, Sir Walter, governor of Edinburgh Castle, 58, 82; surrenders, 74–75
Dundee, 62, 92, Charles II at, 8; English conquest, 158–160, 161, 162, 165, 166, 170, 172; Scots government at, 157–158
Dunfermline, 105, 107, 110
Dunglass Castle, 59, 61
Dunkeld, 165, 166, 167
Dunnottar castle, 8, 162–163, 172–173; Map 8
Durham, 19; and Scots prisoners, 55, 57, 145

East India House, Scots prisoners at, 144
Eastern Association (English), 78
Edinburgh, 8, 11, 14, 16, 22, 27, 50, 51, 60, 94, 95; abandoned by Scots, 51; fortified city, 17, 23–24; English rule, 67–68, 97, 104, 148, 150, 156, 161; meeting of ministers, 167–169; shortages, 33; Map 1, 2, 4, 5, 6, 8
Edinburgh Castle, 17, 51; captured by English 73–75; siege of, 58, 59, 64, 67, 80, 151; Spur demolished, 23; Map 1, 2
Edinburgh University, 68

Edinburgh-Leith Lines, assault on, 24–26; Map 1, 2
Eglinton, 87
Eglinton, earl of, 26, 54, 71, 84, 87
Elizabeth I, 175
Empson, Lieutenant, 26
Engagers, Scots party, 8, 11, 13, 14, 52, 149; purged from army, 28, 29, 34; readmitted, 55, 77, 90, 91
England, Charles II proclaimed king of, 6; Engagers' invasion of, 8, 111, 119; Royalist conspiracies in, 77–79, 85–86; Scots invasion of, 81, 109, 113–127
Erastians, 169
Errol, earl of, 157
Erskine of Scottiscraig, Sir Charles, 63, 162, 171
Essex, 142
Evanston, Captain, 26
Evesham, 134; Map 6, 7

Fairfax, Lord, and decision for war with Scotland, 10–12, 15, 19; and invasion of England, 114, 125, 126; resigns as Lord General, 12, 16
Fairfax's Foot Regiment, at Worcester, 140
Falkirk, 33, 59, 82, 100, 102; Map 4, 5
Falkland Palace, 8, 28, 109
Familists, 169
Fast Castle, 84
Fens, Scots prisoners sent to work at, 145
Fenwick, Colonel, commands at Edinburgh, 148, 156, 162, 166, 168; governor of Berwick, 51, 83; and invasion of England, 114
Ferrybridge, 125
Ferryhills, Inverkeithing, 106
Fife, 8, 33, 55, 66, 74, 87, 93; contributions to Scots war effort, 110; English conquest, 107–111, 113, 152, 154, 156, 157, 161, 168; English invasion, 104–106; English landing planned/attempted, 60, 80–81, 97, 98; Scots garrisons, 92, 98; Map 1
Finlarig, 167, 172; Map 8
Fitch, Colonel, commanding in south-west Scotland, 61
Fitch's Foot Regiment, 61, 172
Fleetwood, 122
Fleetwood, Charles, 93; at Dunbar, 42; and invasion of England, 120, 125; lieutenant-general of the English invasion force, 16; at Worcester, 134, 135, 137, 139, 140
Fleetwood's Regiment, at Dunbar, 40, 43–44
Fordell, 110
Forest of Dean, 134
Forfar, 166; Map 8
Fort Royal, Worcester, 132, 141, 142; Map 7
Forth, Firth of, 17, 28, 33, 60; warfare in, 80–81, 84–85, 93, 98, 104–105, 162; Map 1
Forth, river, 97, 102, 103
France, Charles II proclaimed king of, 6; Scots prisoners to be sent to, 57
Frondes, 1
Frost, Mr, negotiator for delivering Scots prisoners, 56

Galbraith, Lieutenant, 103
Gareloch, 166
Garmouth, Morayshire, 5, 7, 13, 28, 111, 170; Map 8
General Assembly of the Scots Kirk, 9, 66, 109, 155
Gerrard, Sir William, 121
Gillespie, Patrick, Scots minister, 54, 88
Gladsmuir, 23; Map 1
Glasgow, civil conflict in, 88–90; Cromwell at, 63–64, 67, 69, 88–90, 92, 101–102; miners from, 68; under English control, 154, 155, 161, 166; in Western Association 54; map 4, 5, 8
Glencairn, earl of, 111
Glencoe massacre, 1
Gloucester, 121, 132, 134; Map 6
Gloucestershire, 78, 132
Goffe's Foot Regiment, at Worcester, 140

Gogar, confrontation at, 34–35, 96, 101; Map 2
Gordons, at Perth, 113
Gowrie, Carse of, 158
Grafton Manor, 131
Great Britain, Charles II proclaimed king of, 6
Great Sconce, North Queensferry, 105
Greenock, 85–86
Greenwich, 144
Grey, Colonel James, 19
Grey of Groby, Lord, 125, 134
Grey, Isaac de, contractor for Scots prisoners, 57
Grosvenor, Colonel, 147, 156
guerilla warfare, in Edinburgh, 68; in south-east Scotland, 60, 69, 83; in south-west Scotland, 80
Guise, tailor of Worcester, 136
Guthrie, James, Glasgow minister, 88

Hacker, Colonel, 26, 65, 140, 147
Hacker's Regiment of Horse, 26; at Dunbar, 49–50; at Worcester, 140, 147
Haddington, 22, 38, 40, 43, 44, 47, 49, 70; Map 1, 4
Hailes, 61
Haines, Major, 26
Halifax, 144
Hall, Captain Edward, naval commander, 18
Hamilton, 72–73, 80, 88, 92, 95, 100, 101, 151; Map 4, 5
Hamilton, Alexander, English spy, 85, 87
Hamilton, duke of, 119, 141, 142
Hamilton, Sir James, 34
Hampshire, 51, 78
Hane (Hein?), Joachim, German gunner, 155
Hanley Castle, 132
Harrison, Thomas, brings reinforcements to Edinburgh, 104, 108; commands in North of England, 90, 94, 95; and invasion of England, 109, 114–122; at Council of State 10; major-general, 16; at Worcester, 130, 134, 144
Hasilrig, Sir Arthur, governor of Newcastle, 18, 19, 30, 42, 51, 58, 147; and invasion of England, 114; and Scots prisoners, 55–56
Hasilrig's Regiment of Horse, 87, 148
Hawick, 118; Map 6
Hazelmoor, 119
Heligoland Bight, 7
Hereford, 134, 138; Map 6
Herodotos, Greek historian, 38
Hessians, mercenaries, 78–79
Highlanders, at Inverkeithing, 105–106; at Perth, 113; at Stirling, 155–156; at Worcester, 140, 141
Hobson, Lieutenant-Colonel Paul, 58
Hodgson, Lieutenant, 22, 39, 48–49
Hoffmann, Captain Augustine, Dutch mercenary commander, 69, 74, 80, 95, 158, 172
Holborne, Major-General James, 59, 82; at Dunbar, 42, 47; at Inverkeithing, 105–107; lieutenant-general, 90
Holden of Gleneggies, Colonel Sir John, regiment destroyed at Dunbar, 49
Holland, 6, 52, 54, 62
Holyroodhouse, 24, 68
Home Castle, 83, 84; Map 4
Honours of Scotland (regalia), 55, 172–173
Howard, Captain, wounded at Worcester, 143
Howard of Escrick, Lord, 117
Hubbold, Colonel, 156
Hull, 70, 114
Huntly, marquis of (Lewis Gordon), 156, 157; in Northern Band, 65–66; resistance of, 163–164, 165, 166, 171; and Start conspiracy, 62; submission, of, 172
Hyde, Edward, 79, 111

Inchgarvie Castle, 81, 85, 98, 105, 108, 109; Map 4
Independents, English, 14, 67, Scottish, 169
Ingoldsby's Foot Regiment, at Worcester, 140

Inveraray, 157, 162, 164
Inverkeithing, 81, 105–106, 110, 151; Map 5
Inverness, 172; Map 8
IRA, 1
Ireland, 1, 5, 6, 12, 16, 51, 57, 119, 169–170
Ireton, Henry, Lord Deputy of Ireland, 51, 116
Irvine, 154

Jacobites, 1, 174, 176
Jaffray, Alexander, provost of Aberdeen, at Dunbar, 50; surrenders Aberdeen, 160–161
James VI, 175
Jedburgh, 83, 90; Map 4
Jock's Lodge, Edinburgh, 24
John, English ship captured by Scots, 80, 84
Johnson, captain, contractor for Scots prisoners, 57
Johnston of Wariston, Sir Archibald, Clerk Register, 9, 28, 29, 37, 52, 62, 64, 68, 82, 85, 87, 110
Jones, Captain, killed at Worcester, 143

Keith, Colonel Sir William, 140, 141
Kelso, 83, 90, 119; Map 6
Kendal, 119; Map 6
Kenmore Castle, 79
Kenmure, earl of, 144
Kennedy, John, 167
Ker, Colonel Gilbert, 88; and Bothwell Brig fight, 72–73, 101; at Dunbar, 42; leader of Kirk Party faction, 52; and Western Association, 54, 64, 71
Kerr, Captain Alexander, 69
Killin, 164, 167; Map 8
Kilmarnock, 95
Kilsyth, 63, 82, 94, 102; Map 4, 5
Kilsyth, Lady, 90
Kinross, 109
Kirk o' Shotts, 72
Kirk Party, 3, 90, 148; and the coronation, 76; loses power to Royalists, 76–78; policy after Dunbar, 52, 61–62, 65–66; purges army, 17, 28; regime of, 8, 11, 13–15, 33, 36; split into Resolutioners and Protestors, 82
Kirkcudbright (county), 54; Map 4
Kirkcudbright (town), 79
Kirkmen, *see* Kirk Party
Kirriemuir, 157; Map 8

Lambert, John, and Bothwell Brig fight, 72–73; commands invasion of Fife, 104, 107, 108; at Council of State, 10, 11; at Dunbar, 42–50; given a new regiment, 20; at Glasgow, 88; and invasion of England, 118–122, 128; at Inverkeithing, 105–106; lieutenant-general, 93; major-general, 16, 151; meets Strachan, 34; patrol to the fords of the Forth, 102; reconnaissance by, 23; and Scots houses, 70; secures Edinburgh, 58; at Worcester, 130, 134–139, 143; wounded, captured and rescued, 26
Lambert's Foot Regiment, formerly Bright's, 20, 27; at Dunbar, 48
Lambert's Regiment of Horse, 26; at Dunbar, 47
Lammermuir Hills, 70; Map 1
Lamont, diarist, 169
Lanark, 51, 72, 80; Map 4, 6
Lanarkshire, 52, 88; Map 4
Lancashire, 19, 86, 95; earl of Derby and, 77, 121, 122, 131, 132; and Scots invasion, 118, 119, 121, 125, 127, 129, 134, 144
Lancaster, 119, 144; Map 6
Lauder, 72; Map 4
Lauderdale, earl of, 143
Lechmere, Sir Nicholas, 132
Leicester, 19
Leith, 33, 85, 87, 169; bombarded from the sea, 26; captured by English, 58, 67; English base, 60, 81, 97, 104, 114, 115, 117, 118, 119, 148, 153; fortified town, 17, 23–24; king arrives at, 29
Leslie, David, 22; capture, 143, 144;

defence of Edinburgh, 33–34; at Dunbar, 40–50; invasion of England, 108, 149; lieutenant-general, 90; options following invasion of Fife, 107, 108; retreat to Stirling, 51–52; sent to establish control in the Highlands, 65–66; strategy, 17, 19, 23, 28, 30, 31, 37–38, 129; at Torwood, 103; at Worcester, 139, 142
Leven, earl of (Alexander Leslie), Scots commander-in-chief, 17, 42, 58, 90, 149, 157, 158
Leven, Loch, 109
Libberton, Lord, 50
Lidcott, Colonel, attempts to land at Rosyth, 97–98
Liddesdale, 118
Lilburne, Colonel Robert, 27, 85–86, 88–90; in Lancashire campaign, 122–124, 125, 129, 134, 144; at Shrewsbury and Bewdley, 134, 138
Lilburne's Regiment of Horse, 27; at Dunbar, 47; in invasion of England, 120, 121, 122–124
Linlithgow, 33, 59, 61; English garrison at, 59, 63, 67, 71, 82, 85, 100, 101, 102, 104, 105, 107, 148; Scots raid, 80, 84–85, 87; Map 4, 5
Liverpool, 102, 123, 144, 145; Map 6
Lomond Hills, 109
London, 51, 81, 116, 120, 121, 124, 125, 127; Scots prisoners at, 55–58, 144–145; Map 6
Longtown, 116
Lorrainers, mercenaries, 78–79
Lothian, earl of, 29, 69, 71
Lothian, Lady, 69
Loudoun, earl of (John Campbell), and coronation of Charles II, 76; and English conquest, 157, 164, 167, 172; Lord Chancellor of Scotland, 8–9, 59, 63, 111, 149
Ludlow, 138
Lumsdaine, Colonel Robert, 158–159
Lumsden, Colonel Sir James, at Dunbar, 42, 50, 81
Lynn, New England, 57
Lynn, Norfolk, 78, 145
Lysons, Thomas, mayor of Worcester, 128

Mackenzie of Pluscardine, Sir Thomas, 65–66
Maclean, Sir Hector, 106
Macleans, at Inverkeithing, 106
Madresfield Court, 137; Map 7
Man, Isle of, 77, 85, 86, 118, 121; Map 6
Manchester, 122–124, 125; Map 6
Mansfield, 123, 125; Map 6
Marischal, earl, 77, 111, 158
Market Drayton, 144
Marston Moor, battle of, 17, 32, 42
masons, English, sent to help fortify Leith, 58
Massey, Major-General Daniel, 85, 86, 90; in Lancashire, 122–124, 125, 127, 129; raids English camp, 101; at Worcester, 132, 135
Mattingly, Garrett, 174
mercenaries, Dutch, in Scots service, 65–66, 69, 74; Hessians and Lorrainers, 78–79; *see also* Druschke, Hoffmann
Mercurius Politicus, quoted, 22, 60
Merse, the, 23
Mersey, river, 95, 122
Middleton, John, lieutenant-general, 90, 143, 144; in Northern Band, 65–66,
Middleton, Sir Thomas, 127
militia, English, 117, 118, 120, 125, 127, 138, 142
miners, at siege of Edinburgh Castle, English, 73; Scots, 68; and Scots invasion, 134
Moffat, 115, 116
Monck, George, and attacks on Scots houses, 70–71, 84, 85; attempts on Fife, 80, 104; capture of Dundee, 158–160; capture of Stirling, 138, 150–156; in command in Scotland, 115, 117, 144, 146, 147–148, 158; at Dunbar, 45–49; final conquest, 162–168, 171; given a new regiment, 20;

lieutenant-general, 93; and the Restoration, 111
Monck's Foot Regiment 20, 172
Monkland, 102
Monmouth, 138
Monro, Sir George, 65–66
Montgomery, Colonel Robert, 54; captured, 144; at Dunbar, 42; in Fife, 113; major-general, 90; raids English at Musselburgh, 26–27, 28; raids Linlithgow, 87–88; sent to establish control of Western Association, 71–73; and Start conspiracy, 63; in the west, 92, 94–95, 102, 116, 117, 148; at Worcester, 140, 141
Montgomeryshire, 127
Montrose, 160, 166; Map 8
Montrose, earl of, 8, 14, 17, 26, 77, 149
Moorfoot Hills, 70
Moray, 172
Moray, earl of, 68
Moray Firth, 5, 7
Morgan, Colonel, dragoon commander, 147, 160
Morpeth, 55
Moseley, Quartermaster-General, killed at Worcester, 143
Mosse, John, English spy, 81
Musselburgh, 27; English attacked at, 26–27, 29, 47; occupied by English, 23, 24, 30–31, 32, 35, 37, 39, 87–88; retaken briefly by Scots, 26; Map 1, 2
Myerscough, 119

Nantwich, 20
Navy Commissioners (English), 18
navy, English, 18; and Firth of Forth, 80–81, 85
Neidpath Castle, 72; Map 4
New England, Scots prisoners sent to, 56–57, 145
Newark Castle, 101, 103
Newbattle Abbey, 69; map 2
Newbridge, 100
Newcastle, 18, 19, 20, 22, 30, 42, 51, 81, 147; rendezvous of English army, 16; and Scots invasion, 114, 117, 118, 119, 121; and Scots prisoners, 55, 57, 145; Map 6
Newtyle, battle at, 65
Nicholas, royal Secretary, 51
Nicoll, diarist, 80, 160
Niddry, 35; Map 2
Niddry Rows, 59
Norfolk, Royalist rising in, 78, 86, 93, 129
North Queensferry, 104
North Sea, 7, 18, 176
North Wales, 86, 95, 117–118, 124
Northampton, 19, 120; Map 6
Northern Band, 65–67
Northern Ireland, 1
Northern Isles, 176
Northesk, river, 70
Northumberland, 55
Northwich, 122; Map 6
Norwich, 78

Ogilvie, Lord, 77
Ogilvie, Sir David, defeats Kirk Party force, 65
Okey, Colonel, 147, 154–155, 156, 159, 160–161, 163, 165, 168
Okey's Regiment of horse, 153
Orange, Prince of, 6, 54
Ordnance Committee (English), 30
Orkney, 7, 172
Ormskirk, 123
Osbaston, Lord, 154
Overton, Colonel Robert, at Dunbar, 46; at Dundee, 158; governor of Edinburgh and Leith, 58, 67; and invasion of Fife, 104, 154, 157; at Montrose, 160, 166; at Perth, 148, 156, 158

Paisley, 54, 154, 155; Map 8
Pakington, Sir John, 131
Paris, 6
Parliament, English, 9, 16–18, 136, 143, 160; and government of Scotland, 169, 170
Parliament, Scots, 8, 13, 17, 66, 75, 91, 164, 167, 172

Peebles, 51, 72, 80, 83; Map 4
Pennines, 144
Penrith, 90, 117, 118, 119; Map 6
Pentland Hills, 100; Map 1, 2
Perfect Diurnal of the Army, quoted, 60
Perry Wood, Worcester, 135, 141; map 7
Perth, archers for, 105; attacked by English, 108, 109; captured by English, 111, 113–114, 115, 151, 156, 157, 158, 165; Charles II at, 8, 32, 40, 51, 92; English spy at, 81, 85; and Start conspiracy, 62–63; Map 4, 5, 6, 8
Perthshire, 102, 165, 166
Philiphaugh, battle of, 17
Pinchebanke, Colonel, 155
Pitchcroft, Worcester, 130, 131, 132, 142; Map 7
Pitscottie, Major-General, 140, 141
Plymouth, 18
Popham, Admiral, 7
Port Glasgow, 101
Port of Menteith, 102
Powick, 135, 136, 140, 141; Map 7
Presbyterians, English, 10, 14, 119, 121, 123, 130
Prescott, 123
President, English frigate, 80
Preston, 11, 123; Map 6
Prestonpans, 68
Pride, Colonel, at Dunbar, 46
Pride's Purge, 17
Pride's Regiment, 20; at Dunbar, 40, 44, 48
prisoners of war (Scots), 27, 55–58, 124, 143, 144–146
Protesters, Kirk Party faction, 82
Purging Committee (Scots), 28–29

Quarry Holes, Calton Hill, 26
Queensferry, 33, 81, 84, 85; *see also* South and North Queensferry

Reading, 121, 125; Map 6
Records of Scotland, 82, 156
Red Hall, 34, 35, 61, 101, 103
Red Hill, Worcester, 135, 136, 141; Map 7
Rede, Colonel, 147, 156
Rede's Regiment of Horse, 147
Remonstrance (Western Remonstrance), 65, 67, 88
Remonstrants, 67
Renfrewshire, 52; Map 4
Resolutioners, Kirk Party faction, 82
Restalrig, 24, 29
Restoration, the, 79, 111, 131
Revolution, English, 2–3; Scottish, 2–3
Rich, Colonel, 78, 114
Richard II, 6
Richardson, Scottish moss-trooper, 83
Rippon, Major Thomas 30
Rochdale, 144
Rookby, Colonel, contractor for Scots prisoners, 57
Roslin, 70; Map 2, 4
Rosneath, 166; Map 8
Rosse, Lord, 155
Rosyth Castle, 97–98
Rothesay, 167; Map 8
Rotterdam, 18
Rowe, William, Scoutmaster General, 22, 59
Roxburgh, earl of, 39
Royalists, English 3, 27, 29, 111; conspiracies of, 77–79, 85–86, 130; in Lancashire, 119, 123, 144; and Scots invasion, 118, 126, 129; in Worcester, 131
Royalists, Scottish, 8, 14, 29, 33, 34, 55, 65–67, 76–77, 86; return to power, 91; strategy, 95–96
Rushworth, John, Secretary of the Army, 18, 39, 49
Rutherglen, 73; Map 4
Ryton, 119, 120, 121

St Albans, 125; Map 6
St Andrews, 109–110, 154, 157, 158, 159; Map 5, 8
St John, Oliver, 10, 13
St Leonard's Crags, 24
Sandbach, 143
Sanders, Colonel, 114, 119
Saugus Iron Works, Lynn, New

England, 57, 145
Scone, 158
Scott, Major, 161
Scott of Pitscottie, Walter, major-general, 90
Seaforth, earl of (George Mackenzie), 65–66
Seaton, Alexander, 84
Seekers, 169
Selkirk, 83; Map 4, 6
Severn, river, 129, 131, 132, 134, 137, 139, 140, 141; Map 7
Sexby's Foot Regiment, 61
Shettleston, 101
Ship Money, 10
ships, Dutch, 5, 18; English, 18; Scots, 18
Shotts, 101, 102
Shrewsbury, 124–125, 134, 138, 145; Map 6
Shropshire, 125, 127
Sidlaw Hills, 158
Skidam, Dutch ship, 5
Skippon, Major-General Philip, 120
Skipton, 119; Map 6
Solway, river, 95
South Queensferry, 108
Southern Uplands, 115
Southesk Castle, Charles II at, 8
Southesk, earl of, 8
Southesk Glen, 62
Speaker, English frigate, 157, 158
Spetchley, 131, 135
Spey, river, 5
Spur, the, *see* Edinburgh Castle
Staffordshire, 122
Start, the, conspiracy, 62–63, 170
Stevenson, David, 2
Stewart, Lady, and Cromwell, 89
Stewart, Sir Walter, 89
Stirling, attacked by English, 115; Charles II at, 8, 92, 111; conquest of, 150–156, 157, 160, 162, 164; Cromwell theatens, 58–59, 61, 63, 65; Cromwell unwilling to assault, 93, 96, 97, 108; English garrison, 157; factions at, 82, 91; Scots base, 51, 80, 84, 94, 100, 107–108, 111, 113; Scots government settles at, 52, 54, 66, 72, 110, 167; Map 4, 5, 6, 8
Stirlingshire, 102
Stoney Hill, Musselburgh, 32
Strachan, Colonel Archibald, 82, 88; at Dunbar, 42; meets Lambert, 34; raids English at Musselburgh, 26–27, 28; surrenders, 73–74; and Western Association, 52, 54, 64, 71
Stratford-on-Avon, 134; Map 6
Strathbogie, 67
Strathtay, 165
Sydenham, Major, 87
Sutherland, 8
Sutherland, earl of, 113–114

Talbot, Lord, 131
Tantallon Castle, attacked by English, 70, 71; base for sea-raiders, 70, 80, 81; captured by English, 84, 151; Map 5
Tay, Firth of, 157
Tay, Loch, 164, 166, 167
Teesdale, 118
Teme, river, 135, 136, 139, 140, 141; Map 7
Teviotdale, 23, 90, 114
Tewkesbury, 132
Tiltyard, Greenwich, Scots prisoners at, 144
Tolbooth, Edinburgh, 174; Glasgow, 89
Torphichen, 101, 102
Torwood, 100–101, 105; Map 5
Tothill Fields, Scots prisoners at, 144–145
Toynbee, A. J., 174
Tullibardine, earl of, 157
Tweed, river, 19; Map 1, 5
Tweeddale, 90, 115
Tweedsmuir, 115
Twistleton, Colonel, 114
Tyne, river, 119

Ulster, 66
Union, political, of England and Scotland, 2–3, 169–170, 172–173,

174–176
Upton, 131, 132, 135–136, 137, 139, 140; Map 7
Unity, transport ship for Scots prisoners, 57

Vane, Sir Harry, 102
Virginia, Scots prisoners to be sent to, 56–57, 145

Wainman, Colonel, 119
Wales, 125, 127, 129, 134
Walker, Augustine, contractor for Scots prisoners, 57
Walker, Sir Edward, 29
Wariston, *see* Johnston
Warrington, 119, 121, 122, 142, 144, 151; Map 6
Warwick, 125, 134; Map 6
Water of Leith, 32, 34; Map 2
Watt, Captain, guerilla leader, 70
weather, its effect on events, 7, 26, 59, 60, 73, 74, 80, 82, 86–87, 94
Western Association (English Royalist), 77–78, 129
Western Association (Scottish), 52–54, 59, 64–65, 73, 74, 77, 79, 88, 153
Western Remonstrance, *see* Remonstrance
Westminster, 144
Westmorland, 119
Westwood Park, 131
Whalley, Edmund, 16, 23, 26, 65, 72, 80, 92, 109, 152
Whalley's Regiment of Horse, at Dunbar, 47
Wharton, Lord, 51
Whiggamore Raid, 8, 52
Whitehall Palace, 5, 10
Whitelocke, Bulstrode, 10–12, 94
Wigan, 123–124, 125; Map 6
Wigtown, 54; Map 4
William III, 6
Windsor, 120
Wogan, Colonel, 119
Worcester, battle of, 2, 126–127, 128–146, 161; captured by Scots, 126–127, 157; defences to be slighted, 86; refortified, 132; Scots army heads for, 125; Scots prisoners, 143, 145; Map 6, 7
Worcestershire, 130, 143
Wyre, river, 122, 123

York, 19
York, Maine, 57
Yorkshire, 12, 30, 32, 118, 126, 144